Introduction

+ DEFINING THE DREAM

Thirteen years ago, I huffed and puffed my way to what I could only hope was the top of my climb up Mt. San Jacinto in California. Instead, I found a trail intersection and sign for the Pacific Crest Trail (PCT), Mexico to Canada. I had a hard time believing that one footpath could go from where I stood all the way to Canada, but when I got home, I immediately googled the PCT. And that is when long trails became an obsession for me.

For years after, I dreamed about long trails. I pictured myself out on the trail, accompanied by the sound of my footsteps crunching the leaves underfoot and the smell of fresh dirt. I spent my free time (or procrastinating time) reading hikers' blogs. I wished I could make it happen. But there were so many skills I didn't have. I didn't have the time or money. I was scared. But mainly, as much as I wanted to hike a long trail, I didn't know where to begin.

The book you hold in your hand is the one I wish had existed back in 2004. It is designed to give you the familiarity, confidence, and case studies needed to make informed decisions when you set out on your first long-distance hike. If you are anything like I was, the idea of hiking a long trail has inserted itself in your mind. But you have some questions.

Fast forward to present day. After completing twenty distance hikes, I breathe and sleep long trails. But I always keep one foot rooted in where I came from.

Unlike a lot of thru-hikers, I didn't grow up backpacking. By the time I wanted to go on my first thru-hike, I was an adult learning the how-tos of thru-hiking from the bottom. As a result, I keenly remember all the fears and anxieties I had before ever stepping foot on the trail. And, even more painfully, I remember the numerous mistakes I made on the trail—money wasted on gear and food I didn't need, painful foot injuries, awkward social interactions, and, most of all, having to explain to the folks back home that what I wanted to do wasn't crazy. I know there are others out there like me, and I want to help get them and you on the trail feeling prepared and confident.

Whether you plan to be out there for five days or ten months—whatever distance you consider a "long-distance backpacking trip"—this book will help you develop a plan to succeed. Be it an end-to-end thru-hike, a section of a long trail, or simply an individually crafted longer route, there's something here for everyone.

PHOTO CREDIT: STEVEN "TWINKLE" SHATTUCK

Finding your inspiration is easy with views like this.

BACKPACKER
LONG TRAILS

MASTERING THE ART OF
THE THRU-HIKE

BY LIZ THOMAS

An imprint of Globe Pequot

Falcon and FalconGuides are registered trademarks and Make Adventure Your Story is a trademark of Rowman & Littlefield.

Some text reproduced from *Backpacker* magazine and backpacker.com. Copyright page: A special thank-you to Paul Magnanti, Erik Johnson, Emelie Frojen, Sarah Stewart, Corey Buhay, MattHayes, Maggie Wallace, Cat Leipold, Heather Balogh, Mattie Schuler, and Heather Anderson.

Distributed by NATIONAL BOOK NETWORK

Copyright © 2017 Rowman & Littlefield

British Library Cataloguing-in-Publication Information available

Library of Congress Cataloging-in-Publication Data available

CIP data on file.

ISBN 978-1-4930-2872-6

ISBN 978-1-4930-2873-3 (e-book)

♾™ The paper used in this publication meets the minimum requirements of American National Standard for Information Sciences—Permanence of Paper for Printed Library Materials, ANSI/NISO Z39.48-1992.

Printed in the United States of America.

The author and Rowman & Littlefield assume no liability for accidents happening to, or injuries sustained by, readers who engage in the activities described in this book.

TABLE OF CONTENTS

Like most people, my inspiration to hike a long trail came while I was on a day hike. In this book, you'll learn to transition from day hiker to thru-hiker.

This book encapsulates not only the lessons I've learned from twenty different long-distance hikes but also the perspectives of other long-distance hikers, to capture a wide variety of thoughts from people of different ages and backgrounds, who have different paces and different goals. Keep an eye out throughout the book for these perspectives in the Hike Your Own Hike sidebars. "Hike Your Own Hike" (HYOH) is a core tenet of the long-distance hiking community, and a phrase you'll hear often. It's the belief that there's no one right way to do a long hike. What's important, rather, is that you hike in a way that's authentic to you.

On the trail, you're the boss. The HYOH philosophy says, "Hey, being outdoors is the one chance I get in life not to have to fit into someone else's box and someone else's schedule." This book is aimed at empowering you to create your own hike, and to give you the information to help you form your own opinions on how to do it. Instead of telling you exactly what to do, I offer tips on what has worked for me and what works for others. By planning, prepping, and reflecting on your hike before you go, you'll set yourself up for success in your goals—whatever they may be.

FIND YOUR "WHY?"

There are a lot of things you can't predict about a thru-hike, but here's one thing I guarantee will happen: At some point on your journey, you will ask yourself, "Why am I here?" The honeymoon phase when you're just psyched to be out there will have worn off. Maybe you're slogging through your third day of rain while missing your family's annual trip to the beach, with no prospect of a warm bed for weeks ahead. What's to stop you from just quitting right then and there?

A lot of hikers quit when it gets hard. Seventy percent of folks who start the Appalachian Trail don't finish. The biggest difference between those who meet their goals and those who don't? It's not that they're younger or fitter or richer or more disciplined. It's that they're better at winning the mental game that thru-hiking demands.

You're already planning to exercise your body and get fit for your hike. But you also need to exercise your mind. And the most important mental exercise of all is one you can do right now, today: Take the time to truly understand why you want to hike. Spend some time thinking about your motives. Unlike many other situations in life, the only person you're accountable to on a thru-hike is yourself. No one else will tell you what to do or why you have to keep going. No one else

A wonderful world awaits those willing to try a thru-hike.

Sentinel Peak, Olympic National Park

will be there in the rain reminding you that defeating obstacles is an amazing way to grow as a person. That's why you need to be super clear before you begin about what you hope to get out of all this hard work.

Set aside at least 30 minutes of quiet time alone to invest in the hard work of understanding what's important to you. Remember: Successful long-distance hikers aren't necessarily the strongest physically, but they are the strongest mentally and emotionally. Here's how you start getting strong.

PHOTO CREDIT: WHITNEY ALLGOOD LARUFFA

Reflection Lake is one of the most iconic spots on the Wonderland Trail.

THOUGHTFUL REFLECTION: QUESTIONS TO ASK YOURSELF

By finding your meaning for your hike, you give yourself the mental tools to succeed. The more time you put into creating a thoughtful reflection, the more it will serve you when you need it the most. If you're not sure about your answers right now, think it over for a few days and then write something down.

1. Why do I want to take this journey?
2. Why do I want to do it now (or next year, or in a few years)?
3. What rewards will I get if I meet my goals? Be positive and as specific as possible. This is your vision for what your hike can achieve for you.

4. What will I be giving up to do this hike? Am I truly willing to give that up for a while to make this happen?

5. If I weren't hiking, what would I be doing? (e.g., working 80-hour weeks, mowing the lawn)

6. What are my fears or apprehensions about this hike?

7. What am I most excited to learn about?

8. What parts of my personality are going to help the most on this hike?

9. What parts of my personality may get in the way of my success?

10. What can I do before this hike to set myself up for success?

Now, take what you've learned by answering these questions and write yourself a letter to read when times get tough on the trail. Practice visualizing the moment of success for yourself, as if you've already achieved your goal. Be as detailed as possible. How does it feel? What do you see? Who's there with you? What do you hear? It sounds hokey, but there's strong scientific evidence that this type of visualization technique really works.

Being explicit with yourself about your motivation and goals helps give you a reason to push through the hard times. When I set off to thru-hike the first time, I didn't quite know what the trail would give me, but I knew I wanted to find out. Hiking gave me plenty of time to ask and answer questions like, "What do I want to do with my life?" and provided me with the pause to reflect on my transition from one phase of life to another.

As I learned after the fact, prepping for a thru-hike is not just about picking the right gear. It's also about gearing up mentally and physically, prepping resupplies, managing schedules, and establishing budgets. This book gives you the tools you need to turn your dream into reality. It gives you the confidence to start at mile zero of your hike with the knowledge and skills that most hikers usually get only after a thousand miles of hiking. Thanks for picking up the book, and see you up the trail!

—LIZ "SNORKEL" THOMAS

PLAN
&
PREP

A thru-hike is not just about the photo at the finish point, but the journey required to get there. This book will help you understand what is involved on that journey and prepare for success along the way. Pictured: Liz Thomas at the northern terminus of the Appalachian Trail.

Chapter 1

PLANNING TIME
AND BUDGET

For years I dreamed of thru-hiking the Pacific Crest
Trail or the Appalachian Trail, but I couldn't get past
the "no time, no money" part. Not feeling confident in
my skills or my ability to complete the hike (or, heck,
even make my way out of the airport to the trailhead)
didn't help. Finding time and saving money for the
hike became such a wall in my brain that I continu-
ally postponed seriously pursuing my dream, saving
it for "one day." Since you have this book in hand,
however, you likely want "one day" to be "as soon as
the snow melts at the trailhead."

One of the most encouraging things in my quest to
find the time and money to hike was hearing stories from
other people—from a variety of professions and backgrounds—and gleaning what strategies they used to
make their thru-hike dreams happen. Frank discussions
about finding time and money are almost never found in
hiking guides. For some reason, authors have found the
quest for money and vacation trivial when compared to
the natural obstacles hikers may face on the trail. But to
the hiker these human-caused obstacles are often a bigger hindrance than bears or wildfires; money and time are
such obstacles that they keep many people from even
starting their trip.

We all have the same dream to thru-hike, but the hur-
dles we face to meet our goals aren't just thrown at us
by nature. This chapter is about learning to use the same
strategies seasoned hikers use to get out of job and financial obligations.

WHAT IS THRU-HIKING?

To understand how to plan for a long-distance hike, you must first understand what it is and what skills you need to have to complete it. Just as marathoning requires a different set of physical and mental skills than sprinting, long-distance hiking and thru-hiking also have some differences from traditional backpacking. A lot of the skills are similar, but long-distance hiking is trickier than a typical backpacking trip.

The skills unique to thru-hiking include:

- Finding the necessary time, money, and support from loved ones to follow your dreams
- Resupplying your food and consumables and switching out gear
- Getting your mind and body committed for the long haul
- Learning how decisions you make today on the trail will impact what happens to you tomorrow (or even weeks from now) on the trail

Defining Backpacking Lingo

We use the term thru-hiking and thru-hiker throughout this book to refer to any long-distance hiking and hikers, but there are many ways to backpack. Here are a few terms you will hear both in this book and in your hiking life that are useful to know:

Thru-hiker: A hiker attempting to walk from one terminus of a trail to another terminus, all within one season. This can also apply to a backpacker who is walking a loop trail that starts and ends in the same place. Thru-hikers connect all their footsteps so that even when they get off the trail to resupply, they have walked a continuous hike. While this term is usually reserved for those walking trails over 90 miles, it can be used for trails as short as 40 miles.

Section-hiker: A hiker attempting to walk from one terminus of a trail to another terminus over many seasons or even a lifetime. Section hikers do not need to hike all sections in geographical order or even go into a hike with the intention of one day hiking the whole trail.

Flip-Flopper: A hiker attempting to walk an entire long trail in one season, but not necessarily in geographical order. Flip-floppers connect all their footsteps so that even when they get off the trail to restart their journey in a different direction, they have walked a continuous line.

Make sure you know your route well ahead of hitting the trailhead.

CHOOSE YOUR ROUTE

The very first step in budgeting time and money for a long-distance hike is choosing what route you'll take. We'll discuss this concept more in chapter 4, but touch briefly on it here to help you better manage your time and money. Maybe you're already sure of exactly where you want to explore, but there are more variables and options than you've probably thought of. Here are some things to consider when choosing a trek.

TIME OF YEAR

Do you have the summer off from school, or the winter off from your raft guide job? Or are you retired and have no time restrictions? Whatever time you have, a long hike is out there for you. Most long hikes have a "window" during which conditions are the most favorable and safest, but if you can't fit your hiking schedule into that window, you can always break a thru-hike into a series of long hikes over multiple seasons or years. For example, if you can't fit in the time

The PCT and CDT start in the desert, where water can be scarce and temperatures can soar even in April. Plan your trip according to the weather of the climate you plan to hike in.

window for a northbound hike, you may be able to swing a southbound hike. They tend to start and end later in the year.

Depending on the weather window, you can then plan out your per-day mileage. On some trails, like the PCT, you may have to pull consistently bigger miles to finish before your weather window closes. Water sources also come into play. Depending on the season and trail, water sources may be farther apart on some trails, so you have to be either fit enough to walk between them in a day or fit enough to carry water for two days

SOCIAL GOALS AND NEEDS

Long-distance hiking can be filled with days of solitude. When planning a long hike, ask yourself: Are you okay with not seeing anyone for a few days? Will you feel lonely, or will you feel free? How connected do you want to stay? How important is daily cell reception and Internet access? What about exit points—are there a lot of them, in case you need to leave the trail or meet a family member in a support vehicle?

Consider the environment around the trail. Are you looking for a cultural experience or a natural experience? While long trails are everywhere, many hikers who have traveled internationally say that the United States boasts some of the longest, wildest established trail systems anywhere. What kind of scenery are you most excited about?

The Triple Crown Trails

The most famous long-distance hiking trails in the United States are the Big Three: Appalachian Trail (AT), Pacific Crest Trail (PCT), and Continental Divide Trail (CDT). These are called the Triple Crown Trails because the few who have completed all three in their entirety are bestowed the Triple Crown Award by the American Long Distance Hiking Association-West at the Annual Gathering. Think of it as the Academy Awards for hiking—except recipients are dressed in puffy jackets and trail runners instead of tuxes and ballgowns, and it's held at a camp instead of in a theater.

PHOTO CREDIT: AMERICAN LONG DISTANCE HIKING ASSOCIATION-WEST

American Long Distance Hiking Association-West President Whitney "Allgood" LaRuffa hiked the AT in 1996 (this photo), and, twenty years later, he hiked the CDT. He jokes he'll finish the PCT in another twenty years to complete his triple crown.

Liz Thomas on Sentinel Peak, Olympic National Park.

PRACTICALITIES

When choosing a trail, consider permits—are they needed, and how will you get them? How experienced do you need to be for that particular trail? What kind of skills do you need to master—like navigation, setting up campsites, using an ice axe, fording raging rivers, and so on?

FINANCIAL PLANNING

Figuring out how to get away on a hike—both financially and time wise—is one of the most daunting puzzles a prospective thru-hiker faces. I worked for three summers and all throughout college saving for my first long thru-hike on the Appalachian Trail. I set it as my goal and was sure to put away one week's pay-check per month for my hike. For me, slow and steady saving was the key to financing a long-distance hike. I found time to thru-hike by choosing to do my

PHOTO CREDIT: LIZ THOMAS

Whitney "Allgood" LaRuffa may not be rolling in money, but he is rolling in chocolate.

first long walk at a transition point in my life when I didn't have a full-time job or many responsibilities.

To help you save for a hike and stay financially healthy, here are some age-appropriate tips for you, whatever your current life status.

TEENS OR JUST STARTING OUT

I started my first thru-hike a year out of college. For me, hiking a long trail was just the transition I needed before finding a career and planning the next move in my life. The trip and everything I took away from it have stayed with me throughout my life.

For centuries, many cultures have had rites of passage for their young people before they entered adulthood. These rituals helped young people cope with the transition and build confidence and character. Our society, on the other hand, has rushed young people into making decisions—often before they know what they want in life.

As a young person you may not be rolling in wealth, but you should not let a lack of cash get in the way of making your dream trip a reality. I started hiking during this period of life and found these trips to be worth their weight in chocolate.

☐ **Stash your stuff.** Whether you're taking a gap year or waiting for your career to begin, you probably have fewer assets than older hikers. This can be a good thing: Little furniture and no mortgage can make cutting ties to the off-trail world simple. However, make sure you can afford a storage facility ($50 to $100 per month) for the things that won't fit in your kind, generous relatives' attics or basements.

☐ **Defer your student loans.** If you've just tossed your grad cap, you probably have more than a few dollars of debt to your name. Fortunately, government-sponsored student loans will grant extensions. "They're really flexible about giving you even a year's deferral without many questions," says 1999 AT thru-hiker and Certified Financial Planner (CFP) Tom "Katmandu" McClean. You'll continue to accrue interest during that time, though. If you have loans from a private firm, deferral isn't always possible, says John Zachary, a CFP and member of the Appalachian Trail Conservancy. You're better off taking a short-term or seasonal job until you've saved enough money to keep up payments while on the trail.

☐ **Don't let your credit lapse.** It's tempting to throw responsibility to the wind and dive into the woods right after graduation, but defaulting on loans or credit card debt could haunt you. A bad credit score can make it difficult to secure a job or lease when you return to civilization. Make sure you work credit card and loan payments into your trail budget.

MID-CAREER

If you hate your job or are feeling burnt out, going for a long hike mid-career can be just the jump start you need. Going for a long walk gives you time to reflect on your mid-life goals and strategize how to achieve them. Many of my best friends (who you will meet in the Hike Your Own Hike sections of this book) started

My friend Naomi "The Punisher" Hudetz went on her first thru-hike at age 39 in the middle of her career as an actuary. She came back refreshed, focused, and rejuvenated: "Employers see value in someone who can plan and follow through on a big trip like this."

hiking mid-career and have found that when they return from their adventure, they are energized and focused on their jobs in ways they never would have been had they not gone hiking. Think of it as career development.

☐ **Make a tactical exit.** If you've held the same job for years, talk to your employer about taking an extended vacation or sabbatical. Larger corporations will often grant a leave of absence to a veteran employee, possibly with continued benefits. This could mean major savings on health insurance. "You'll continue to pay a reduced cost as part of a group plan rather than having to pay an individual health plan," says CFP John Zachary.

□ **Rent out your digs.** If you own a home, consider renting it while you're gone. This will help defray some of the cost of your mortgage payments during the four to six months you're unemployed. At the very least, find a house sitter to make sure everything remains in working order while you're gone. Make sure you factor the sitter's fee into your trail budget and set up automatic bill pay for your mortgage before you leave home.

□ **Look into refinancing your mortgage.** But be cautious, says CFP and 2004 PCT thru-hiker Scott "Stormtrooper" Jacobsmeyer. If you started a thirty-year mortgage ten years ago, you can significantly lower payments by taking out another thirty-year mortgage. However, this extends the life of the loan, possibly into retirement age when most people want to be debt-free. If you decide it still makes sense to refinance, go ahead and do it. "Just make sure you do the refinancing before you quit your job, since banks require up to two years of earnings history," Jacobsmeyer says.

APPROACHING RETIREMENT

If you've dreamed of hiking a long trail your whole life but have done the so-called responsible thing and stuck it out until retirement—now is your chance! Soon, you'll have the time to make your goal come true. Make sure you have the money to do it—and to still be able to enjoy retirement afterward.

□ **Start eyeing your 401k.** Dipping into retirement savings before you're 59½ years old will slam you with a 10 percent penalty for early withdrawal on top of income taxes, says CFP Tom "Katmandu" McClean. If you're within six months of 60, though, you can start withdrawing without the penalty, and CFP John Zachary actually recommends doing so. "If you wait until you're 70, when the government mandates you start withdrawing, that might bump you up a tax bracket," he says. Taking money out sooner will smooth the spike in income and could reduce taxation.

□ **Stop eyeing your social security.** At age 62, you can start taking money out of Social Security savings—a second government benefit coming in on the heels of your 401k availability. However, taking money out of Social Security before you're of "full retirement age" (either 66 or 67, depending on when you were born) means a 30 percent reduction in monthly benefits for the rest of your life. "It's a big decision," warns Zachary.

□ **Consider holding out for Medicare.** The older you get, the more expensive health insurance is. If you retire before 65, when Medicare kicks in, you'll be

Dean "Ghost" Krakel retired from his job as a photojournalist at the *Denver Post* so he could hike and occasionally sit out rain storms on the Colorado Trail.

in a pricey age bracket. Consider waiting, and make sure you figure any premiums into your budget.

SAVINGS TIPS WE CAN ALL USE

Unless you're an excellent saver already, chances are you'll need to start putting money aside specifically for your hike. You'll have a better sense of how much you'll need to save each month after you calculate your trail budget (see "Calculate Your Budget" in this chapter). For example, if you decide you need $6,000 to hike your long trail and plan to start a year from now, you'll need to save $500 a month. Here are some tips for making it happen, no matter the amount.

☐ **Eliminate things you don't need.** Living on the cheap prior to your hike will help you carve savings out of your existing budget and put aside more for the adventure ahead. Make your own coffee instead of stopping at your local cafe. Eat out less. Repair your clothes instead of buying new. Be creative in looking at what areas of your life you can trim. After all, you can't take all the stuff you buy with you when you're hiking—so you may as well hold off to get it until after your trip.

☐ **Open a savings account just for your hike.** Vow not to withdraw from it. Shop around at different banks and find one that pays the highest interest.

☐ **Stop using credit cards.** People who pay with plastic have less of an emotional connection to the money leaving their hands and tend to spend 12 to 18 percent more annually than those who pay with cash.

☐ **Don't rely on the stock market.** Investing might be advisable if you have a loose and distant idea of when you want to hike, but not when you have a specific start date in mind, warns Tom McClean. "The market could be in a downturn in eighteen months. It's much better to have the money than to need it when the market's down," he says.

☐ **Create a visual reminder of your goal.** Put that poster of Jennifer Pharr Davis over your mantelpiece. Set out a big jar for change next to the kitchen sink. Having something tangible will help keep you on track.

☐ **Get insured.** If you leave your job, you can get a continuation of your health insurance for up to eighteen months through COBRA. "It's often the most convenient, but maybe not the lowest cost," CFP Jacobsmeyer says. Younger hikers can often find better deals through a broker or on the public exchanges. Either way, make sure you have insurance. "The penalties for being uninsured grow more onerous by the year," says CFP McClean. "Besides, you might need medical care along the way." If you're shopping for new insurance, try Healthcare .gov. According to John Zachary, you might be able to get government subsidies based on your prior income.

☐ **Deal with any debt.** One of the best ways to eliminate stress from your thru-hike is to minimize your financial burdens. If you have credit card debt, you might be able to talk the credit card company into new terms. According to McClean, it might require some pushing, but companies oftentimes will accept a reduced payment agreement rather than lose more money by letting their customer declare bankruptcy. Taking the extra time to pay off debt is worth it. "You are planning for this great, amazing journey. You shouldn't be worried about these obligations," says McClean. Make sure you can afford not to be.

HIKE YOUR OWN HIKE

WHY WE CHOSE SECTION HIKING

PHOTO CREDIT: PHIL HOUGH

Phil Hough and his wife, Deb Hunsicker, section-hiked the CDT in 2008, 2009, and 2010.

Deb and I are Triple Crowners. After thru-hiking the Appalachian Trail and Pacific Crest Trail, we chose to tackle the Continental Divide Trail as three sections—each 1,000 miles, and each over three consecutive summers. By doing it this way, we were better able to manage our work lives. We hiked each section during a time when we were least subjected to weather extremes or uncertainties. We didn't want to be forced to make route selections—such as the high San Juan sections—based on weather and snow conditions. We wanted to see high sections, like the San Juan Mountains, in all their wildflower glory, not covered under feet of snow. By hiking the CDT this way, we were able to have three summers' worth of long-distance adventures, and we were able to do it in a way that we could keep our jobs, manage our work lives, and manage our trail experience. By section hiking, we could decide where we wanted to be and when we wanted to be there.

—Phil "Nowhere Man" Hough

CALCULATE YOUR BUDGET

So how much money do you really need to do a thru-hike? This is an important question to answer to make sure you truly can complete your hike. Sadly, there is no perfect equation for how much a thru-hike will cost. It depends on a lot of things: your goals, what you can do without, and how long it will take you to complete your hike.

My first long thru-hike of the Appalachian Trail was the most expensive of all twenty of my long hikes. I thought camping in the woods for months would be a frugal way to travel, but I made some rookie mistakes that drove up the

Thru-hiking requires planning and budgeting before and during your hike. Kate "Drop 'N Roll" spends a zero day on the Hayduke Trail looking over maps, preparing boxes, and refueling.

sticker price on my adventure. I wasn't happy with the gear that I started with, so I ended up buying all new gear at full price at gear stores along the way. I wasn't used to camping, so I ended up spending every opportunity I could in a hotel or hostel. I didn't buy my plane ticket home until the very last minute, so I paid for a very expensive flight. Before I left for the AT, I was so focused on doing everything I could do just to start hiking the trail that I didn't think enough about money. When I discuss budgets with other accomplished thru-hikers, I realize how common it is to go over-budget—even among some of the most budget-minded people I know.

WAYS TO ESTIMATE YOUR BUDGET

Here are a few simple equations commonly used by thru-hikers as measuring sticks. They don't always add up to the same number, but will give you a ballpark range of dollars you should expect to have available.

- Minimum of $2 per mile, not including gear
- $1,200 per month, not including travel or gear
- $100 minimum per resupply town, not including travel or gear

When creating your budget, don't forget to include health care costs—medical insurance, prescriptions or OTC medicines, and post-hike physicals (especially tests for Lyme disease, if needed). Also take trail-related costs into consideration. This includes food, hotels, and travel, as well as gear replacement and shipping costs, cell phone bills, and SPOT or DeLorme (now Garmin) satellite tracker bills. Ongoing bills on the home front should also be rolled into your budget: mortgage, car bills, student loans, child support, utilities and rent, storage unit and parking space rental, and vet costs for pets that are being watched by friends or family. Consider canceling monthly or even annual subscription services, such as Netflix, magazines, and cable TV. Make sure any automatic bank transfers are covered.

Here are some more tips from financial planners.

☐ **Budget for practice runs.** "You might want to go on some trail hikes to test gear and get in shape," says Tom "Katmandu" McClean. If this is part of your plan, make sure you include the gas expenses and days off work in your thru-hike budget.

☐ **Prepare for the unexpected.** "Have a contingency plan for if you get injured," Zachary says. He recommends a 10 percent budget increase to provide wiggle room for emergencies. McClean echoes the advice: He had to spend two weeks at a hotel in Damascus resting a stress fracture during his thru-hike. And unforeseen costs aren't just about getting hurt. You may discover you need a warmer sleeping bag. At some point your shoes may become too small for your swollen feet. It's possible a resupply box won't show up, and you'll have an unexpected extra resupply to pay for.

☐ **Set aside a fun fund.** "I was surprised by how much I enjoyed the social aspect of thru-hiking the AT," says McClean. The people you meet are part of the experience, and it's easier to savor that aspect when you can participate in occasional movies or town days. And no matter how much you plan your budget at home, you will have a hard time saying "no" to food and a hotel when you finally make it into town after a hard day and are hungry and wet. Budget well for times like that—or set up a plan that will satisfy your need for food and warmth without hurting the bank. It's not uncommon for a hiker to want to eat two entrees while in town. Don't budget based on your appetite now. You're going to be one hungry animal later.

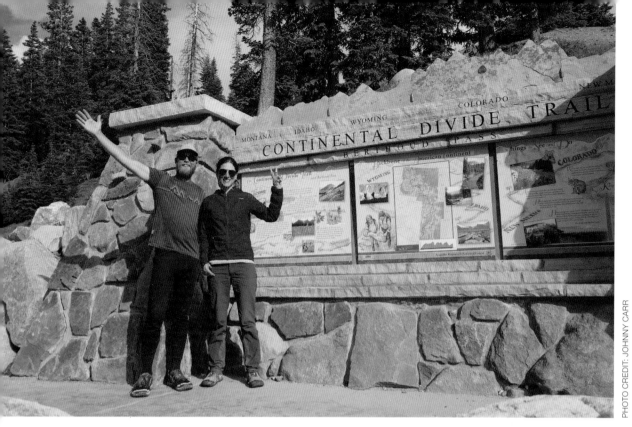

Getting your finances organized before thru-hiking will make you more relaxed on the trail.

☐ **Account for post-hike expenses.** McClean recommends including a post-hike unemployment period (unless you're taking a sabbatical) in the trail budget. It's important to save up money for when you finish your hike too. It may take some time to find a new job when you return. Try to leave yourself a cushion to cover, at the very least, one month's cost of living when you return. If you plan to change careers or fields after your hike, it make take even longer to find a new job. This includes money for a housing deposit, rent, utility turn-on fees, and a car if you don't have one waiting for you. "If you're a businessperson looking for a job, you might also need to shop for a new suit. A lot of us lose weight on the trail," he says.

WAYS TO LOWER YOUR THRU-HIKING BUDGET

Since my expensive first trip on the Appalachian Trail, I've learned the hard way how to keep my thru-hiking budget down. For me, long hikes are made of emotional ups and downs, so splurging now and then is essential to keeping my sanity. Much like dieting, the trick to budgeting on the trail (and off trail) is never to feel like you are denying yourself an experience. Instead, it requires making

A hiking parter can increase your confidence on tricky terrain.

choices that enrich your life (while opting out of the extras that don't bring you maximum joy). For example, finding a good hiking partner is a great way to save money, and it can sometimes make your trip more enjoyable. On the other hand, an extra beer at the bar while in town has diminishing marginal returns and isn't going to maximize your joy.

☐ **Share gear with other hikers.** Having a partner to share gear, like a tent and stove, can be a big advantage—provided the two of you don't have a falling out. There is risk in sharing big gear items. But, in general, splitting bulk purchases (such as boxes of Ziploc bags or Clif Bars) with other hikers makes for a more efficient use of everyone's funds.

☐ **Stay out of town.** Town time is money. Staying at a hostel or splitting a motel room with other hikers definitely lowers your budget, but the best way to save money is to skip the bed altogether. By camping close to town, you can do laundry, pay a few dollars to use the shower at a hostel, resupply at the store or post

office, and be back on the trail by afternoon. For those times when you do stop in town, go through a mental checklist. Is the weather miserable? Are you sick? Are there other hikers who want to share a room? Does it seem like a valuable experience to stay at this particular hostel or town? If you can't say "yes" to at least one of those questions, reconsider the pricey room and stick with the tent you've already paid for.

☐ **Avoid restaurants.** Of course, the lure of a lumpy hostel bed is nothing compared to the siren call of real food. I know it's hard, but if you really want to keep a tight budget it's better to walk past those greasy spoons to the grocery store. When you do eat out, remember that breakfast is the cheapest meal and doesn't (usually) tempt you with a beer menu. Similarly, comparison shopping has its place even in tiny trail towns, where Dollar General often sells the same instant potatoes, oatmeal, or pasta that the grocery store carries—only for a lower price.

☐ **Ignore the party scene.** The AT and PCT are social trails, and after a long week of hiking, it's tempting to get a beer with other hikers inside a warm, bug-free bar. But alcohol is an expensive way to make up for a caloric deficit—and it increases the odds that you'll get a room for the night. You don't have to live like a monk to stay on budget, but set yourself a limit. If you must buy beer, get it at a grocery or liquor store to save a lot of money (but remember to consume it some place legal and preferably indoors—not the park).

☐ **Shop smart for gear.** A little research can save you a lot of money. Check out hiking forums, read gear reviews, and visit physical hiking stores before you decide what you want to buy, so you aren't spending double the money replacing that gear mid-trail. (For much more on choosing gear, see chapter 6.) After you narrow down your gear list, wait for deals, keeping an eye on sales and used gear exchanges. Or try making your own gear. Homemade alcohol stoves are growing in popularity and cost only the price of a tin can (but check restrictions on them in certain wilderness areas before you bring them). But you don't have to stop at stoves if you want to get crafty. Several online sites sell lightweight materials to build your own backpack, sleeping bag, and tarp. A whole world of instructional videos, blogs, and books is available to help you get started. (Note: Make sure to test any homemade gear before relying on it.) And know that making some items (like sewing a pack) takes a lot of skill and time; if you go this route, realize that what you save in money, you'll be investing in time.

☐ **Ignore marketing.** The entrance of any outdoor store is replete with shiny things you can do without. You don't need a pricey first-aid kit from an outfitter

Karluk the Dog has been Whitney "Allgood" LaRuffa's hiking partner for many day hikes and shorter backpacking trips, but, as a responsible dog owner, Allgood knew the CDT was too long and tough for them to hike together. Allgood made arrangements for Karluk to stay at home for five months while he was on the CDT.

when you can make one for free out of your bathroom first-aid supply. You don't need a backcountry French press or plastic wine glasses, and an old Swiss army knife is nearly as useful as any new multi-tool (or better yet—just use a razor blade). Instead of buying two different temperature-rated bags, buy a single 20°F bag and get a silk liner for the cold months. Although there is a lot of cool camping gear on the market, most of it costs money you don't need to spend and adds weight you don't need to carry.

☐ **Don't spend a lot on clothing.** Unlike high-tech tents or down sleeping bags, which often deliver worthwhile performance gains for the extra money, low-priced hiking clothes often work almost as well as the more expensive competition. Used gear stores, thrift stores, and box stores such as Walmart or Target have wicking and synthetic hiking shirts for under $20 that will work almost as well as that $80 shirt from a high-end brand.

☐ **Trust people (within reason).** You can't build a budget around people's kindness—but you can open yourself up to it. The fact is, people want to help travelers. You'll be offered rides, food, and spare gear. People will open their houses to you. You need to use your best judgment in these situations, and it will feel strange at first and maybe a little uncomfortable. Just keep in mind that when someone offers you something on the trail, it's a gift that you will eventually return by paying it forward to another traveler. Donating $20 to stay with a trail angel who will give you a roof, feed you, and do your laundry is a lot less expensive than paying $50 for a hotel room plus $5 for laundry plus $20 on food. It's not only good for your budget, it's also good for your faith in humankind.

SET THE HOME FRONT TO AUTOPILOT

Imagine the thrill of reaching the crest of a hill on your hike, realizing your phone has service, and then seeing a dire text message from a friend. Disaster has struck at home, and you need to return immediately to sort it out. Whether the pipes froze, your cat got sick, or your neighbor wants a new fence, your needing to leave the trail to deal with it is often preventable. It just requires working with your support team before you go to make sure that they have the resources and information to

Pets on the Trail

If you decide to take your pet on the trail with you, realize that almost all dogs that start thru-hikes don't make it the whole way. Responsible pet owners realize that a thru-hike isn't usually a dog's dream as much as the owner's dream. Work your schedule around your dog's needs. After all, Fido didn't make the decision to come out here, you did. If it gets to a point where the miles, terrain, or trail tread is too tough on your pup, it's probably time for him to go home, chow down on food, and enjoy town life while you finish your trek.

Before going on the trail with your pet, budget for its food, potential medical bills, replacement doggie gear, any kenneling or shuttling that may occur (for example, national parks do not allow dogs, but many kennels will shuttle your dog around the park for a fee), and for the high likelihood that your dog may need transportation back home while you're still on the trail. Hotel rates tend to be higher for people with pets, so factor that into your budget too. For more information on distance hiking with your dog, visit allgoodsk9adventures.com take care of almost any disaster that could happen while you're gone. Make sure you consider and secure all potential issues before leaving home.

If you have a pet, find a friend or family member to care for your animal. Make sure you leave any meds or special feeding instructions, as well as emergency numbers and protocol, including what to do if your pet gets sick, who your vet is, and limits on pet medical bills. Discuss before you leave who is responsible for expenses, and leave enough money to cover all costs.

For longer hikes, many hikers move out of their home or apartment completely. Others rent out their home or apartment while they are gone. Renting out or subletting your place can be a good way to get some passive income while you hike—or at least make sure you will have a place to come back to when you're done. One problem here is if you quit your hike, you may be homeless for a while. (Or it can be another way to make sure you don't quit!) If you live with a spouse or other family members, make sure they are prepared to properly take care of the home (including plumbing, heating, air conditioning, etc.) and care for your things (including pets and houseplants) while you are gone. This may involve leaving phone numbers of trusted repair people, and so forth.

If you're planning to give up an apartment or move out of your house completely while you are on a longer hike, consider giving your belongings away or putting them in storage. Find houseplants a new home or someone willing to water them while you are away. If you are renting your house out, consider renting it furnished so you don't have to deal with moving as much stuff. (You'll still probably want to store your clothes and other personal items elsewhere.) If you don't have a friend or family member willing to keep your stuff in an attic or basement, factor the cost of storage into your hike's budget.

If someone is taking care of your bills for you while you're away, leave them cash before you go on your trip. Many banks, phone companies, and other places allow you to set up autopay for your bills. This is a good way to make sure you get your bills in on time without having to rush to town to pay by phone.

LEGAL MATTERS

Long-distance hiking has an extremely low rate of fatality—especially compared to almost any other outdoor activity. That said, leaving for your trip is a good excuse to get your will in order in case something happens to you out there. If you're going on a longer trip, you may consider giving someone you trust power of attorney. Think about life situations and legal issues you deal with on a regular basis. Do you own your business or real estate? If you can think of a good reason, it may be worth talking with an attorney to figure out how to set this up.

Whether you start solo or with another hiker, be prepared to form some very close friendships during your thru-hike.

In summer 2015 I pioneered a 300-mile route across the Wasatch Range in Utah. Two days into the trip, I turned on my phone and realized I had cell service when I saw a text in all caps from my boyfriend: "CALL ME ASAP. EMERGENCY." While I was gone, I'd left my car with my boyfriend. He was co-listed on the insurance, but the car was registered in my name. The night before, the car had been towed. The towing company refused to release the car to him because it was registered in my name. I had to backtrack to the nearest road, hitchhike to town, and find a notary willing to sign a letter releasing the car to him. What a hassle! He was lucky I had cell reception and could deal with it quickly. I should have thought about giving him power of attorney before I left.

RALLY YOUR TEAM

Thru-hiking is rarely a truly individual pursuit. Whether you hike solo or with a partner depends first and foremost on whether you have a partner you want to hike with, followed by how experienced you are, how hard the trail you chose is, and what the conditions are like. Time spent alone on the trail helps you connect more to nature, see more wildlife, and practice your outdoor skills without relying on others. I personally love hiking solo because it gives me the freedom to

A good hiking partner can share gear weight and help with trail tasks like navigation.

set my own pace, decide on my own breaks and camp, and really enjoy nature. If you're hiking a trail that gets a lot of traffic, like the AT, PCT, or John Muir Trail (JMT), chances are that even if you start hiking solo, by a week in you're going to meet some great people—some of whom you may even want to hike with for hundreds or thousands of miles. I've met some of my closest friends that way.

Starting a thru-hike solo gives you the advantage to choose your friends and hiking partners along the way, and not to feel too bad if you ditch them to spend an extra day in town. While many folks are afraid to start alone, the reality is that hiking trails is statistically a lot safer than walking around cities. Thru-hikers create a bond—we become family. If you're hiking solo and you fall or something happens to you, if you're on a major trail, thru-hikers you don't even know will go to extremes to make sure you're safe and all right.

Having a partner on the trail means having someone who can share the gear weight, or who can help out in a rescue if you get injured or sick, or who can double-check your navigation to make sure you stay on course. And, of course, it's always fun to have someone to share the adventure with. If you decide to go with a partner, make sure it's someone you know really well—not a random someone you met on the Internet or a friend of a friend who also happens to want to hike your trail. Hiking with a bad partner can sometimes be more harmful than almost anything that could happen to a solo hiker. You didn't come to the woods for drama, and sticking with a bad hiking partner can be psychologically and emotionally painful.

A caveat for couples: I often see romantic partners hiking together where one person is not considerate of the other person's needs, fitness, skill, or comfort level. These couples often argue loudly in the backcountry—impacting other hikers' serene experiences. The trip is clearly not good for their relationship. If you go out as a couple, prioritize your relationship over any other goal on the trip—including walking every mile and finishing. If you're not willing to do this, don't go together—many outdoorsy couples actually decide to do separate hiking trips so they can enjoy the woods in their own style and avoid conflict with their partner.

PLAN FOR PARTNERSHIP SUCCESS

If you decide to go on a thru-hike with a partner—romantic or otherwise—spend a few weeks or months having meetings to talk about your expectations for the trip. Aside from familiarizing yourself with each other's skill levels and what to do in emergencies, ask questions like:

- Are you and your partner sticking together no matter what?
- Are you going to be with each other 24-7, or meet every night in camp?
- What if your hiking partner befriends someone you don't like?
- What if one of you hikes at a much faster pace?
- What if you're ready to camp and the other person isn't?

Writing down your questions and answers, brainstorming scenarios, and having honest conversations before you go will set you and your partner up for a better trip.

PICK YOUR SUPPORT TEAM

Whether you hike solo or with a partner, you'll need a support team back at home to help you logistically, physically, mentally, and emotionally. Your team doesn't have to be just one person, though it could be. On my first hikes, my dad sent my resupply boxes, but my boyfriend was the person I called on the hard days. A strong support team ensures that your journey is about more than yourself. Your support team will see your emails, photos, and blogs while you're on the trail and start to believe that they could do it too. But they'll also call your BS if you want to quit. With loved ones' support, you'll be less tempted to quit. Here are the key support team roles to fill with one or more people.

☐ **Resupply support.** This person can send you gear, food, or the latest issue of your favorite magazine when you're in the middle of nowhere on the trail. (See chapter 5 for more on resupplies.) This person should be good with details and someone you'll trust with your money.

☐ **Home front support.** This person will watch your dog, cat, plants, and car while you're gone, make sure your bills are paid, and deal with that jury duty letter. Again, this needs to be a core, trustworthy team member.

☐ **Emotional support.** This person will cheer you up on a hard day and his or her excitement about what you're doing will fuel you through the lows. The best people are those who are good at answering their phone and email, who rarely go on trips, and who are generally enthusiastic about your hike. Look for positive people who make you laugh. You may want to find more than one person who can do this.

GATHER YOUR SELECTED TEAM

Your support team plays a huge factor in your success. You'll rely on them for big favors, of course, but that doesn't mean the work and appreciation needs to flow in just one direction. Once you've decided on your team, you need to employ some tactics to get them on board and to show your appreciation once they've committed.

Start early—feel out for potential team members at least three months in advance. Make an initial "ask" as early as you can. The best team members are the ones who offer before you can ask. Sit down with each team member individually and go over what kind of tasks they will be responsible for. You may want to make a list and give it to them. Make sure they are clear about their responsibilities and willing and able to do them. If not, find someone else. Make sure they have all the resources they need at least a week before you head out on the trail, including important phone numbers, worst-case scenarios, and, when applicable, cash money. Make sure they have a copy of your itinerary, including important addresses along your trip. And make sure they feel confident they will be able to do their part on the team.

Once you've gathered a committed team, throw a party for your team before you go. Stay in touch while you're on the trail. Let them know your blog address or where you'll share photos. Send them postcards from the trail. Call regularly to keep them abreast of whether you are on schedule. Give a slideshow and make them dinner when you get back.

In a few cases, friends and family may look at your hike as crazy and refuse to support you. If you don't have family, friends, or partners willing and able to support you, know that there still is a way to make your dreams come true. With good planning on your part, you can do many of the functions of a support team remotely. You can also pay companies or individuals that specialize in resupply logistics. Lastly, and perhaps most importantly, attend a long distance hiking community event at least a year in advance of your trip. It's quite likely you will befriend someone there who has walked in your shoes and will be willing to help with your support.

KEEP YOUR TEAM ON BOARD—AND IN THE KNOW

A big, long hike isn't just tough on the hiker—it's also a challenge for those left at home. But with proper planning and communication, even parents of young kids can complete one. If others are relying on you financially, make sure you have plenty saved up to take care of them while you are gone, or have passive income that can help support them. But money in the bank isn't the only thing your loved ones are going to miss about you. Making sure that others know they are loved even when you are away is important, and being as interested in their day-to-day life as you are excited to tell them about your trail life is key. Here's how to get—and keep—your team on board.

COMMUNICATE EARLY AND OFTEN

Communication is important both on the trail—how many days will the family go without a phone call, and what should they do if that deadline passes?—and at home. Even though you as a hiker might be 100 percent invested—and aren't asking for permission—don't spring the idea of a thru-hike on your family. (This goes for adult children and their parents as much as for spouses and kids.) Involve them in it from the beginning. Start casually mentioning the idea and buying some guidebooks. A good way to bring it up is by sharing popular (or more realistic) books or movies about thru-hiking. Show your loved ones why this is important to you.

Often the biggest concern from family and friends is safety. Validate and quell concerns by explaining what a thru-hike is, where you are going, and how you'll stay in touch. Let them know that this is not the unknown. Others—in many cases thousands or tens of thousands—have done this before.

Sometimes it's nice to rest and replenish calories in town like these hikers in Stehekin, WA.

PREPARE WELL—AND VISIBLY

Demonstrate just how prepared you are by getting loved ones involved with food shipments and any extra research you need. Show them planning documents, or get a wall map and show them how knowledgeable and well-prepared you are for this journey. When your family sees you're not just walking out the back door with a hobo bindle and a pocketknife, they'll likely feel better about what you're attempting.

GET TO THE HEART OF THE REAL CONCERNS

Even after educating family and friends, you might still find hesitation and negativity from others. It's important to realize that their negativity is most likely stemming from their concern for the relationship and their fears about what will happen while you're gone and when you come back. Talk with your partner about what his true worries are and how you will handle that before, during, and after the hike. Help him understand what he will get out of this—such as less conflict in the relationship in the long run—and why he should buy in.

ACCOMMODATE WHEN POSSIBLE

Ted "Scarecrow" Warren completed the Triple Crown (PCT, AT, and CDT) while married with children (his youngest was just three and a half during his AT hike in 2001). Ted and his wife, Carole, a high school math teacher, knew that his hikes would work best over the summer when Carole and the kids were out of school. Ted planned accordingly by starting a few weeks later than normally recommended, so that he was gone when Carole was home for the summer. You may find that splitting a long trail up into a section hike and being gone for shorter periods over several years may be another way to be flexible with your time while still achieving your dream.

If the trip is what you really need at this moment in your life, overall it will benefit everyone. "It's not my dream or goal, but if he is happy achieving this dream, that's a benefit for the whole family," Carole said of her husband's three thru-hikes. "And I was more than happy to hold down the fort. Don't get me wrong—there were times I was frustrated that he was not home to help with one thing or another, but I had to remind myself that this is a blink in a lifetime. Ted came home from each of these trails fulfilled and inspired to achieve more great things."

Plus, as Carole stressed to her kids, their father couldn't do this without their support. "Daddy wouldn't be a successful Triple Crown hiker without you," she'd tell her kids. "Each of us had a piece of his success. He was the shining star, but it wouldn't have happened without your support."

As the hiker, be appreciative and show it. Ted found that validating and acknowledging his own feelings about the hike—as well as those of his family members while he was away—was a way to keep the communication honest and authentic. "It is when you don't check in, or say a simple thank you, or offer guidance when asked, that things may fall apart."

PLAN VISITS—AND FOR EMERGENCIES

Maybe your family wants to join in for a few days of hiking, or perhaps they are more comfortable meeting you in a town. Whatever the location, planning trips that are fun and accessible for all parties is key to an invested visit. Know that you might not be completing as many miles as normal with a visitor in tow. Find

Liz preparing for the Chinook Trail, Columbia River Gorge, Oregon, and Washington, 2014

a good way to compromise: Hike a few miles during the day, but stay in a hotel at night, or have visitors meet you from town to town while you continue to hike and the visitor explores the surrounding cities.

Emergencies, deaths, births—events will happen during a months-long trek. Discuss ahead of time what counts as a "get off the trail"–level incident. Ted knew he wouldn't come home for emergencies or deaths of distant relatives, but committed to coming home immediately for any crisis relating to his kids. Especially if you have a lot of people depending on you, be mentally prepared that a pause in your trek might be necessary. Just know that the trail is always there, waiting to be finished.

TAKE ADVANTAGE OF TECHNOLOGY

Before you start your hike, invest in a camera that has WiFi built in, or get a WiFi-enabled memory card. That way, when Internet is available, you'll have an easier time sharing your photos and keeping loved ones in the loop. Also, get a satellite messenger device, such as a SPOT or a DeLorme InReach, which allows you to send out location information even when you don't have cell service. Ted clipped his SPOT onto his backpack while hiking (SPOT devices also have emergency rescue buttons); each night after he set up his tent, he'd send out a location message letting his family and friends know where he was and that he was okay.

AT HOME SUPPORT AND POSITIVITY

Remember those chain crafts back in elementary school? Carole uses them every time her husband heads on an adventure. She and the kids make a paper loop for every day that their dad is away (with different months represented in different colors) and connect them in a (very) long chain. Then, to keep up with their family dinnertime traditions, each night they remove a link and write a high and low about their day on it, to share with their father the next time they chat with him. "It visually shows the time ticking down," Carole said, noting that it helped when the kids were young, and still helps now that they are teenagers. Carole also kept up the positivity around the house. "I did not speak negatively about Ted's hikes and I would never let any negativity into where my kids would hear it," Carole said. Instead, she looked at his hike as just another adventure for the family. She and her kids sent Ted care packages, talked with him every five or six days, and tried to stay busy with fun trips and adventures themselves.

THE IMPORTANCE OF PLANNING

When I started my second hike on the AT in 2011, I was pretty broke. I had this dream to hike the AT again, but I knew I had to make every last dollar get me as many miles as it could. By training a lot before I left and being smart about planning my budget before I even stepped foot on the trail, I was able to manufacture one of the most fun hikes I've ever done, and on a super limited budget. Thanks to all that preparation, I even set a speed record on that hike, and completed it with one-third the budget of my first thru-hike on the AT. Good planning can help remove some of the frustrating unknowns from your hike, like the time I ended up sleeping at a halfway house. Don't worry—even the best planned hike will still provide plenty of surprises to keep you on your toes.

IDEAL PLANNING TIMELINE

Here's what your timeline for planning a thru-hike would look like in an ideal world. This is a rough sketch that should work for most hikers, but will differ from hiker to hiker depending on your responsibilities. For example, some aspects of a thru-hike (such a getting your legal issues in order) may take a lot longer for a mid-career business owner than a college student. Use this timeline as guidance, but don't panic if you're not on schedule—you can definitely plan a great hike in less time. I planned my first AT hike in less than a month, for example.

MORE THAN ONE YEAR OUT

As soon as you can, mention (or at least hint) to your spouse or family that you may want to one day hike this particular trail. Watch some hiking movies and read some hiking books. Sketch out a rough budget (see "Calculate Your Budget" in this chapter) and calculate out how long it will take you to save the money you need. Start saving. Resist the temptation to buy gear for your trip. Finally, hike. It doesn't matter if it is a day hike or backpacking trip, the more time you spend in nature, the better prepared you will be for spending a lot of time in it. Join a Meetup Group, the Sierra Club, or local outdoors group like the Mountaineers or Mazamas that takes hikes regularly.

ONE YEAR OUT

Take classes like Wilderness First Aid, Snow Travel, Map and Compass Navigation, and read as much as you can about outdoors skills and safety. (See the Resources for a list of helpful material.) Read trail blogs to get an idea of what day-to-day life on your trail is like. Start looking at gear lists of others who have hiked your trail, and research specific items you'd like to buy. Resist the temptation to buy anything yet. Use this time to get opinions about specific models and to hunt down physical versions of the gear you want in stores or at hiking festivals. If you can, take a short practice hike or backpacking trip on your dream trail. Attend hiking festivals like Trail Days. Keep saving money. Do a backpacking trip. The best training is at least one three- to four-day backpacking trip the summer before you go. Plan your job exit strategy. Keep open communication going with family and friends.

SIX MONTHS OUT

Order maps and guidebooks. Decide on an approximate start/end date (more on this in chapter 4) and discuss ideal timing with family and friends. Get permits and apply for visas if necessary. Consider making reservations for shuttles to your trailhead and your hotel/hostel for the night before you start. Ground transit and hostels for popular trails fill up as many as 6 months in advance. Sketch out a detailed budget with your family (see "Calculate Your Budget" in this chapter) and keep saving money. Go on walks daily, even if they are just in your neighborhood. Use a pedometer or fitness tracker (like a Fitbit) and write down or use a phone or Web-based platform to track your progress. Make it a goal to up your weekly average. See chapter 2 for tips on how other hikers have found time to integrate hike training into their busy lives. If you've made some decisions on specific models of gear you would like, start looking for deals on the model or on used gear forums.

FIVE MONTHS OUT

Flesh out your itinerary. Ask friends and family to be a part of your support team. This will give you important info on how much you can count on them for resupply. Decide where you may want to resupply. Identify tasks that need to be completed to get your home front ready, especially those that may require getting others involved (resupply person, pet sitter, house sitter, etc.). Start carrying a pack on your daily walks. You don't need to buy any fancy new gear yet—your old-school backpack should do just fine.

FOUR MONTHS OUT

Continue to reach out to friends and family and ask if they will be part of your support team. Tell them a little about your trip, hope that they offer to help, and, if they don't, find someone else. Talk with your family/spouse about contingency plans in case of emergencies when you're gone. Continue carrying a pack on your daily walks. Add some minor weight to your pack (5 pounds or less). Order any gear on your list that you haven't been able to find used. Ultralight gear made specifically for thru-hiking by cottage companies can take up to 12 weeks. Walk in the shoes you plan to wear on trail.

THREE MONTHS OUT

Get the last of your gear so you can start practicing with it—even if you are just setting up in your living room. Research health insurance options for when you leave your job. Many hikers find that travel insurance covers their trip. If applicable, make sure your plans to vacate your home and find a replacement are secure. Get your legal and financial issues sorted. As you get closer to your departure date, you don't want to have to worry about this. Buy the plane ticket to the trail location. Increase the amount of weight on your daily walks to 10 pounds.

TWO MONTHS OUT

Practice setting up your shelter and breaking it down. Aim to get it up in 5 minutes. Pack up all your gear before your daily walk. Go on your walk and then unpack all your gear. This trains you on the best way to pack your pack, as well as how to pack and unpack quickly. Cull any gear in your system that you think is less important. Research modifications that you can make to your gear so it suits you better. Replace anything that does not work for you. If you plan to use a mail drop resupply strategy, develop a list of all the things to pack in your mail drop boxes and start ordering food in bulk. (You get a much better price this way.) Do more backpacking or a simulated backpacking trip.

ONE MONTH OUT

Give important contact information and contingency plans to your support people. Make sure you like your itinerary. Share it with your support people and make sure all their questions are answered. Put together your mail drops—the resupply boxes you will have sent to you over the course of your trip (for more on this, see chapter 5). If you haven't already talked to your employer about leaving, this is a good time to do that. Cancel monthly services or subscriptions you will not use while you are gone. Set up autopay for bills while you're on your trip. Continue practicing shelter setup, packing your pack, and walking.

ONE WEEK OUT

Move the last of your stuff into storage. Throw your support team a party that doubles as a going away party. Hand over plants, pets, cars, and keys to your place to your support people.

NIGHT BEFORE YOU LEAVE HOME

Pack your backpack with your gear list next to you. Check off everything on the list as you put it in your pack to make sure you do not leave anything behind. Check that you have all the maps, guidebooks, permits, and databook info you need for the first section of the hike. Pack the food you need to complete the first section. Make sure you have plane tickets, hostel reservations, and anything needed to get to your trailhead.

DAY BEFORE YOU START HIKING

Unpack your pack and make sure you have everything you need. If you see anything that is missing, try to replace it. Many hostels or trail angels near trailheads offer to take hikers on last-minute runs to REI or Walmart. Charge your electronics and make sure that cameras, satellite trackers, external batteries, and such are at full charge. Fill up your water bottles. Make sure you have the food you need to complete your first section. Pack your pack completely with everything but the clothes you plan to wear the next day. Send home the clothes you wore on the plane or any gear you decide you won't need. Get a good night's rest.

THE MORNING OF YOUR HIKE

Shower—it may be the last time for a while. Eat a good breakfast. Pack extra snacks and drinks for your ride out to the trailhead—you don't want to start your hike hungry. Leave civilization feeling hydrated. Don't forget your electronics chargers or your hiking poles. Get ready to make new friends, see new places, and start the adventure of a lifetime.

Don't worry if you are behind schedule. It's not likely to be your biggest obstacle on the trail.

WHAT IF I'M ALREADY BEHIND SCHEDULE?

Behind schedule already? Don't worry. Simply by reading this book, you will be a lot more prepared than most hikers. The ideal timeline schedule allows you to leisurely put together a plan for your hike. But that doesn't mean it can't be done in less time. I planned for my first Appalachian Trail hike in one month—but it was three weeks of research and prep without interruption (though as noted earlier, I made lots of costly mistakes).

Many hikers without a lot of time to plan ahead opt to "plan on the go" and only do what's needed to complete the first section. This still requires some prep, but can take a lot of pressure off figuring out your exact resupplies. After you've hiked the first part of the trail, you will likely take a zero day (a rest day) anyway—that's a prime time to plan out the next few sections of your hike. If you have less time to prepare, here's what you should prioritize:

- **Permits:** These take the longest to get, and land managers' quotas may already have been met. Check this first before you do any more planning. Make phone calls instead of sending emails. Be prepared to call (or in some cases, fax) every day until you can get a permit.

- **Trail-specific guidebooks and maps:** The more research and data you have on your trail now, the better prepared you will be. Start reading books and studying maps—especially about the first part of your trip.

- **Transportation:** Get your plane tickets, shuttle reservations, and hotel/hostel reservations early, as these can be completely booked up to 6 months before thru-hiking season.

- **Support team:** If you need a support person to help you, talk with him or her now.

- **Fitness:** Depending on your chosen trail and how quickly you want to do it, you want to start training now. On most trails you can ramp up your miles per day as you get stronger. Start training—but don't overdo it. There's no way to make up six months of training in three weeks—that's only asking for injury. The physical activities I've included in chapter 2 are a good guide for what you should do if you're leaving soon. Accept and plan that you will start your hike significantly slower than other hikers and realize you'll make up the miles later in the trip when you have walked yourself into shape.

- **Gear:** Start doing gear research now. Many accomplished hikers put their trail-specific gear lists online. Many garage grown companies that specialize in ultralight gear for thru-hikers have a long wait list (some even make gear to order). Find out how long it may take to get your ideal gear. If there's a twelve-week wait on your first choice, you may have to settle for a second choice item that ships immediately. You also may end up spending more than you might have if you'd had more time to scope out deals and sales.

- **Resupplies:** If you're leaving very soon, I suggest resupplying locally if at all possible and not planning to mail yourself anything. (See chapter 5, "Resupplies.")

- **Route plan:** You'll learn how to set up an itinerary in chapter 4. First time hikers often spend too much time planning food and resupplies. Spend more planning time on the first leg or two of your trip now. You can do planning for later in the trip while you're on the trail during a rest day.

- **Study up:** Read everything you can about your trail. The more you know about your trail and its unique challenges, the better prepared you will be (in terms of gear and physical and mental skills) to take on the obstacles.

"Bubs" is in peak shape to hike the Hayduke Trail across Utah.

Chapter 2

PREPPING PHYSICAL FITNESS

On my first thru-hike of the Appalachian Trail, I met a man who weighed 300 pounds. He was attempting to walk to Maine from Georgia. Some days, he hiked 5 miles, sometimes less. He didn't know if he would make it the whole way, but that wasn't what mattered. He was out there. He was taking it step by step. And he was going after his goal. This is what I love the most about thru-hiking. There are so few sports where people of all shapes and sizes feel comfortable and accepted, and believe that their goal is within reach.

That being said, being physically fit prior to hitting the trail has major advantages. It will save you some pain and huffing and puffing on your journey. Being fit before hitting the trail also reduces your chances of injury, which can take you off the trail or cost you extra money. But most importantly, being fit increases your chances of success.

Part of preparing for the trail is preparing yourself physically. Here is some helpful information to get you ready.

Prepare your body for walking all day with a big pack.

PREPARE YOUR BODY

So here's the million dollar question: Do you need to be in peak physical fitness to complete a long trail? Well, no. You don't need six-pack abs to thru-hike. In fact, sometimes starting with a little weight to lose can be a benefit, because you won't have to worry as much about losing too much weight. But you do need to be strong. Exactly how in shape you need to be depends on the trail you are doing. On some trails that have lots of water and campsites and a large window to finish (think the AT), you can start the trail pretty out of shape and walk fewer than 5 miles a day from shelter to shelter. Of course, you won't finish the whole trail in one season this way and it's going to hurt a lot (if you don't get injured before that), but that may not matter to you. On trails like the PCT, you may need to walk 16–21 miles your first day to reach the first water source—or else be fit enough to carry two days' worth of water. If you're not fast but need to make big miles, you can always put in longer days if you have the endurance to do so. No matter what trail you hike, though, the fitter you are when you start, the happier and more comfortable you will be.

CONFESSIONS OF AN OUT-OF-SHAPE HIKER

PHOTO CREDIT: WILLIAM "PI" MURPHY

Bill "Pi" Murphy of Ann Arbor, Michigan, tells the story of starting his first hike while pretty out of shape.

When I started my first attempt at a thru-hike, I was at a fitness level best described as "North American Computer Programmer." As for my diet, when I expressed my intention to hike the whole Appalachian Trail at the local McDonald's—which I visited about five times a week—one of the clerks expressed concern that I would get lost and never make it back to that McDonald's. In part because of the shape I was in, I only made it some 373 miles before picking up a stress fracture in my right foot. And then another 20 or so painful miles to get to a road crossing before I quit. If you start a long trail in similar shape, you aren't being nice to yourself.

The Appalachian Trail can be started with 6- and 8-mile days that roller coaster steeply up and down hills between shelters. If you're southbound, the first day is a climb 5,000 feet up a mountain and then back down, soon followed by the 100-mile wilderness. It's even a rougher start for PCT hikers: The PCT begins with a 16- to 21-mile-long waterless stretch.

If you want to be nice to yourself, get in shape before the hike starts. Get to where an 8- or 10-mile walk on a Saturday afternoon leaves you wanting a few more miles on Sunday. Once you're on a thru-hike, you'll have all day to hike. So if you can fit in 8 or 10 miles in 3 or 4 hours without a pack, then it's likely that the first 16 or 20 miles needed on the PCT will be possible given the whole day to get it done. Later thru-hikes have taught me that even being in marathon-ready shape isn't the same as being in trail shape. No matter how fit, it's likely you'll be a bit sore—or worse—for the first few weeks on the trail. Around week three your muscles will feel better, but it isn't until week four or five that your tendons and bones will have caught up. So hold back when you first start to feel good around the end of the third week. Back to my first thru-hike: Six weeks after leaving the trail to heal up, on my second attempt and with lighter gear, I completed my first thru-hike.

—Bill "Pi" Murphy

Super hikers don't just have strong muscles, but strong feet, tendons, bones, and ligaments.

TOUGHEN YOUR FEET

I always tell prospective hikers that the best way to train for a hike is by hiking (or walking). Although running is great for cardio, some hikers find it develops muscles that you don't need walking and your body just starts eating away once you're on your trip.

Get a pedometer, Fitbit, or other fitness tracker and start writing down your mileage at the end of the day. Over a six-month period, try to ramp up mileage per day by at least one additional mile each week—even if this means walking laps in your house. Walk on trails or uneven surfaces to prepare physically and mentally for obstacles such as rocks, roots, or branches in the trail. If you're going for a walk around your neighborhood, try to walk on grass or lawn. This strengthens your ankles and legs more than simply walking on sidewalk.

Go for training walks in the rain or on windy days—even just around your neighborhood—to prepare physically and mentally for what to do when the conditions get tough. It will also teach you how to dress and layer your clothing during less-than-ideal conditions.

PHOTO CREDIT: LIZ THOMAS

Strong ankles and core will help keep your balance on unsteady ground, as Brian "Mr. Gorbachev" Davidson shows here on the West Highland Way.

Train in the brand, model, and size of shoes you plan to use for your hike. This can help break in your shoes to prevent blisters, or reveal that those particular shoes are not a good choice for a long hike.

BUILD ANKLE AND CORE STRENGTH

A strong core helps with balance and stability as well as your pace on the trail. Strong feet and ankles are important too; foot and ankle injuries are among the most common injuries that take people off the trail for good. Try the exercises on pages 311–313, or substitute others you know and like.

Public stairways can be a great way to train for elevation gain if you live in a city and can't make it to the mountains.

A Bosu ball helps you work on your core and ankle strength at the same time. A free substitute is standing on one foot for an extended period, then standing on your other foot. You'll feel your ankle wobble a little at first, but as your ankle and core get stronger, it'll become easier. It seems silly, but this "exercise" can be done while you're standing in line or greeting a friend on the street.

TRAIN FOR CARRYING WEIGHT

There is a big difference between walking 10 miles with and without a pack. Your back, core, and shoulders need to adjust to having the weight of a pack on your back all day. Start by walking with an empty pack. The next week, add a small amount (5 pounds or so) to your pack. Ramp it up each week in small intervals.

You can add weight to your pack using actual gear, or by using water bottles, rice bags, or sandbags. You can also use dumbbells, but they don't distribute weight across the whole pack as well. I carry a small weighted day pack wherever I go in town—shopping, on errands, and during my commute. It can be a bit uncomfortable and you may get some looks, but it's a great way to sneak some

Training before you hit the trail increases endurance and strength during your hike while reducing chances of injury.

training into an otherwise busy schedule. Many hikers train by walking during lunch breaks with weighted packs or ankle weights.

If you have your gear ahead of time, try doing your walking exercises with a fully loaded pack. At the beginning of each exercise, pack your pack as you would on the trail. When you're done, unpack your pack. This will help you find an efficient way to pack your pack and increase your pack-up speed.

TRAIN FOR ELEVATION GAIN

Training for elevation gain can be hard—especially if you live someplace without mountains. Walking hills—even short ones—and repeating the climb several times is the best way to train. If you have access to a treadmill or stair climber, these are solid substitutes. You can also use public stairways, like those found in a parking garage, or even the stairs in your own home. If you don't have access to these machines or want to train in your home, consider doing stair step-ups. I've enjoyed them in my training, and all you need is a step stool. And you can even do this exercise while watching TV. Aim for at least 2,000 feet of elevation gain per week, or more depending on your trail.

PHOTO CREDIT: HEATHER ANDERSON

Personal trainer and record-breaking thru-hiker Heather "Anish" Anderson shares her at-home training tips on pages 311–313.

ADD IN WEIGHTLIFTING AND YOGA

Squats and deadlifts can help you develop stronger quads and glutes (big-time hiking muscles), as well as hamstrings. They also help develop your back and shoulder muscles, which is important since they will be holding your pack for hours each day. Sign up for a class or a personal training session at a local gym or YMCA if you're not familiar with these techniques and want to try them.

Yoga is not just for hippies and soccer moms anymore. Like hiking, yoga is not just a physical practice, but also a mental one. One mental skill you can learn from yoga is how to ride the fine line between pain and discomfort, and to use that information to avoid injury. The physical practice of yoga also strengthens muscles that traditional weightlifting may not hit, like ankles and deep core muscles, both of which work to keep you from falling or slipping as you hike. Good yoga practices also teach breathing techniques that are beneficial to hikers on uphills or during stressful moments, such as during storms or wildlife encounters.

AVOIDING OVERUSE INJURIES

Many section-hikers say that the hardest thing about section-hiking is that they're finally fit by the end of their section, but then they have to go back to work. When they return to the trail later, they have to get in shape all over again. The best way to address this is by staying in shape even off the trail. On the plus side, overuse injuries are less common on section or shorter hikes.

Overuse injuries are among the top reasons people quit the trail—and it usually happens early in the trip. I see it time and time again, even among some very skilled, fit, and well-trained former military members. Avoid the temptation to overdo it by setting your daily mileage lower at the beginning, ramping it up after a week, and then ramping it up more. Even if you're training 20 miles per day at home, start your hike off at a lower mileage—after all, you have to get up and do it again the next day. I advise starting with one-half to two-thirds of the distance you can easily hike at home, then ramping up slowly over the course of three or four weeks.

KNOW THE DIFFERENCE BETWEEN SORENESS AND INJURY

Avoid injuries that will take you off the trail for good by being able to tell soreness from injury. If anything feels off in your first few days of hiking, stop and slow your pace or call it a day. Take a zero (a day off). A day off may mess up your schedule, but injuries can take you off the trail for good. We'll talk more about soreness versus injury and zero days in chapter 9.

View from the Pacific Crest Trail

///

Chapter 3

+ THE LONG TRAILS

When people think about long trails in North America, they most often think about the Big Three—what's known as the Triple Crown of Hiking—the Pacific Crest Trail (PCT), the Appalachian Trail (AT), and the Continental Divide Trail (CDT). It can be argued that these are the most well-known trails, particularly with the success of such books (and subsequent movies) as *Wild* and *A Walk in the Woods*. But, while these three trails together go through a total of twenty-two states, there are a number of other trails out there that are deserving of your attention.

This chapter gives you a sneak peek into the varied long trail options in North America and even internationally. Take this time to dream, to think about what you want to accomplish, and to learn more about the beautiful terrain this world has to offer. Be open to trying new routes or even giving a previously tossed-out route a second chance.

The trek you choose depends on your availability, skill level, and—of course—what you want to see. Some of these trails are loop hikes—meaning the starting point is the same as the ending point. Other trails are hiked one-way northbound or southbound (or, in the case of a few trails, east- or westbound). All of these hikes can be done as section hikes over many seasons or years. Almost all of the trails have an associated trail organization that can provide you with information on required permits, local regulations, and best weather windows. Visit their websites to learn more (see Resources). As you spend your time planning and dreaming, consider donating your time or money to help sustain these trails, too.

While I have done twenty thru-hikes, I have not yet done them all. So I've enlisted the help of Sarah Stewart, Emelie Frojan, and Rachel Zurer to introduce these trails to you.

The Appalachian Trail travels through eastern hardwood forests where trees flower in early spring, leaf into green by summer, and turn red and gold in the fall.

PHOTO CREDIT: ISTOCKPHOTO/ THEBIGMA

APPALACHIAN TRAIL

Nickname(s): AT, Green Tunnel

This iconic trail runs along the Appalachian Mountain range from Georgia to Maine. It's 2,190 miles long, making it the longest hiking-only footpath in the world, and usually requires four to seven months to hike in its entirety. Built in the 1920s and 1930s, the trail covers fourteen states. After the National Trails System Act passed in 1968, some of the trail was relocated onto more scenic areas.

The AT is strenuous but highly populated, with shelters and blazes (painted white rectangles that serve as confidence markers to indicate you are on the correct trail) the whole way; thus it's a decent choice for a beginning thru-hiker. You can expect to traverse wooded slopes and ridges, as well as a few valleys and farmland, and you'll cross over hundreds of roads (great for access points) and through about a dozen small towns.

The PCT hits six major ecosystems, including high desert, temperate rainforest, and alpine.

PHOTO CREDIT: STEVEN SHATTUCK

PACIFIC CREST TRAIL

Nickname(s): PCT, PCNST (Pacific Crest National Scenic Trail), or Pretty Cushy Trail

This 2,650-mile trail runs from Mexico to Canada through the mountains and deserts of California, Oregon, and Washington. Its stats are pretty impressive—it crosses over fifty-seven major mountain passes, goes through nineteen major canyons, and passes more than one thousand lakes. It cuts through five national monuments, five state parks, and six national parks.

Along the way, you'll hike through the snowy Sierra Nevada, into deep forests, and over the Cascade Range of volcanic peaks. The PCT was officially completed in 1993. In some ways the terrain is less strenuous than the AT, but its remoteness, high altitude, and lack of facilities make it a more advanced trail.

The logistics of hiking the PCT can be more challenging than the AT, including everything from obtaining permits to planning for enough water. The route also offers less signage, but signs are present at all trail junctions and road crossings.

View from the Continental Divide Trail

PHOTO CREDIT: JOHNNY CARR

CONTINENTAL DIVIDE TRAIL

Nicknames: CDT, The Continental Divide National Scenic Trail (especially when used in conjunction with the "official route," often used with the tagline "Embrace the Brutality")

This approximately 3,100-mile route is the roughest and least-traveled of the Big Three. The path, from New Mexico to Montana via Colorado, Wyoming, and Idaho, isn't even complete the whole way and offers major challenges to hikers, including navigation, lightning, long water carries, grizzly bears, steep snow travel, and hundreds of miles over 10,000 feet.

The CDT was officially founded in 1978. But, due to budget difficulties and shrinking private funding, trail building has been in fits and starts. Unlike the AT or PCT, as of publication, 5 percent of the CDT is still incomplete—meaning trail users must walk on a road to connect non-contiguous sections.

This trail isn't generally a good choice for new thru-hikers and is best tackled by those with significant backcountry experience. The CDT was designed to be a wilder experience than the PCT or CDT, so sometimes it is more of a route than a trail. Expect to find portions that require you to travel cross-country from cairn to cairn or post to post. Intersections may be purposefully unmarked; you are responsible for your own navigation.

Those who attempt the CDT in a year should be able to walk and navigate through hundreds of miles of snow-covered mountains, as well as desert areas with limited water sources. Experienced thru-hikers enjoy the four-to six-month challenge.

The lake-studded John Muir Trail traverses the Range of Light through the Sierra Nevada.

JOHN MUIR TRAIL (CALIFORNIA)

Nickname(s): JMT

BACKPACKER magazine readers have voted the John Muir Trail as the "Number One Trail to Do Before You Die." It's not hard to see why. Its 211 miles extend from Yosemite Valley south to Mount Whitney, the highest peak in the Lower 48. Though 170 of those miles follow the Pacific Crest Trail, the JMT is a thru-hike in its own right, and many PCT hikers say the two to three weeks they spent on the JMT were the most beautiful of their 2,650-mile trek.

The trail starts in Yosemite National Park and winds through the Ansel Adams Wilderness, Sequoia National Park, and Kings Canyon National Park. It ends at the highest peak in the continental United States—Mount Whitney (14,496 feet). Expect to see alpine and high mountain scenery and breathtaking views—the trail is largely above 8,000 feet (the last 30 miles sit at 10,000 feet).

Despite some serious elevation gain and high altitudes, this is a great, bite-size trek for new thru-hikers—if you can get your permits worked out.

The gentled-graded TRT has an easy walk-up permit system to gain access to Desolation Wilderness. Water is plentiful on the west side but can be dry on the Nevada side, especially during a drought.

TAHOE RIM TRAIL (CALIFORNIA AND NEVADA)

Nickname(s): TRT, the "Neiman Marcus of US Trails"

This 165-mile hike was my first thru-hike, and is a great one to warm up with. It generally takes most hikers about two weeks to complete. The trail circles Lake Tahoe, hitting all the major high points penning in the Tahoe Basin. The trail ranges in elevation from just over 6,000 feet to just over 10,000 feet, and part of the trail overlaps with the PCT. The trail was first proposed in 1978 and was completed in 2001.

A few perks make this a great thru-hike for beginners. This is one of the few long trails that forms a loop, making drop-off and pick-up plans logistically convenient. It also crosses roads every 40 miles or so, where you can access towns with food and hotels, get medical help, or decide to go home.

The WT takes you close to glaciers; you occasionally cross their outflow, usually on well-maintained bridges.

WONDERLAND TRAIL (WASHINGTON)

Nickname(s): WT

You can't see Rainier from its summit—so why not spend 93 miles circumnavigating its base for maximum admiration? This five- to fourteen-day journey tours Rainier's diverse surroundings, from alpine ridges to rushing rivers winding through marmot and bear territory. The trail sports eighteen wilderness campsites and three non-primitive campgrounds. It's especially awe-inspiring in the summer, when world-famous views of blooming paintbrush and lupine are abundant and soften the 22,000-foot total elevation change.

The Wonderland Trail was built in 1915. The average length of a trip here is ten to fourteen days. The trail's biggest challenge? Getting permits from the national park, which you'll need for the entire trip, due to the growing popularity of the trail.

PHOTO CREDIT: ISTOCKPHOTO / KEVINMWALSH

A day hiker on an open ridge walk, a highlight of the LT.

LONG TRAIL (VERMONT)

Nickname(s): LT

These 272 miles of Green Mountain State trail form the oldest long-distance foot-path in the United States, having been constructed between 1910 and 1930. The trail starts at the Massachusetts border and runs to the Canada-US border, along the backs of the Green Mountains. It overlaps with the AT for about 100 miles.

The Green Mountains are rugged territory, and this challenging trail usually takes about three to four weeks to complete. Go in the summer when the northern latitudes have warmed to a reasonable temperature, or in the fall to immerse yourself in Vermont's vibrant autumn colors. With seventy primitive shelters and numerous adorable towns along the way, this can be a great first trail for the physically fit.

Views of the Connecticut River along the New England Trail

NEW ENGLAND TRAIL (CONNECTICUT AND MASSACHUSETTS)

Nickname(s): NET

The New England woods have drawn wilderness pilgrims since long before Henry David Thoreau made escapism stylish, and this 215-mile trail offers enough deep forests and waterfalls to inspire another back-to-nature movement. The paths are over 500 years old, and the scenery reflects it.

Since the trail was designated in 2009, it has expanded to include a 4-mile extension to Long Island Sound and a 22-mile eastward deviation in Massachusetts. You'll hike from the shores of Connecticut to the southern border of New Hampshire through a pine-thick reverie of lush ferns, mossy tombstones, and crumbling stone walls. This two- or three-week hike will carry you through trail easements on a number of private land holdings—so make sure you're overnighting in designated campsites.

The expansive Colorado Trail has great views of Colorado's high summits.

COLORADO TRAIL (COLORADO)

Nickname(s): CT

The Colorado Trail is no cakewalk, as it courses past some of the most venerable Rocky Mountain summits in North America. The Colorado Trail travels from Denver to Durango for over 500 miles and nearly 90,000 total feet of elevation gain. You'll cross the Sawatch Range, Collegiate Peaks, and San Juan Mountains. The CT is perfect for an experienced backpacker with four to six weeks available. Bring your trekking poles—and a good camera. Summer travelers may see snow, wildflowers, and afternoon lightning storms. Autumn hikers can watch the Aspen turn golden and hear elk bugling.

The PNT offers up some of the most breath-taking views.

PACIFIC NORTHWEST TRAIL
(MONTANA, IDAHO, AND WASHINGTON)

Nickname(s): PNT, the 4th trail

This is your chance to go against the grain—while the Triple Crown trails and the country's dominant mountain ranges fall north-south, the Pacific Northwest Trail defiantly takes an east-west trajectory. Cross the wild, sparsely populated land just south of the Canadian border on an undulating path that carries you up and over those north-south ranges. The route starts in Montana's Glacier National Park and flows west to the Pacific Ocean and the ancient old-growth rain forest that greens the feet of Washington's snowcapped volcanoes. This 1,200-mile hike sees around fifty thru-hikers per year, so this is one for lovers of solitude. Low traffic means following the Pacific Northwest Trail is a challenge that should be reserved for experienced navigators. Most hikers finish this trail in sixty to seventy days.

The hiking-only SHT has one of the best signage and fee-free shelter/campsite systems of any of the long trails.

SUPERIOR HIKING TRAIL (MINNESOTA)

Nickname(s): SHT

The Superior Hiking Trail's name aptly describes this 310-mile footpath, first established in the mid-1980s, both for its quality and its location, as it runs primarily along ridgelines above the North Shore of the United States' largest lake, Lake Superior. Combine this with the hardwood lowlands and boreal highlands of the surrounding Sawtooth Mountains and the rapids, waterfalls, and gorges of the streams along the way, and you have one of the most scenic trails in the Midwest. Give yourself at least two weeks to hike from Jay Cooke State Park at the trail's southern terminus to the Pigeon River at its north end.

An autumn campsite at Potawatomi State Park, a highlight of the Ice Age Trail

ICE AGE TRAIL (WISCONSIN)

Nickname(s): IAT (not to be confused with the International Appalachian Trail), IANST (Ice Age National Scenic Trail)

The Ice Age Trail is the perfect trail for any science buff. Tracing the moraine line (glacial debris) of the last ice age (about 12,000 years ago), the trail is the most scenic way to see Wisconsin. The route, which was founded in the 1950s, is 1,200 miles long, half of which are yellow blazed. (The other half of the route is unmarked but easily navigable.) While the trail isn't yet complete, it does occasionally overlap with state biking trails, and some parts of the trail lead directly through small Wisconsin towns. The trail stretches from Potawatomi State Park in Sturgeon Bay to Interstate State Park in St. Croix Falls.

Views from the Ouachita Trail

OUACHITA TRAIL
(ARKANSAS AND OKLAHOMA)

Nickname(s): OUT

The fact that many folks have never heard of this 223-mile trail—much less know how to find it—is one reason why the Ouachita (WA-she-ta) Trail can guarantee crowd-free hiking. The fact that it straddles the Arkansas-Oklahoma border (not exactly a backpacking epicenter) is another. The trail follows the Ouachita Mountains and wanders elevations between 600 and 2,600 feet. It plows through the heart of the Ouachita National Forest, which is the largest national forest in the South.

It's a good trail for a beginner thru-hiker, although the elevation gains can still be tricky. Take two or three weeks to hike through this window into America's forested, creek-crossed heartland.

Travel through two federally designated wildernesses on well-maintained trail and generally well-signed trail.

ARIZONA TRAIL

Nickname(s): AZT

Desert-lovers will revel in traversing 800 miles along the north-south length of Arizona. Starting at the Mexican border, the route connects sky islands—rugged mountain ranges rising up from the desert sand—and demands a rim-to-rim of the Grand Canyon. Visit unique historical and cultural sites and travel through billions of geologic years, viewing everything from stark red desert to cool boreal forest. This well-marked trail is a gem of the Southwest, but knowledge and skill in desert travel is required for this one- to two-month-long spring or fall thru-hike.

Tirell Pond and the colors of birch and maple forests are a highlight of the NPT. Enjoy uncrowded shelters as you travel through numerous remote areas.

NORTHVILLE-PLACID TRAIL (NEW YORK)

Nickname(s): NPT

The Northville-Placid Trail bisects most of the 6 million-acre Adirondack Park from north to south, a journey of 133 miles. The path connects one serene mountain lake after another—you'll hear loons every night—and in autumn passes through an amber forest of innumerable birch and maple trees. Give yourself one to two weeks to complete this remote trail, and expect to have it mostly to yourself.

Thru-hikers say that Big Cypress Preserve and the sunsets are what make the Florida Trail.

FLORIDA TRAIL (FLORIDA)

Nickname(s): FT, FNST

This relatively flat trail skirts sandy beaches, palm-shaded forests, ancient sand dunes, and the Everglades ecosystem—but don't expect it to be a walk in the park. Hikers seeking plants and wildlife unlike any other in the United States will enjoy this approximately 1,300-mile hike along the north-south length of the Sunshine State. It's a perfect trail for winter travelers escaping snow elsewhere, but expect hiking challenges you won't find on other long trails: wading through swamps with alligators and snakes, long road walks through rural communities, and hiking in winter and peak hunting season. A highlight of the typically two- to three-month trip includes the Big Cypress Preserve, home to a high diversity of plants and wildlife, including several endangered species.

INTERNATIONAL LONG TRAILS

Long established walks are a satisfying and unconventional way to visit new countries. While this list is not anywhere near exhaustive—especially of the 37,000-plus-mile Grandé Randonnée (GR) trail system in Europe—it should give you an idea of the opportunities to explore on foot abroad. Long trails exist on almost every continent and often surround a culture of staying overnight in huts and hostels instead of wild camping.

CAMINO DE SANTIAGO (SPAIN AND FRANCE)

The trail began as a spiritual journey to the shrine of St. James in Santiago de Campostela, near the northwest coast of Spain. On the Camino Frances—the most popular of several possible routes—you'll follow the trail's scalloped-shell insignia 485 miles though the French Pyrenees, numerous towns, the Spanish countryside, and the Cantabrian Mountains. It takes most hikers a month to walk from the trailhead at St. Jean Pied du Port to the cathedral in Santiago de Campostela. With inns, towns, and friendly locals along the way, this is an excellent route for beginning thru-hikers.

TE ARAROA (NEW ZEALAND)

Although New Zealand is only about the size of Colorado, its two islands host one of the best treks in the Southern Hemisphere. The Te Araroa is a 1,864-mile trail that starts in Cape Reinga on the tip of the North Island and ends in New Zealand's southernmost town, Bluff. The trail acquaints hikers with a unique country by connecting settlements, towns, and indigenous *marae* (meeting houses of the Maori people). The Te Araroa also winds across Mount Tongariro, an active volcano on the North Island. You'll need about five months plus some hefty airfare for this culturally and ecologically diverse hike.

GR20 (CORSICA, FRANCE)

On the GR20, your finish line is the Tyrrhenian Sea. So is your starting line. This 112-mile trail crosses the French island of Corsica on a diagonal from the northwest to the southeast coast. Don't be fooled by the sea-level beginning and end; total elevation change across the middle of the island is about 33,000 feet. Most people take about fifteen days to complete this sun-soaked Mediterranean hike. Mountain huts offer food and lodging along the trail from June to September, and the path crosses through several villages with more luxurious accommodations.

The Camino de Santiago is both a physical journey and a spiritual one.

WEST HIGHLAND WAY (SCOTLAND)

Scotland's iconic long-distance path makes a perfect first thru-hike for those who love nature and culture. Footed in some of Scotland's finest green country, this well-marked trail travels from the lowland sheep farms over gently rolling terrain past fields, villages, pubs, and fog-draped ruins. You'll follow centuries-old footpaths and roads to the foot of Ben Nevis, the UK's highest peak. This one- to two-week 96-mile trip is a top pick for beginner backpackers looking to have gear delivered to a hotel every night.

TOUR DU MONT BLANC (FRANCE, ITALY, AND SWITZERLAND)

You'll need more than one phrasebook on this high mountain circuit, which crosses three international borders and circles 15,770-foot Mont Blanc. But even armed with a handful of languages, you'll struggle for words to describe the ridiculously beautiful vistas gracing this 105-mile, seven- to ten-day journey. It dips into France, Italy, and Switzerland, with steep, snow-frosted mountains towering 10,000 feet over the valleys the entire way. On trails ranging from ancient cobblestones to dirt, the route tops seven alpine passes. Camp along the route to save as much as $50 per day, but spend at least a few nights in mountain huts and inns to immerse yourself in the local flavor.

Route planning skills you learn here translate to all types of trails—from short and well-marked to the Hayduke Trail, shown here.

Chapter 4

+ ROUTE PLANNING

What is the importance of route planning? Why bother in the first place? On my first thru-hike, which was the 165-mile-long Tahoe Rim Trail, I decided to "wing it" and did pretty minimal preparation and no itinerary planning. I figured I could just hop on the trail, walk however far I wanted each day, and—eventually—I'd finish the loop hike back at my car.

Several times on that trip, however, I ran out of water and had to beg some off others because I didn't know where the water sources were. I didn't know where I could find flat places to camp, so I had some of the worst campsites imaginable, which led to some of the worst sleep imaginable. There were days when I was ready to stop hiking, but I couldn't because there were no campsites, so I kept going, and when I finally found something not even decent, my feet were ready to rebel. They were in so much pain that it made getting up and walking the next day even harder. I didn't know where resupply opportunities were or how often I'd come upon them, so I ran low on food.

If nothing else, I learned from that trip that good route planning ahead of time saves a lot of grief on the trail. Most advanced thru-hikers invest the time to set approximate plans for each day and make ballpark estimates of their mileage. This information becomes the basis of all your trip planning—like deciding how much food to carry or when loved ones can join you.

Here we'll explore the resources you need to start thinking about for your hike on the micro level. Itinerary planning looks like a daunting task, but we'll walk through the same process I've used to make itineraries for nineteen of my twenty hikes.

The Arizona Trail is routed so that thru-hikers must hike a rim-to-rim of the Grand Canyon. This requires thru-hikers to get permits to stay in designated campsites.

THINK ABOUT PERMITS

Some trails don't require permits. But for many long hikes in the United States and around the world, you will need to have a permit to legally hike your hike. If your planned hike does require permits that are in high demand, once you have an idea of the dates you want to be hiking, securing your permit should be the first concrete step you take in your route planning. Some trails have a maximum number of permits that can be issued, so getting a permit early helps reserve your spot. Permit systems and reservation methods differ from trail to trail. Be prepared to call, fax, or email in your permit and to have backup starting dates and trailheads. You may have to try for a permit multiple times.

THRU-HIKER PERMITS

Many land management agencies have special permit systems for long-distance hikers. For example, the Pacific Crest Trail (PCT) issues one permit that is good for all eight national parks the PCT goes through. A John Muir Trail (JMT) permit is good for Yosemite, Sequoia, and Kings Canyon National Parks and US Forest Service land. These permits often have special restrictions, such as limiting you to camping along the corridor of your long-distance trail.

SELF-ISSUE AND AREA-SPECIFIC PERMITS

For some long trails, like the CT/CDT and FT, permits may only be required before you enter certain wilderness areas. These walk-up permits don't require advance planning and can be collected 24-7 at kiosks right outside the wilderness areas. For other long trails, like the AT or CDT, permits may only be required before entering national parks. You may need to call the Park Service a few weeks ahead of time or print out/apply for a permit online before you enter the park. The Park Service is generally knowledgeable about how unpredictable thru-hiker itineraries can be, and are usually flexible in working with your schedule.

CAMPSITE-SPECIFIC PERMITS

Some permits may require you to know where you will camp every night and tell the land management agency this information. You may need to plan an approximate route before you get your permit. The Wonderland Trail permit is like this, for example. The Yellowstone and Glacier National Parks permits for the CDT also require knowing your camps ahead of time. To know dates or which campsites you will stay at, you will need to know a lot about your itinerary in advance. Plan your schedule first and then apply for these kinds of permits or plan your entire schedule around your permit.

DECIDE ON START AND DIRECTION

Picking a start date is the next step in planning your route. As a general rule, start as early as reasonable for your trail, depending on your personal commitments and the snow year. But there's a twist: For many long hikes, such as the AT, PCT, and CDT, your start date will be different depending on which direction you're heading. Here are some factors to consider when picking a start date and hiking direction.

Plan your start date to minimize the chance you'll run into snow like this, but maximize the chance you won't get snowed on at the end.

IDENTIFY WHEN TO START

First, figure out what your own personal time restrictions or obligations may be. Is your schedule dictated by school? Did you promise an employer you will stay until busy season is over? Do you need to wait to start until after a loved one's wedding or a family reunion? Ask your family or friends if they need you in town on certain dates. These "real world" issues are the first layer that dictates your start timing.

Next, consider weather and seasonal factors. Ideal starting times differ from trail to trail and from year to year based on weather conditions. If you start too early, you may hit snow in high-elevation areas. Walking in snow is much more

Standard Weather Windows for Common Trails

Depending on your skill level and comfort walking in snow or in the desert, you may be able to start your trail earlier or later than the "ideal" starting time listed here. If you can't start during the ideal window, remember that you can always hike in a different direction or hike as far as you can until you are stopped by snow. Figuring out how these seasonal windows interact with your personal timing is a big part of deciding which direction to hike. While dates depend on that year's weather patterns and your skill level and experience, here is a helpful weather table showing ideal windows for first time hikers on the Triple Crown trails.

Trail	Ideal Start Window	Ideal Finish Window
AT Northbound	March 1- May 1st	Before October 15
PCT Northbound	April 15-May 10	Before October 1
CDT Northbound	April 15-May 5	Before October 1
AT Southbound	June 15-July15	Anytime, though before Thanksgiving
PCT Southbound	June 20-July 10	Out of the Sierra by October 5
CDT Southbound	June 15-July 1	Out of the San Juans by October 1

difficult and dangerous than walking on dry trail; "too much snow" is a common reason why hikers quit. Conversely, if you start too late, you may finish your trip in the snow, or not be able to finish at all. If you start too late on a trail like the PCT or CDT, you may find yourself walking through extreme heat in the desert sections at the beginning of a northbound trek.

Figure out your motivations and goals, and then decide which direction to hike.

HIKE DIRECTION

Most hikers on the Big Three trails go northbound. But that's not to say you cannot hike southbound. For everyone, it's a personal preference combined with weather knowledge and practicalities. One of my southbounder (SOBO) friends hiking the AT wanted to get the hard part done first. Another doing the PCT couldn't get a permit for the start date he wanted. Crowds also play a factor. Some northbound hikes can be crowded, and people may choose to go southbound to avoid the traffic on the trail.

For some hikes, one starting point may be better suited to easing into the rigors of thru-hiking. For example, the CDT in New Mexico is a lot flatter than in Montana. CDT hikers who start at the Canadian border often walk through snow for days, which can be a rough way to start a 3,000-mile hike. If you're coming from sea level and don't have much time to acclimate, you're probably better off choosing a starting point that is at a lower elevation to give your body time to adjust. For example, if you are hiking the John Muir Trail, it's easier to acclimate if you start in Yosemite Valley (around 4000 feet) than if you start on top of Mt. Whitney (more than 14,000 feet).

Logistics also should be factored in, even details as simple as hitching a ride to the terminus. Some trails, like the CDT, have easy-to-schedule shuttles for northbound hikers. Figuring out logistics of getting to the Waterton Lakes northern terminus can be trickier—requiring trains, shuttles, or hitchhiking to get across an international border. If you live near a terminus, starting at the trailhead near your home can be a logistically easier starting point. But be warned: The temptation to go home when times get rough can be great. That's one reason I decided to walk the Colorado Trail from Durango to Denver—even though I live in Denver. I wanted to walk home and not have an easy bailout during those first few days of the hike where transitioning into backpacking from "normal life" can be difficult.

PLAN YOUR HARD STOP DATE

Planning your end date can be tricky. After all, it is hard to know your pace before you head out on the trail. Even if you're an experienced hiker and think you know your pace, you may surprise yourself. Maybe you'll become fitter than you expected. Or maybe you'll befriend someone who is slower than you and

PHOTO CREDIT: LIZ THOMAS

My finish photo from my thru-hike of the PCT in 2009. I had to get back to school in September, so my hard stop date was Sept. 6th, the day I finished.

Section Hiking

Don't forget when choosing your trail that you don't have to do the whole trail at once. Section hiking (tackling pieces of a trail over many years to connect a whole trail) is one popular option. And hiking a section of a big trail can be smart even if you never plan to hike the whole thing. Here are some of my favorite portions of long trails that make great section hikes:

Pacific Crest Trail: Oregon (about 460 miles)

Tunnel through dense fir forests, peer into the jeweled depths of Crater Lake, and spy a volcano-studded skyline that includes the craggy heights of 11,239-foot Mount Hood. This relatively flat section (compared to the rest of the PCT) starts near Siskiyou Summit on the California border and continues north to the Bridge of the Gods (of *Wild* fame).

Appalachian Trail: White Mountains Traverse, New Hampshire (54–75 miles)

Tackle some of the most epic and difficult terrain on the AT—the exposed granite backbone of the White Mountains. By day you'll bag endless views and life-list summits (including the East's tallest peak, 6,288-foot Mount Washington); by night you'll cozy up in the eight historic AMC huts dotting the route.

Appalachian Trail: Great Smoky Mountains National Park, Tennessee and North Carolina (71 miles)

Have a week to spare? See the best of the nation's most-visited national park on foot. You'll summit 6,643-foot Clingmans Dome, sleep in trailside shelters, and score views of the park's verdant valleys and undulating peaks.

Continental Divide Trail: Colorado Trail Collegiate Loop (about 160 miles)

This is a circuit for peakbaggers with a big chunk of bucket list to get through. Hike two 80-mile sections of the Colorado Trail and CDT to make a 160-mile loop that passes by eleven fourteeners along the way (summits are optional). The full loop takes most hikers twelve to eighteen days to complete. Beware of high altitude and afternoon thunderstorms, and get ready for some serious quad burn and 360-degree views.

Pacific Northwest Trail: Boundary Trail, Washington (about 80 miles)

Delve into the heart of the half-million-acre Pasayten Wilderness, home to gray wolves, old-growth forests, and the largest population of lynx in the Lower 48. Deep in the North Cascades just below the Canadian border, you'll find both water and solitude in abundance.

On the Oregon section of the PCT

Arizona Trail: Gabe Zimmerman to Picketpost, Arizona (185 miles)

Traverse sky islands that soar from cactus-filled desert bottoms to 8,000-foot aspen-shrouded peaks on this easy-access route from Tucson to Phoenix. Enjoy the Sonoran scenes of Saguaro National Park and ideal hiking temperatures in winter and spring—off-season for most other long trails.

John Muir Trail: Bishop Pass to Mount Whitney, California (about 90 miles)

Hiking north to south, the latter half of the JMT climbs like a staircase through Sequoia and Kings Canyon National Parks, its successively higher passes culminating with 14,495-foot Mount Whitney. Highlights include top-of-the-world terrain and turquoise lakes by the thousands.

you'll choose to stick with them. What is important is that you know what your must-stop date is and do everything you can to finish before that.

Ask yourself: What do I need to be home for? Does school start September 1? Does your job start on October 15? If so, you probably want to finish at least a week before that to get your head back into the "real world" and to allow plenty of time for transit from the trail to your home.

Does your trail have end dates built in? On the AT, at the time of writing, hikers are not allowed to camp inside Baxter State Park after October 15. The AT goes through Baxter for about 30 miles, so unless you plan to pull a 30-mile day (plus 5 miles to get back to the trailhead), then you should finish your hike by October 15. Other built-in end dates may not be as explicit, but believe me—you don't want to be finishing the PCT or CDT in December.

CAN YOU REALISTICALLY FINISH THE TRAIL AT YOUR PACE?

Now that you have a rough sense of your start and end dates, think about whether you're setting yourself up for success or not. Starting too early or still being on the trail too late in the season are both common reasons for quitting hikes. We'll get more in-depth on how to figure out your daily pace in chapter 7, but you can use this simple calculator to play around and get a sense of the average miles per day you'll need to cover to finish your selected trail in the amount of time you're imagining.

- Total planned days from start to finish
- Divided by total miles on the trail
- Equals average daily miles required

Remember that the average doesn't mean that you will hike that many miles per day. The average takes into account zero days (days where you hike zero miles) and nearo days (when you hike near zero, such as days when you get into a trail town around noon or days when you start later in the day than usual). For example, imagine you are on a 100-mile hike averaging 10 miles per day. On your sixth day, you decide to take a rest day in town. At the end of the day, you've hiked a total of 50 miles. You have 50 more to go—but only four full hiking days to do it. For the rest of your hike, you need to walk 12.5 miles per day to keep up your average. How averages work may seem obvious, but you'd be surprised by how many hikers I meet who think that if they hike big miles, they can take as many zero days as they want.

Start with a rough calculation:

Your miles per day will be a function of how many hours per day you hike multiplied by your miles per hour.

Most people hike around 2 miles per hour when backpacking, plus an extra 30 to 60 minutes for every 1,000 feet climbed. Thru-hikers in top shape can approach 3 or 4 miles per hour.

Remember, just because you're awake for 15 hours a day doesn't mean you'll be hiking 15 hours a day. Calculate in plenty of time for setting up and breaking down camp and food breaks. Calculate "off-time" every time you're in town. I usually take at minimum half a day to eat, shower, and resupply.

Now refine your estimate. Take a day hike carrying a pack similar in weight to what you'll carry on the trail. It's best if you can use the actual trail you'll be thru-hiking, but finding a real trail (not a sidewalk or track) that has varied terrain or topography similar to your trail also works. Get a sense of how many miles you can hike in an hour—but don't sprint. Remember, you'll have to keep this pace up all day, day after day. Use this information to update your pace estimate.

Finally, measure your maximum daily mileage. On the same or a different day hike, see how far you can reasonably hike in a full day (say, 8 to 10 hours). Take that number and reduce it by half to two-thirds when you're planning the mileages at the start of your long hike. Plan your trip by starting with small miles toward the beginning (first 2 to 3 weeks), then slowly adding more miles per day.

Remember that other variables impact miles per day, such as:

- Your miles per hour
- How long it takes you to climb 1,000 feet
- Terrain (flat, mountainous, etc.)
- Trail tread (rocky, rooty, soft and sandy, etc.)
- How many breaks you take during the day and how long those breaks are
- What time of day you start and what time of day you finish
- Weather and snow conditions
- Weight of your pack (which can differ depending on how much food and water you need to carry)
- Any injuries, like blisters or knee pain
- Pace of hiking partners
- Navigation difficulties

DECIDE WHETHER THE AVERAGE IS REALISTIC

We'll get into more detail about how to estimate your pace in chapter 7. For now, just do a gut check on the mileage you just estimated: Does it seem realistic to hike that far, day after day? Knowing what you know about your training and the amount of time you've been training, only you can answer that question. Don't

Zero Day: A Definition

Zero day: A day you hike zero miles. A day of rest from hiking. It can be taken on the trail, or you can hike into a trail town and take a day of rest in town. Also referred to colloquially as a "zero." How it is used in a sentence: "My foot was feeling achy, so I decided to take a zero in town and see if it got any better." It's definitely wise to schedule zero days. See page 94 for more.

forget, you'll want some rest days, and you'll lose part of a day every time you go into town. Unless you have significant experience, if your estimated average is outside the range of about 9 to 15 miles per day (at least to start the trip), you might need to rethink your plan.

PLAY WITH OTHER MILEAGE CALCULATORS

It's always good to take a second look at something before making a final decision. So I suggest you explore other online mileage calculators. Even if you are not hiking the PCT, I highly advise checking out Craig's PCT Planner (www.pctplanner.com). This free online calculator shows how your trip can change depending on your pace, how much time you lose gaining elevation, the terrain of the trail, and break times. It's a much more sophisticated version of the simple calculations I describe above.

I'd also advise playing ATThruHike.com, a free Web-based Oregon Trail–style game. It's very difficult to win (even for me, and I've hiked the AT twice), but it does give you a good idea of how pacing can impact your health, energy, money, and ability to finish the trail before it closes for the season.

ESTABLISH TRANSPORTATION TO AND FROM THE TRAIL

Trailhead transportation is a small part of your planning process, but it's one I get a lot of questions about. For me, like finding time and money, figuring out how to even start the darn trail was a big mental block. I'm a beginning-to-end kind of planner, so having a big hurdle right at the beginning was a mental barrier to planning the day-to-day of my hike.

Catching a ride on the narrow gauge train to the trailhead at Cumbres Pass in the South San Juans, CDT

Unlike a day hike or normal backpacking trip, if you plan to hike for four to six months, chances are you don't want to leave your car at the trailhead. To make things harder, long trail starting points are often in places not serviced by public transit. Worse yet, sometimes these trailheads are so obscure you can't even find them on Google maps. There's often not a lot of information out there about how to get to and from the trail, and local transportation providers change almost annually. As a result, one of the biggest obstacles people face when planning their thru-hike is uncertainty about getting to and from the trail. Here are some options.

Many local outdoor gear shops and hostels will pick you up from the airport or train station and take you to your trailhead for a fee.

- Pros: Reliable, safe, usually familiar with hikers and their needs
- Cons: Expensive, not always available, requires reservations

You can always hitchhike to the trailhead.

- Pros: Free, no reservations needed
- Cons: Slow, unreliable, safety concerns

Ask a family member or friend to drive you to the trailhead.

- Pros: Reliable, safe, lower cost, can be a way to include family and friends in your hike, can be a nice way to say good-bye
- Cons: Requires finding someone willing to spend a day or more driving you to the trail, adds temptation to call your family and friends to bail you out when the first hard thing happens

Some hikes can be accessed by public transit, including the Colorado Trail and PCT.

- Pros: Generally reliable, safe, cheap
- Cons: Takes a long time, service can be infrequent to rural locations, may require many transfers, not available for most trails

Many local taxis (or Lyfts or Ubers) can take you to trailheads.

- Pros: Reliable, door-to-door service
- Cons: Very pricey, driver often unfamiliar with the area and will be unhappy about the distance, often do not go to dirt-road trailheads

Trail angels are friends of the trail who help hikers out. Some trail angels are listed in guidebooks as people who can help hikers in need of rides or a place to stay. Other trail angels may not even know what a thru-hike is, but after talking with you and hearing your story may offer to help you get to where you need to go or give you some food. Trail angels may be able to help you get to the trail-head. For example, Barney and Sandy Mann thru-hiked the PCT in 2007 and, after their hike, wanted to give back. They live in San Diego and are happy to pick up hikers at the airport or train station and take them to the PCT's southern terminus. Trail angels ask that you let them know your travel details as soon as possible so that they can make transportation arrangements for you. Barney and Sandy's contact information is listed in many guidebooks. If you're hiking other trails, you may find people like Barney and Sandy who can help you get to your starting point.

- Pros: Low cost (please provide a donation and ask your driver what a reasonable amount may be), trail angels understand hikers
- Cons: Not always available or reliable, you're operating on the trail angel's time and good graces (so be respectful)

What about getting home? Be sure to save enough money at the end of your hike to afford to go home. If you're hiking a shorter trail and need to be back by a certain time, book your flight home ahead of time and make sure that you have arrangements or reservations for ground transport to the airport that will get you there in plenty of time. I personally like to use airlines that allow free changes or cancellation to my itinerary. If you're hiking a longer trail, don't make your return flight reservations until a few weeks before you finish. You may hike the trail a lot faster than you expected. Or a lot slower. Or you may not finish at all. It's best to book your flight when you know that you'll finish and already have a good idea of the speed with which you'll finish. Alternatively, you can always book a flight on an airline that allows free changes and cancellation and ballpark your finish date, updating your tickets as you get closer to finishing.

Most guidebooks for common trails list the best options to get from the finish point to an airport. Unless you have a family member picking you up, expect to take many buses, trains, and taxis to get to the airport. It may take you all day to get there, but by the time you finish your hike, any transit that happens on wheels will seem fast.

ROUGH OUT YOUR ITINERARY

Now that you understand the fundamentals involved in route planning, let's go through the steps required to truly sketch out your route. Making a day-to-day itinerary of your trip is a lot of work. But route planning is actually the number one way to help you become familiar with the trail before you go and to keep yourself safe. I know there are many unpredictable moments on a long hike, and to be honest, whatever itinerary you make at home probably won't be exactly what you walk. The longer you're out there, the less likely you are to stick to the timeline you make for yourself now. But believe me, by familiarizing yourself with the day-to-day, week-to-week level of what your route looks like, you will walk that trail feeling like you know what's coming. An itinerary is a great way to establish good practices, like being well hydrated, getting good sleep, and having plenty of food. And remember, you don't have to figure it all out at once. Just take it one day, one week, one chunk at a time—just like you will on the trail. Think about

Maps, a databook, and guidebooks are important planning tools.

your thru-hike as many back-to-back shorter trips. Before you know it, you'll have your whole route sketched out.

☐ Step 1: Pick Your First Resupply Point

You won't carry all your food with you for any trek longer than about ten days at the most. Instead, you'll resupply, either by picking up things you've mailed to yourself, or by buying things in town. Figuring out where to top off your supplies is the first step in roughing out your plan. For the purposes of this exercise, let's focus on how to plan your first few days on the trail, from your starting point to the first place you will resupply.

Choose a resupply that is a reasonable distance from your starting point or last resupply. My ideal resupplies are three to four days apart. On many trails you don't get a choice, and there may be no resupplies for seven days. The best resupplies are right on the trail. This does not happen often (Damascus, Virginia; Cascade Locks, OR; and Lordsburg, NM are among the few). Occasionally you can hike a sidetrail to town. Otherwise, most resupply towns are accessed when your trail crosses a road used by cars. From there, you leave your trail and take the road to town.

You can walk to town, catch a ride in a car, or (rarely) take public transit into town. Most hikers do not walk into town unless it is less than 2 miles away. Walking on a hard, paved road can be painful after days on softer dirt, and there are often better options to get to town. Some hostels, outfitters, taxis, or trail angels are willing to run shuttles to and from the road/trail junction. Most hikers access town by hitchhiking (more on hitchhiking safety in chapter 8). If you have to hitchhike to town, choose towns that are easier to hitchhike to (your guidebook will often give you an idea of how frequent traffic into a town may be).

The ideal trail town has groceries, restaurants, laundry, a library (for computer access), a gear store, hostels, outfitters, and a post office. A hiker can easily get from the hostel to the grocery store to the post office by walking, taking public transit, or biking (some hostels or trail angels have bikes available). Some towns' services are very spread out and are not set up as well for a hiker on foot. When picking resupply towns, think about what makes the most sense for your needs.

☐ Step 2: Estimate Your Daily Mileage

Start with an idea of how far you'll go each day, even though that will certainly evolve over the course of your hike. Use the tools and variables discussed earlier in this chapter to estimate what that mileage will be, at least for the first part of your trip.

☐ Step 3: Think Through Your Campsites

It's not enough just to know you can hike 12 miles per day and decide to do that every day no matter what. You also need to plan around where you can and cannot camp for the night (and what's going to be most comfortable). If your permit requires you to camp somewhere specific, then that's where you have to stay, even if it means pushing a big day or ending your day early.

It's easy to plan where to camp each night if your trail has shelters. At shelters, you can find a roof out of the rain, guaranteed flat tent sites, guaranteed water, a fire pit, a privy, and other hikers (so you won't have to camp alone). Shelters can also attract things that may prevent you from a good night's rest: snorers, mice, and partiers. You may plan your camping itinerary to purposely avoid these shelters, too.

The beautiful stone group shelter at Indian Bar Camp on the Wonderland Trail

Water sources play a major factor in planning out your campsites. Especially in the desert, there may not be many water sources. Camping near the water (at minimum, 200 feet away) means you'll have the water you need to cook your meal, clean up, and rehydrate both at night and in the morning.

Although your permit (or lack thereof) may say you can camp anywhere, you will often find trails are routed through steep, rocky, or thickly vegetated areas where setting up a tent is basically impossible. When you find a good flat spot toward the end of the day, it may be worth calling it a day. You may not find another good spot for a while. If it's getting dark but nothing flat is around, keep pushing on until you find something. If you hammock instead of camp (more in chapter 6), this is less of a problem.

Although you may be able to find a tent site in an area above treeline, these camp spots tend to be exposed. That means your tent may rattle or bow in the wind, and you may get more condensation in your tent in the morning. I prefer to camp below treeline to avoid these conditions. Since most hammock set-ups require trees, hammockers usually plan around camping below treeline, too.

Most trails have short sections that are routed on paved roads—usually because there is no public land nearby. These roads are usually lined with private property on either side, which means you can't camp there. Even if you're tired, pass through the road section and get back on public land to camp. Even if you're not ready to call it a night, if you won't be able to get past the whole road section, it's best to find a nice camp spot at least a mile from where the road section starts, where those traveling by car will be less likely to spot your camp and try to mess with you.

Based on your mileage and where water sources can be found, figure out all your campsites between your starting point and your first resupply. Ideally, the campsites should be evenly distributed.

☐ Step 4: Plug It into Your Spreadsheet
Log this information into your spreadsheet template (see Resources).

☐ Step 5: Repeat
Pick your next resupply, figure out the campsites along the way, and plug it in again. And again. And again. I know this step is time-consuming. I also know it's worth it.

Take a Nearo Day

If you're on a tight budget, here's a money-saving trick: Plan to camp just outside of town and spend a "nearo" (near zero) in town. You'll get almost all the benefits of a rest day at a fraction of the cost. By definition, a nearo day is one in which you hike significantly fewer miles than you typically do. It is used as a day of partial rest from hiking. In hiker lingo: "I walked 2 miles into town, hung out there all day, and walked 2 miles out of town after getting dinner. I saved so much money neroing."

Make sure you're accounting for neros as you plan your itinerary. I usually plan to take one about once every week or so. Why you want them:

- Your body needs time to repair.
- You need a day to replenish calories you burned on the trail.
- Your friends and family want to visit (and you don't want to hike with them if they're slower).
- You have a lot of "town chores" to do (get new gear, do laundry, go grocery shopping, visit the post office, use the Internet at the library, charge your electronics, etc.).
- Your favorite team is playing and you want to watch the game.
- You just feel like it.

Eating dinner in a hot spring—doesn't get any better than that! (Unless you use hot spring water to rehydrate your food. Then you'll feel sick for hours afterwards, which may have happened after this photo was taken.)

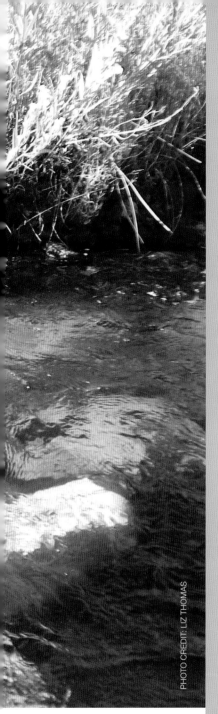

Chapter 5

+ RESUPPLIES

What you put in your tank for fuel is even more important than the gear you carry. That's why we're covering it first. While hikers infamously fuel themselves on PopTarts, Snickers, and ramen, I've found that the adage "you are what you eat" is especially true when you have a lot of miles to cover. Sure, I've eaten my share of cookies and chocolate for breakfast while I'm hiking. Heck, it's one of the many reasons that I hike. But, ultimately, the foods you choose impact performance, energy levels, and recovery.

In this chapter we'll discuss how to choose foods that will stay tasty and nutritious throughout your hike (and yes, sometimes part of your resupply option is cookies and chocolate). Then you'll learn how to get that food to yourself on the trail. We will also discuss sending yourself non-edible consumables on the trail and tricks to make sure you have just what you need when you need it.

What food you eat and how you resupply are personal choices. Most hikers discover the system that works for them through trial and error. Resupplies are one of the big differences between normal backpacking trips and thru-hiking—and it is important for would-be thru-hikers to learn the nuances. In this chapter, we outline guidelines to better direct you towards a method that suits your needs.

Try not to obsess about resupply. While some trails, like the CDT, are not forgiving if you make a resupply error, other trails, like the AT, have bailout options. Know the basics, understand how to get the items you need while you are on the trail, and then move on to physical training and backcountry skills.

PHOTO CREDIT: CAVEMAN COLLECTIVE

This is typical of hiking food as you buy it from the store.

FOOD RULES FOR THRU-HIKERS

Yes, there are food rules for thru-hikers. These are overarching principles and rules about eating on the trail. They're important to understand as you plan for your trip. Because food is the heaviest thing in your pack, it's important to make sure everything you bring is something you're going to love that can also fuel you.

RULE 1: KEEP IT TASTY

Choose foods you already know you love. On the trail, it's almost impossible to get too many calories. This is your chance to eat some of your favorite junk foods relatively guilt-free. Remember: The real key to keeping your food tasty is variety. One good way to make sure you're getting a true variety is to think of all your food, especially snacks, in terms of a "flavor matrix." Each food is either salty or sweet, crunchy or chewy. "You really want a balance of those textures and tastes in what you're packing," explains Claudia Pearson, the rations manager for thousands of students at the National Outdoor Leadership School's Rocky Mountain branch. "That way you can choose what you're in the mood for at that moment, and you won't get totally sick of whatever you've got."

See the chart below for some examples of snacks that fit into each "quadrant" of the matrix. If one of the quadrants is empty, I recommend you try to find a snack you like that would fill it.

Food Flavors Matrix

Keep these four tastes and textures in mind when planning your snacks for the trail. Having options from each quadrant will let you choose what you're in the mood for and keep you from getting totally sick of what you're carrying. We've given you an example for each; fill in your own favorite snacks as you plan and pack.

SALTY

• Jerky

• Roasted, salted peanuts

CHEWY

CRUNCHY

• Dried fruit

• M&M's

SWEET

Gummi bears (sweet and chewy), almonds (crunchy and salty), M&Ms (sweet and crunchy), and pretzels (crunchy and salty)

RULE 2: MAKE EVERY RESUPPLY DIFFERENT

Even though it's easier to make resupplies that look homogenous with all the same four foods, chances are you will tire of them quickly. If you're resupplying by mail drop (more on that soon), make every box a bit of a surprise. It'll make each package feel like a birthday present instead of a bill.

RULE 3: MAKE SURE YOU GET THE NUTRIENTS YOU NEED

Yes, thru-hiking is a great chance to indulge in junk food. But that doesn't mean you can get away with only eating junk. If you eat nothing but candy on a day hike, your body will still be able to perform. But if you eat nothing but candy, day after day, week after week, on a thru-hike, it's going to cause trouble (not to mention cavities). The info in the next few pages comes from *Pack Light, Eat Right* by Brenda Braaten, Registered Dietitian, PhD in Biochemical Nutrition, thru-hiker (AT and LT), and trail angel. This is the only scientific article created by a registered dietitian that addresses endurance nutrition specifically for thru-hikers. I advise reading it slowly, perhaps several times, before buying any food for your trip. She goes into much more detail on her website, but if you're curious, it's a great resource. Here are the key vitamins and minerals thru-hikers need to worry about, and good ways to make sure you get them:

HIKE YOUR OWN HIKE

MY BIG FOOD FAILURE

PHOTO CREDIT: DEAN KRAKEL

Dean Krakel learned the Rule 2 lesson the hard way on his thru-hike of the Colorado Trail.

I'm a 63-year-old photojournalist, and in 2015 I walked the Colorado Trail from Durango to Denver, including the Collegiate West loop. When I decided to walk the Colorado Trail, I did a lot of research on food, and I spent the whole winter and spring making my own trail food. I had two dehydrators going full blast 24 hours a day, day after day. I made huge batches of energy bars. I bought bulk freeze-dried food and put it into individual ziplocks. I also made pemmican, the food that I was going to rock the Colorado Trail with. Pemmican is a blend of 50/50 lean beef of buffalo and fat that, some say, tastes like a beef-flavored candlestick. It's very lightweight and incredibly calorie dense, and I thought it would solve my calorie to weight conundrum. I made 24 pounds of it.

I packed every resupply box with my pemmican. When I got into the field and on the trail, I only ate a pound of pemmican before I was totally sick of it. I had to go into towns to restock my food. As I walked on the trail, my needs in food changed dramatically. Going into town allowed me to buy the food I wanted and the food that I was craving, and it also allowed me to buy as much food as I knew I would need because, by that time in the journey, I knew exactly my daily mileage. The moral of the story? Food is about flavor. If it doesn't taste good, you won't eat it. And you gotta eat. And if you need pemmican, I still have a freezer full.

—Dean "Ghost" Krakel

VITAMIN C

Why you need it: Vitamin C is critical for building healthy connective tissue (muscles, ligaments, blood vessel walls—everything that keeps you going, mile after mile)—and for preventing oxidative damage in the water-soluble compartments of your body. It is also beneficial in assisting iron absorption and use.

PHOTO CREDIT: GRANT SIBLE/GOSSAMER GEAR

Wild berries can provide Vitamin C at least part of the time.

Where it comes from: Normally, fresh fruits, fruit juice, and vegetables. But because Vitamin C is not stable to heat, light, and air, dried fruits and dried vegetables have lost over 90 percent of their natural Vitamin C.

Your trail strategy: Because fresh oranges are not likely to be included in your menu, and wild berries along the trail are not to be depended upon, to get the recommended 60 mg/day you will have to make a conscious effort to find Vitamin C–fortified foods or drink mixes (spiced cider, Tang, instant breakfast, some cold cereals—read the labels) or take a supplement (a "one-a-day").

VITAMIN E

Why you need it: Vitamin E is an antioxidant in cell membranes and organelles. It is of major concern because exercise may promote more free radical damage within the tissue and Vitamin E protects cell membranes from oxidative damage.

Your trail strategy: Since you may need more on the trail, look for good sources of Vitamin E: vegetable or olive oil, nuts, whole grain cereals, wheat germ, seeds, peanut butter. All you need is 10 to 15 mg/day, so it only takes three or four servings of Vitamin E–rich foods each day.

IRON

Why you need it: Iron is involved in delivering oxygen to muscles and turning fuel into energy. As you exercise more and put more demands on your muscles, you need even more of it. This is one very good reason to train before you hit the trail.

Where it comes from: Meat (beef, tuna, chicken—even jerky) has a readily absorbable form of iron (heme iron). Other food sources do not supply iron in a form that is most readily absorbed, but Vitamin C will aid absorption if you drink or eat it along with your iron-rich food. Other non-meat sources: iron-fortified cereals, beans and peas, tofu, dried fruit, and even dried broccoli.

Your trail strategy: Supplements are not necessary for individuals on a balanced diet, but if there's a nagging doubt about how "balanced" your diet is, and you opt for a one-a-day multiple vitamin with iron, be forewarned. Supplemental iron is not readily absorbed—most will go right through you, turning your stools black and making you constipated. Never exceed the recommended daily allowance (RDA: 10 mg for males and 18 mg for females "of child-bearing age") or you may "rob Peter to pay Paul." Minerals are delicately balanced within your body. If you get too much of one, you'll inhibit absorption of other important minerals such as calcium and zinc. So stay within the RDA. And be consistent. The iron transport proteins will adapt to a certain normal level of incoming iron. If you vary radically from that level, most of the iron will be wasted on days when you take a larger-than-normal dose.

CALCIUM

Why you need it: Calcium warrants special attention, since it is critical for muscle contraction, nerve transmission, and the obvious—building strong bones. Even if you think you're not building strong bones, subtle changes are going on as you hike. By carrying an unaccustomed load on your back, the skeletal system will be receiving messages to increase bone density in your spine and lower extremities. The pull of the muscles on your skeleton will also send signals to lay down thicker bones. (Women: Backpacking is a wonderful way to decrease your risk of developing osteoporosis because it strengthens your skeleton. Exercise can be as important as getting enough calcium for building strong bones, so do both!)

Where it comes from: Milk or dairy, salmon, sardines (or any fish with bones in it), eggs, dried beans and peas, and dark green vegetables (broccoli again!).

A Note on Fiber

Although fiber is very important in a normal off-trail diet, many hikers find that eating foods fortified with extra fiber can be detrimental. A favorite hiker joke is "I accidentally picked up the high-fiber cookies and spent the whole next week having to poop every hour." Many hikers find the mechanics of hiking itself provide many of the benefits of fiber.

Your trail strategy: With the additional demands on your system, you'll need more calcium than usual. The "usual" is supposed to be between 800 and 1,200 mg calcium/day. Set 1,200 mg/day as a reasonable goal. That is easily achieved if you eat or drink three to four servings of milk or dairy.

Try to add 1 to 2 tablespoons of powdered skim milk to every meal. If you don't "do" milk, nuts and seeds (including sesame seeds) are rich sources of calcium, so eat some every day. In baking trail goodies, use blackstrap molasses rather than white sugar. Molasses is a good source of most minerals—calcium, iron, zinc, copper, chromium—you name it.

If you normally take a calcium supplement at home, continue to take it on the trail. Familiar lesson, repeated: Enzymes need a consistent message. In this case, it's the calcium transport molecules that need a consistent message, but the outcome is the same. The transport molecules get accustomed to seeing a certain level of calcium and adjust their activity accordingly. Don't send them mixed messages, or your bones will pay the price. Be consistent!

Can I know if I'm not getting enough calcium? Although there are other causes, "charley horses" or muscle cramps are often caused by inadequate calcium, so your body may send you a message loud and clear if you are not getting enough calcium. Fortunately, the calcium deficiency can be quickly remedied by boosting your calcium intake.

MACRONUTRIENTS

Staying healthy as a thru-hiker isn't just about micronutrients, though. We are out there for months—so how our bodies convert food into energy and muscle is different than other athletes. Here are some key rules to keep in mind:

FAT IS YOUR FRIEND

For a long duration hike, boost the fat to 35 to 40 percent of your daily calories by selecting high-fat foods. Besides keeping your pack weight down, more fat will make your food taste better. And your breakfast will hold you longer since fat slows down digestion, giving you a more even distribution of fuel being absorbed.

YOU NEED LESS PROTEIN THAN YOU THINK

Proteins contribute a little, not a lot, to your energy needs—10 percent at most (although more in males than in females). Protein will not make a perceptible difference in your performance level, so it's not the fuel needs you're concerned about, but the building of tissue—especially muscle tissue—that is taking place.

For the muscle-building/restructuring that is going on, an adequate supply of protein is necessary. The general recommendation for athletes is 1 gram protein/kg body weight or 12 to 15 percent of your diet, only slightly higher than what is recommended for the general population.

Most Americans regularly consume twice that much protein, so your trail diet can have considerably less protein than you normally eat at home and still supply more than ample protein for the muscle building and energy needs of your body.

TIMING MATTERS FOR CARBS

Eat frequent carbohydrate snacks, especially during and immediately after a hard workout (15 minutes to 1 hour after quitting for the day). During the day, about 20 to 30 grams of carbohydrate per hour is a reasonable goal: 20 grams for easy hiking; 30 grams for more challenging terrain.

That fuel should come from complex carbohydrates (starch, whole grains, high fiber foods), which are better nutrients all around. Complex carbohydrates release sugar over a longer period of time, rather than giving one big dose all at once. A second benefit of complex carbohydrates is that they are more likely to supply the B vitamins and minerals you need.

NEVER EAT A HIGH SUGAR SNACK JUST BEFORE EXERCISING

Insulin, a hormone released when sugar is eaten, stimulates cells to absorb glucose from the bloodstream, thus causing blood glucose levels to fall. If you then begin to exercise, glucose levels will further plummet, thus decreasing your endurance. Drinking water or milk would be better than drinking a sugar-laden soda just before you exercise, since the sugar will cause you to run out of energy faster. If you must mainline sugar, eat it in small doses during or after exercise, but not before!

For long-distance hikers: Half the fat that you burn is from storage, and half is supplied by the food you eat. To minimize pack weight, choose a higher fat menu. A 50-35-15 diet on the trail is reasonable:

- 45–55 percent calories from carbohydrates
- 35–40 percent calories from fat
- 10–15 percent calories from protein

RULE 4: DENSITY MATTERS

Do the math: If you need 4,000 calories of food per day, you could carry 40 ounces of food that has 100 calories per ounce. Or you could carry 30 ounces of food that has 125 calories per ounce. Ultimately, by choosing more calorie-dense foods, you can get similar nutritional benefits while carrying 10 ounces less food. Backpackers often spend hundreds of dollars on gear items that are 10 ounces lighter than other gear. By choosing more calorie-dense food, you can get the same weight savings benefit for free.

Remember that density doesn't just refer to calories per pound—it also refers to bulkiness. Potato chips, for example, have a high calorie-to-weight ratio (usually around 150 calories per ounce). But because of their shape, they can take up a lot of room in your pack. Many hikers reduce the bulk of their potato chips by crunching them into potato chip dust, and eating the dust either with a spoon or by sprinkling it on top of other dinners. (I personally prefer to only minimally crunch my chips, if I carry them at all.)

If you're not accustomed to thinking through the density of your food, here's an easy trick: Remember that you want to be carrying as little water in your food as possible. Water is both heavy and calorie-free, so foods with lots of water in them (fresh veggies, for example, but also, say, applesauce) are choices that aren't very calorie dense. Dehydrated or freeze-dried versions of water-heavy foods are almost always a lighter weight choice (dried apple rings, for example).

RULE 5: BALANCE QUICK ENERGY AGAINST SLOW RELEASE

Not all foods are created equal, even if they have the same calories and weight density. Calories are not the only way to measure nutrition. Foods with a lot of processed sugars tend to give you quick energy. These are great for when you are bonking (hitting the wall)—but ultimately your body runs through the sugars very quickly, and you will crash if this is all you're eating. Slower-release sugars and carbohydrates found in complex starches like whole grains are used by your body less quickly. When you eat these on the trail, you will have sustained energy for a longer time than if you were to only eat quick-release sugars.

How fast or slow sugar is released from a particular food is its glycemic index (GI). You can find a database of the glycemic index for many foods, plus tons more information on the concept, at www.glycemicindex.com. The short version: Foods with a lower glycemic index release their energy more slowly and stay in your system longer. Foods with a high glycemic index give you an instant hit of energy (which can be good on the trail, but reduce overall endurance if you start your day with it). Make sure your rations include both kinds, but especially lean toward low-GI foods at meals and the beginning of your day.

This isn't just fancy theory; you can feel it for yourself. On the AT, I decided to do a comparison with my trail food, testing how much energy different foods gave me. I compared a normal toaster pastry to a whole-wheat toaster pastry. While fairly similar items with similar calories per packet, they had a big difference on my energy levels in a way I never would have noticed at home. One day

What Is a Resupply?

Hikers spend more time thinking about food than pretty much anything. And no, unless you're hiking just a section of a long trail or one of the shorter long trails (seven to ten days), you won't start your hike with enough food to last you for the whole trip. Instead, you're going to learn to resupply, which means going into a town and getting the food, fuel, gear, and medical supplies you need to cover you until you hit the next town.

Planning your resupplies can be a little tricky. You never really know how much food you're going to eat until you get out there. I usually lose my appetite for the first two weeks of hiking, and then my "hiker hunger" kicks in, and suddenly I can eat twice as much as I do normally. You never really know what your body is going to be interested in eating either, until you get out there. I've carried homemade granola bars that I thought would be awesome, only to ditch them for candy bars. Knowing how much and what food to carry is an art, so don't worry about getting it perfect. The more you hike, the more you'll know what you like and how much of it. But the tips you'll learn here will help you make better decisions.

For me, planning resupplies and thinking about what to eat is one of my favorite parts of prepping for a long hiking trip.

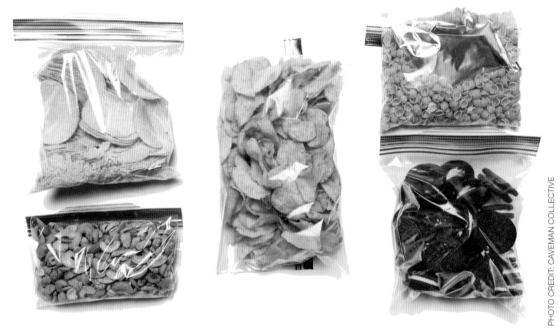

PHOTO CREDIT: CAVEMAN COLLECTIVE

Typical hiking food after you remove excess bulky packaging

I would eat two normal toaster pastries and have energy for an hour. Then I'd be starving again. Another day I would eat two whole-wheat pastries and have energy for 2.5 hours. The whole-wheat pastries cost a bit more—but I got 1.5 extra hours of energy. This experiment made me realize that on the trail, food is not just what I eat when I'm hungry. It is my fuel, and my body is worth using premium gas.

RULE 6: KEEP IT TRAIL READY

Shelf-stable food often comes in boxes or plastic packaging to make it look prettier. But—along with everything in your pack—if it doesn't serve a purpose, it doesn't need to get hauled up the mountain. Packaging makes food bulky, so if you wanted to keep your food in its original packaging, you'd need a much bigger pack. Master the art of repackaging. Remove boxes and wrapping and dump your food into plastic ziplock bags. Less to carry is, well, less to carry (both in and out), and that's a good thing.

Good food planning means happy camp eating for these PCT hikers.

RULE 7: BE REALISTIC ABOUT COOKING

For most thru-hikers, by the time you get into camp for dinner, you want to eat now. Unlike shorter trips or camping trips, thru-hiking is not a time for back-country gourmet experimentation. It's a time to quickly get warm calories in your mouth. These are the types of meals thru-hikers tend to like:

- Quick
- Easy
- One pot
- Relatively inexpensive
- Quick-cooking or instant
- Simple clean-up

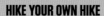

ON NEVER COOKING AT ALL

PHOTO CREDIT: STEVEN SHATTUCK

It's less popular, but there is always the option of not cooking at all during your thru-hike. Hiking stoveless isn't for everyone. I recommend you test it for a week or so before fully committing. My friend Steve "Twinkle" Shattuck explains how he makes it work.

I've hiked roughly 4,000 miles on long trails going completely stoveless. Many people would consider my style of hiking a minimalist approach, going as many miles as I can each a day. To do this, I carry very little, and going stoveless just fits that approach. I eat mainly maltodextrin, a food additive product that is a starch in powder or sugar form. Put some water and juice with it, and it's a drinkable meal. Malto is actually the main ingredient in a lot of name-brand sports energy drinks used by ultrarunners and endurance cyclists like Hammer Nutrition, CytoMax, or Gatorade. It's great as an on-the-go food source for thru-hikers, too. I can get roughly 2,500 to 3,000 calories per day from maltodextrin.

On top of malto, I supplement with bars, such as Probars or Clif Bars, and nuts and a lot of chips. All these are food and drinks that I can eat on the go, which fits well with my approach of hiking as many miles in a day as possible to maximize what I see on my vacation. Cooking takes time and energy and has an added weight cost. Things can go wrong too, including forest fires, which I think are a huge danger on the long trails, especially in desert areas. Without a stove, I don't have to worry if I have enough fuel to cook the foods that I have. If I don't have to worry about that, it's one less care I have on the trail. With my stoveless system, it's pretty easy for me to get into camp and throw food in myself, whether it's a bar or chips, and go to bed. I don't worry about setup and breakdown and cleaning of pots and pans. Going stoveless is just a pretty easy approach to fueling myself on the trail. Don't worry—if you try malto on trail, the Post Office won't give you too hard of a time about the resupply boxes full of white powder.

—Steve "Twinkle" Shattuck

Many thru-hikers tend to prefer foods to which you can add boiling water and then let soak for a while before eating (this system is used by a lot of freeze-dried food companies). This system uses less fuel than cooking or simmering your food for a long time. (Note: You can actually cook a surprising number of foods this way, including pasta. Flat and angel hair noodles cook faster than shell or curly noodles.) If you choose foods that need simmering or boiling for a few minutes, you'll find a canister or woodstove to be more fuel efficient (more on this in the "Gear" chapter). Also, the less water your dinner needs, the less fuel you need.

That said, some thru-hikers like to make more elaborate meals with real vegetables on their first night out of town. And I always stick at least one pricier "treat" dinner into each resupply. This can serve as a motivator and celebratory meal after a hard day.

A majority of thru-hikers do not cook breakfast. You certainly are welcome to start your day with a cooked breakfast, but over time many people decide that it is easier to eat a cold breakfast. I usually do not cook, but on cold mornings I pack up quickly, eat a cold breakfast, and then stop later and cook up hot coffee and hot oatmeal.

You may recall learning in school about water boiling at lower temperatures at altitude than at sea level. This is very relevant when cooking backpacking food. Unless you want your rice, pasta, and veggies to be crunchy, remember that dehydrated and freeze dried foods will take longer to rehydrate at altitude. You'll need to simmer meals that require cooking longer, too. Atmospheric pressure is lower at altitude than at sea level, so while water boils at 212°F at sea level, at 5,000 feet, it is 203°F and at 10,000 feet it boils at only 194°F. Most backpacking food companies suggest adding 1 minute of cook or soak time for every 1,000 feet over 5,000 feet. Water also evaporates faster at altitude—so if you don't use a lid with your pot, you'll need to add 1–2 tablespoons extra per 5,000 feet.

RULE 8: USE YOUR MEALS IN TOWN WELL

Although many hikers are tempted to eat pizza and burgers in town, it's also a great time to catch up on vegetables and fruit. I often make the produce aisle my first stop in town. Then, after gorging on fruits and veggies, I find a restaurant to order pizza and a burger. I try to make a habit of getting at least a side salad with my meals. Most hikers reach town at least a little dehydrated. Start your time in town with a drink more exciting than water.

Men over 50 years old who are long-distance hiking have told me they tend to lose body fat and mass more easily and quickly than other gender/age

Thru-hiking is your chance in life to eat whatever you want, however much you want. Here, Whitney "Allgood" LaRuffa enjoys three barbecue sandwiches at the annual PCT Days festival in Cascade Locks, Oregon.

groups. This is great at first—until the body runs out of fat and starts attacking muscles, including organs. I have met several older men who had kidney problems because of it. They typically notice that it has become an issue because they start urinating blood.

According to some hikers who have suffered this problem, their doctors recommend getting enough carbohydrates and proteins in their diet to replenish glycogen stores and eating frequently so that the body does not start attacking itself for fuel. All hikers—especially older ones—should talk to their doctors about how nutritional choices can safeguard then from falling victim to this or other health issues.

RULE 9: CHECK EXPIRATION DATES

When I hiked the CDT, I purchased a lot of bulk discount food items near their expiration date for the trip. Before leaving, I divided out the items into twenty

PHOTO CREDIT: LIZ THOMAS

A little something to spice up your meal can go a long way.

different boxes, which a friend mailed to me over the course of my five-month trip. I particularly remember opening a bag of chocolate that I received in my last resupply box. The chocolate had clearly gone bad; it was full of spiders.

Many raw or minimally processed foods have short shelf lives. If you intend to send yourself that kind of food, I'd advise not buying all you need before you leave for the trip. Instead, ask your resupply person to get a few batches of the food and refrigerate or freeze them until right before sending them off to you. It may prevent the heartache associated with opening some rotten food.

RULE 10: SIMPLE THINGS MAKE EVERYTHING TASTIER

Thru-hiking food can get boring, which is fine for some people, but unacceptable to a foodie like me. To keep costs down, most thru-hiker dinners are based on five boring simple food groups: instant mashed potatoes, ramen, noodles, beans, and rice. To make every meal a little different, I carry a variety of spices and hot sauces, as well as freeze dried and dehydrated vegetables. I try to bring cheese—especially nice cheese—to make any of those staples a little tastier. Olive or coconut oil or butter makes everything taste better. Bacon bits or store-bought fried onions and garlic turn your meal gourmet.

RULE 11: THINK ABOUT NON-FOOD CONSUMABLES

This isn't exactly a food rule, but it's important to think about as we move on to talking about resupplying. Food isn't the only thing you'll consume/use up as you hike, and it isn't the only thing you'll need to think about resupplying. Here's a list of common non-food consumable resupply items to consider:

- Maps and databook for the next section
- Fuel
- Hand sanitizer
- Sunscreen
- Batteries
- Toilet paper
- Tampons and/or other menstruation-related items
- Medications (over-the-counter and prescription)
- First-aid supplies
- Blister supplies
- Dental care (floss and toothpaste)
- Vitamins
- Ziplocs (you can never have too many)
- Any extra gear you may need for the next section, including shoes, socks, a bear canister, an ice axe, crampons, water treatment drops/pills, etc.
- Crossword puzzles, Sudokus, books, or other fun entertainment

HOW TO DECIDE ON A RESUPPLY STRATEGY

Now that you know some of the basic principles of how to decide what goes in a resupply, it's time to think about the specifics of how you'll get those things on your particular hike. You have a few options when it comes to picking up more food and supplies: mail drops, grocery/convenience stores, a hybrid or combo of those, or friends and family. Each hiker has a preference, so you'll need to

Occasionally, your resupply strategy may involve getting a pizza delivered to a trailhead as I did with another hiker on the AT in 2011. But it certainly isn't something that can be counted on.

figure out what's best for you. We'll go over the pros and cons of each option to help you choose, then explain how to do each type.

Remember, don't forget to think about how you will get into town, which could impact your itinerary and your resupply. If you must hitchhike into town to resupply, you will have a better chance of getting a safe ride before dark. If your itinerary shows you will reach that road after dark, it's best to camp at least a mile from the road and try in the morning. Or choose a resupply where you can walk into town (or call a shuttle) and that will still be open later at night (i.e., not the post office).

MAIL DROPS

This is where you prepare your food and other supplies ahead of time and mail them to yourself at various points along the hike. There are pros and cons to this strategy.

Pros:

- You can choose exactly what you want
- Individual items can be bought cheaply at home or in bulk
- Can be fun to put packages together with friends and family
- Allows for special diets
- Can make homemade dehydrated meals
- Can have a better diet and more variety in general than other options
- Often a place that accepts mail drops is located right on the trail, which helps avoid hitchhiking and saves you time by not having to go into town or spend time shopping in town
- You pay for your food and shipping ahead of time so can budget your trip better

Cons:

- Lots of work and time and organizational skills required
- Hard to know in advance what you want or how much to send
- Requires a friend or family member to send the packages and be responsible enough to send them on time
- Packages could get lost
- Limited pick-up hours, if you choose to send to a post office
- Shipping costs can be pricey (expect at least $200 in postage costs alone for a 2,000+ mile hike)
- You often get tired of the food you send yourself, or food that sounded great before you started is awful on the trail (remember Dean's pemmican)
- If you quit the trail, you end up with a lot of extra food at your house
- Food must be nonperishable (e.g., you can't send yourself fresh fruit or veggies or cheese)

Along with the post office (PO), you can also send your mail drop resupplies to hostels, hotels, trail angels, or businesses. The advantage of sending to a non-PO location is that those businesses tend to be open longer hours (and on the weekend), unlike many POs. On the other hand, any packages you send Priority that you don't pick up from a PO can be sent back home for free (say if you were to decide not to go into that town or to quit the trail). Packages delivered to a business may not be returned at all. Packages sent to a PO using

PHOTO CREDIT: LIZ THOMAS

Whitney "Allgood" LaRuffa resupplying at a grocery store on the Chinook Trail, 2014.

Priority Mail can be bounced to another PO for free. Packages sent to businesses cannot be bounced for free. Call or email any non-PO mail drop point before you leave for your hike to ensure that they accept packages, and if so, how they would like you to label the box. Sometimes, businesses charge a nominal fee to hold your package.

GROCERY/CONVENIENCE STORE RESUPPLY

With this method you buy your food and other needed supplies at stores along the way as you hike. Like mail drops, there are also pros and cons to this strategy.

Pros:

- More flexibility to get the food you've been dreaming of (assuming the store has it)
- You are less likely to get tired of what can be found in a grocery store
- Requires less planning and preparation at home and saves you time
- Grocery stores tend to be open longer than the post office
- If you quit the trail, you won't have extra food around your house

Cons:

- Depending on the store, choices might be limited, which can be especially difficult for those with dietary restrictions or vegetarians/vegans. The "usual" choices can become tiring.
- Options may be less healthy than what you would choose at home
- Individual items are more expensive that what you could buy in bulk or at a store at home
- Can be overwhelming to make food decisions while hiking; easy to end up with too much of one item or a non-balanced diet
- Big tendency to overbuy food (especially when hungry)
- May require hitching into town or hitching from your hotel in town to the grocery store
- More difficult to budget how much you'll spend on food because it is an as-you-go expense. You may run out of money at the end of your trip and have to quit because you can't buy food. In comparison, someone who has sent themselves boxes has paid the cost upfront.

HYBRID

This method uses a mix of mail drops and local shopping. It works well for those who like the convenience of mail drops, but don't have a lot of time to prepare mail drops before starting the trail. It also works well for those who are hiking internationally.

My good friend Brian "Buck-30" Tanzman sometimes works 80-hour weeks during the winter and spring. When summer comes around, he likes to spend all his time on the trail. For that reason, Buck-30 prefers to save putting together mail drops until he has hiked a bit. He uses the hybrid method to maximize his non-hiking/not-working time; he can take care of logistics while giving his body a rest day from hiking.

If you are hiking abroad (or if you are a hiker visiting from another country), you will find that shipping food and gear to yourself from another country is prohibitively expensive. For this reason, international hikers find that the hybrid or buy as you go methods are best.

Many international hikers will bring extra gear or special items with them on the plane, and then create a bounce box (more on this later). The bounce box serves as a wandering garage that allows you to keep a few expensive or harder-to-find items relatively accessible without requiring you to carry them the whole way. For example, my German friend Buttercup hiked the CDT in 2016 and used a bounce box to mail his cold weather gear, special foot-care items, and extra camera equipment from trail town to trail town. He would use the items in town, take what he needed for the trail, and then mail the box ahead. I used a similar strategy in 2016 when I hiked the Great Divide Trail in Canada.

So what does a hybrid system actually look like? Here are a few examples.

SHOPPING SMART

I shop at grocery stores in towns that I know have good supermarkets with wide selections. In towns where the grocery stores are not great or are very expensive, I send mail drop boxes instead.

SENDING MAIL DROPS FROM THE TRAIL

When I reach a big town with a supermarket, I take a zero day (a rest day) and plan, purchase, pack, and ship mail drops for towns I will hit in two or more weeks. When I reach the next big town with a supermarket, I repeat those steps.

EVOLVING SYSTEM

I start with mail drops that I packed at home and use them until I get tired of them. Then I call my resupply person, tell him to stop sending my boxes, and switch to grocery store resupply. This strategy is usually not something I plan in advance but becomes an inevitability when I tire of my boxes.

FAMILY/FRIEND RESUPPLY

This method works best for shorter trails where a friend or family member would only need to intercept you once or twice on your hike. It's best suited for hikes like the JMT, where the trail is very far from trailheads and to get off the trail into a town would require a two-day detour. My family came to visit me on the PCT and brought a resupply with them—but that was only once on the whole trail. I had to figure out other resupplies for all the other towns.

Pros:

- Get to see friends and family
- Often can get exactly the kind of food and the amount you want

Cons:

- Requires a lot of logistics and timing
- Can be easy to miss someone at a meeting place
- Difficult to get a loved one to meet you at every resupply point over a long hike

MAIL DROPS

There are steps and tricks for planning the various kinds of resupply. By definition, a general delivery is a means by which you can pick up a package addressed to you at a post office by presenting a government-issued ID. In this scenario, you or a family member ships you a package to pick up at a trailside post office. Most POs will hold your box for two weeks; some will hold it for longer. Remember to be nice to your postmaster, as he or she controls whether you get your package. Address your box like this:

[Your real name—not your trail name]

c/o General Delivery

Town, State, Zip Code

Please hold for hiker ETA [date]

You can also send boxes to yourself at some businesses or trail angels' houses along the trail. Always call or write to ask a business before you send them a package. Most trail angels or businesses have specific requirements for how they would like mail drops addressed or packaged. Please follow their requests. Some businesses charge a small fee to hold your box. This level of detailed information will be available in your trail's specific guidebook. In general, when mailing yourself a box to a business or trail angel, it is best to address your box like this:

[Your name]

c/o [the business]

Town, State, Zip Code

Please hold for hiker ETA [date]

This method works great if you think you may get into town after a post office closes, on a weekend, or on a federal holiday when the PO isn't open. Remember that if you send a box to a business, like a hotel or restaurant, you are committing to patronize the business. It's just plain rude to use a business to hold your package and then patronize a competitor. If you aren't sure whether you will have enough money to patronize this business, send your box to the PO.

ENLIST A FRIEND TO SHIP YOUR MAIL DROPS

If you assemble your boxes before you leave for the trail, you will need a person back home to ship them to your resupply points. Because the post office and some businesses generally will not hold a box longer than two weeks, that person needs to send you boxes about a week before you arrive. Figure out who this person is before you even start prepping your boxes.

Most gear stores don't sell ultralight gear. Luckily, many gear companies will ship General Delivery to Post Offices along the trail. My Mountain Laurel Designs Apex hood and mitts were shipped to Jasper National Park, Canada, just as it was getting cold.

Be sure you set aside at least 3 hours to explain the entire process to your friend—including how much room these boxes may take up at his or her house!

Make sure your friend knows all the work that being a resupply person will entail, including ensuring your packages get sent out on time.

It's best to choose a friend who won't be on vacation when you need his or her help. But if your friend is leaving town for a while and can't get a package out, be sure to come up with an alternate plan before you go.

ASSEMBLE YOUR BOXES

Once you know you've got someone able and willing to send you your mail drops, it's time to start putting them together. Unlike shipping your sibling a birthday present, hiking mail drop boxes need to be labeled specifically and sometimes have very specific shipping requirements. As a result, experienced thru-hikers sometimes feel like they know postal service regulations even better

Preparing many boxes of resupplies to send to myself for the Appalachian Trail, 2011. This is a messy process best done on a large desk, open floor space, or ping pong table.

than postal employees. I have always found postal employees to be very helpful, but here are a few tips to make sure your box has what you need and to ensure that it reaches its destination in one piece.

STEP 1: PREPARE YOUR BOXES

If you are shipping your box via USPS Priority, you can pick up free boxes at the post office. I like the large flat-rate option. You can also have them shipped to your house for free by going to the USPS website and ordering free priority flat-rate boxes available in their store under "Free Shipping Supplies." Boxes of all sizes and shapes are available, but for most of my thru-hikes, I use both kinds of medium flat-rate boxes or, if I need to send a lot of food or shoes to myself, the large flat-rate box.

I am a very big fan of the post office and have used it extensively over my twenty thru-hikes. I've always thought I would be their ultimate athlete to sponsor—but they haven't gotten back to me yet. I could write a whole book just on how to send food and supplies via the post office, but here are a few tips in choosing which boxes to use:

Flat-rate boxes must always be shipped Priority, but this provides speedier service, tracking, and $50 insurance should it get lost. If I am hiking a trail relatively close to where I live, the regional flat-rate boxes (only available online, but are free) can sometimes save some money. If the trail is very close to where I live, shipping my box first class tends to be the least expensive option. If I choose to ship first class or parcel post (the very slowest and sometimes the cheapest way to ship), I cannot use the flat-rate boxes. Instead, I use empty boxes and cross out names and logos that previously were associated with the boxes' contents. First class and parcel post boxes do not come with free bouncing if I don't pick up my box at its labeled destination. (I learned this the hard way when a friend sent me a package, I bounced them to another post office, and then had to pay shipping for stale cookies.)

Create a box for each resupply destination.

Create an address label for each box. The addresses for your trail towns can be found in your trail-specific guidebooks. Sometimes, rural locations do not receive door-to-door postal service delivery, but UPS or FedEx will work. Take note and label any boxes that need to be sent UPS or FedEx (as opposed to USPS).

Write the number of days' worth of food and resupplies are in each box. You should be able to determine this from the itinerary you put together (see chapter 4).

STEP 2: DO SOME MATH TO FIGURE OUT HOW MUCH YOU'LL NEED

I usually aim for 2 pounds of food per day between resupplies. At the beginning of the hike, I eat less per day. Toward the end of the hike, I may eat more like 3 pounds per day. Your average food per day differs depending on your body size to begin with and metabolic rate, but I've found regardless of what that magic number is, it's easier to think of your resupplies in terms of pounds per day than calories per day (assuming that in your 2-pound resupply, each ounce of food generally contains 100 calories). Make sure you have enough dinners and break-fasts for each day. Most thru-hikers enjoy eating snacks for their lunch, grazing on food every few hours instead of taking a big lunch break.

Here's how to calculate how many pounds of food to add to your box:

Days before your resupply x pounds of food you'll eat per day = pounds of food to carry on the next leg of your trip

STEP 3: BUY YOUR STUFF

If you are putting together mail drop boxes at home, buy the food you need for your trip in bulk at stores like Costco or on the Internet. Don't forget that you will likely get tired of foods that you buy in bulk, so show some restraint. Remember the food matrix (see "Eleven Food Rules for Thru-Hikers" in this chapter)—get a good variety of flavors and textures.

STEP 4: PACK UP YOUR BOXES

Now comes the best part: putting it all together. Start by making your boxes distinctive. You want them to stand out on overly full shelves. One option: spraypainting the boxes a bright color. (Note: In a few very rare instances postal workers will have a problem with boxes that are decorated or made to look distinctive. Check with the postmaster of the local PO before going to town on the ornamentation.) Next, repackage anything that came in bulk or was prepackaged to fit into smaller Ziploc bags. Then figure out what goes in each box.

Let's use my own real-life PCT example of packing a resupply box that I will get at White Pass, Washington, and that will hold me over until Snoqualmie Pass, about 100 miles later. This resupply needs to last me four days. That means that at 2 pounds of food per day, I need 8 pounds of food. First, throw your box on the scale and hit the zero or tare button. This allows you to calibrate your scale so it doesn't include the weight of your box in the weight it shows on the dial. This allows you to get an accurate weight of the food you have without letting the weight of the box throw off the calculation. Next, toss in four breakfasts, four lunches, and three dinners (I'm planning to eat my dinner on the fourth night at the Aardvark Express restaurant). Add some drink mixes. Check how close the box is to 8 pounds. Add in some more snacks if it's low or take some snacks out if it's too high. Sometimes, if I know the section will be particularly cold or difficult, I add a little extra food to the 8 pounds that I'm "supposed" to be eating. Also, toward the end of a thru-hike, I like to have a little extra food because my metabolism gets faster.

STEP 5: DON'T FORGET NON-FOOD CONSUMABLES

Once your food is in the box, add in non-edible items. I like to send myself new shoes every 400 miles. I like getting a new pair of socks in every other box, too. I also add in sunscreen, hand sanitizer, OTC meds, and anything else I need to maintain hygiene. Note that the post office requires you to double-bag any liquids or things that could leak (e.g., olive oil, shampoo, or wet wipes).

I also send myself stuff to use in town, like razors, good shampoo, conditioner, and lotion. If the town I'm sending my food to doesn't have a restaurant, I send myself some heavier food to eat—ready-to-eat entrees (I like Tasty Bites or Fish People food packets), sardines, or shelf-stable tofu. I always pack extra ziplock bags to carry trash and protect electronics, or to sort out my daily snacks. Don't forget to add maps for your upcoming section to each box. You can add some types of fuel to your boxes—but it must be declared to the postal person

Example of stuff you might want to include in regular (or monthly) maildrops. Obviously, you don't need a new pair of shoes every week.

and sent ground shipping, which is a lot slower. I normally don't bother and instead buy my fuel locally.

I also leave my resupply person with gear that I may want added to my boxes when the weather changes. Family members or friends may not always be knowledgeable about what gear you need. To make it easy for them, I gather all my extra gear that I may want on the trail and put the items in labeled and numbered Ziploc bags that reference their color. That way, when I call up my resupply person from the trail asking for "the blue Montbell wind shirt," I won't get the "blue Montbell wool shirt" instead.

STEP 6: HAND IT OFF TO YOUR RESUPPLY HELPER

When I'm done, I prepare a spreadsheet itinerary for my resupply person. This itinerary includes all the locations I need boxes sent to, the addresses, phone numbers, and my ETA. Then, I'll take that ETA and pick a date two weeks before, and ask my resupply person to send my boxes by that date. Trail towns are often in remote areas, so be sure to leave plenty of time for your box to get to your destination—especially if there are holidays like Memorial Day or Columbus Day in between. Update whoever is mailing your boxes if you are ahead of or behind schedule. Leave your itinerary with your friend in both paper and electronic versions. Carry your itinerary with you on your trip—both paper and electronic versions. That way, you both will not lose your shipping plans.

PHOTO CREDIT: LIZ THOMAS

I used the maildrop resupply option for the California part of PCT. Here, my maildrop strategy was supplemented by care packages from . . . pretty much everyone I knew.

When I'm done, I don't seal up my boxes. That way, if I decide that I am tired of a certain food item, my resupply person can take it out and replace it with something good. Be sure to include the cost of shipping your resupplies into your budget, and be prepared to hand that cash over to your resupply person before you leave. Resupplying is a big and very time-intensive job. You may want to look into the USPS's online shipping option like Click N Ship. This can make shipping a little easier for your resupply person, take them less time, and will be less expensive.

STEP 7: STAY IN TOUCH AND SAY THANKS

Call your resupply person regularly to let him or her know if you are running ahead of or behind schedule. That way, he or she can adjust when to ship boxes accordingly. Also, if you decide to quit the trail, let your resupply person know as soon as possible to avoid wasting money sending out unneeded boxes.

Thank your friend many times. Send your friend postcards. Take your friend out to dinner before you leave and after (if you have any money left). Being a resupply person is a huge task, and you should be enormously grateful that someone likes you enough to do it.

WHAT IF YOU MAIL TOO MUCH STUFF?

If you pick up your mail drop box and realize you have things in it that you can't or won't use, you have a few options. You can mail things back home (expensive) or bounce them ahead to yourself (more on that soon). Or you can leave your items in a "hiker box," something many trail-town post offices, trail angels, and businesses have. A hiker box is a place to leave unwanted items for other hikers to use—and a place to take needed items that other hikers have left behind.

GROCERY STORE RESUPPLIES

For most first-time thru-hikers, I recommend that they not use the mail drop method for all their resupplies. Most people learn a lot about themselves, how much they eat, and what they like to eat on the trail while they are hiking. The mail drop–only method works best for those who have a thru-hike or extended backpacking trip under their belt already and know their on-trail eating habits better. Furthermore, it is very easy for first time thru-hikers to obsess about food and let other pre-hiking preparation go on the back burner. I feel that your time is best spent doing other planning, as the food can be done locally (for the most part) once you are on the trail. Statistically, first-time thru-hikers are the most likely to quit. So if you quit the trail, you don't want extra junk food around. I know from experience—12 Costco-size bags of Fritos are hard to get rid of. A better option for first-time thru-hikers is to choose the other end of the resupply spectrum—buying all their food locally at a grocery or convenience store.

First, during a grocery store resupply, make the best of the full store at your disposal. This means grabbing a few fresh foods that you could never get using the mail drop strategy. Think cheese, fresh garlic, or even broccoli. A good rule of thumb (for long trail preparation—and for life!) is not to shop while hungry. Eat first. I will usually enter a store and grab a few fresh foods to eat, leave the store, and eat until I am full. Then I'll return to do my resupply.

Don't buy too much food. You can use the produce section's scale to weigh your resupply. Remember to get a variety. Because grocery store food is sold in big packages, it's easy to buy too much of a single item. For example, two blocks of cheese could easily be half your needed food weight for the next

section. Instead, actively remind yourself of the food flavor matrix (see "Eleven Food Rules for Thru-Hikers" in this chapter).

GAS STATION RESUPPLY

Obviously a nice grocery store or supermarket is ideal for on-the-go resupplies, but you can actually get away with shopping at a gas station. A gas station certainly doesn't have the selection of backpacking foods you'd find at a natural food co-op or even a grocery store or supermarket, but every year thousands of thru-hikers manage to resupply out of convenience stores.

Look for foods with high calories per ounce. Include enough dinners and breakfast choices for all the days you are out—and pick foods you can easily cook on your camp stove. Don't forget—one of the huge benefits of resupplying locally is getting some semi-fresh food. I like to grab cheese, prepackaged hardboiled eggs, lunch meats—even pizza. These "real foods" might be a bit heavier than other backpacking foods, but will feel like a huge luxury and treat once you're 10 miles away from town.

Decide on a set number of snack choices per day. And don't buy all the same thing, like cookies or cheese. Balance your snack choices between crunchy, chewy, sweet, and salty. Don't forget electrolytes and drink mixes.

As you load up your shopping basket, keep track of the total number of pounds of food you've collected versus what you estimate you'll need to fuel your body through the next section. If the store has a produce section, use a scale to check yourself. Otherwise, use the package weights and take notes to keep track. This matters—it's easy to buy way too much. Once you're done with getting all your food, grab some non-food consumables, like sunscreen, hand sanitizer, bug spray, and toilet paper.

Finally—and I've learned this one the hard way—when you leave town, don't forget to top off your water bottles or buy a bottled drink in town to take into the woods with you.

BOUNCE BOXES

Whether you use mail drops, local resupplies, or something in between, consider using a bounce box for at least some of the towns you visit. A bounce box is a box that contains many useful items that aren't found in all trail towns. One box or bucket is used over the course of the entire trail and "bounced" (forwarded) ahead—hence the name. This box or bucket is not sent to every resupply town, only to selected resupply towns. When you get your box, take out the items you need right away, and send the rest ahead.

If you get a bounce box in town and decide you don't need anything, as long as the box isn't opened and hasn't left the post office counter, the box can be bounced ahead for free to another PO. To qualify for free bouncing the box must have been shipped Priority Mail in the first place.

Consider adding town clothes in a bounce box. This is a chance to include the comfy shoes and cotton you'll be craving. And you'll have something to wear while you do laundry. Or consider including gear you need to add along the way or replace, like gloves, socks, gaiters, or a bandana. You may also want to keep cold weather gear in here, like microspikes, an ice axe, and cold weather clothes (we'll talk more about gear in chapter 6).

Sometimes you may want to include replacement gear, like tent stakes, a new spoon, extra buckles or shoelaces, a sewing kit, or even supplies for cleaning up in town, such as shampoo, conditioner, razors, deodorant, and nail clippers. Or include consumables—toilet paper, hand sanitizer, first-aid supplies, Gold Bond powder, bug spray, toothpaste—that are often sold in containers that are too big to carry, but that you can bounce from place to place, topping off smaller containers. Extras of items, like Ziploc bags, are helpful for protecting electronics and maps, or for dealing with trash.

A cheap netbook, laptop, or tablet will let you take care of any computer work you need to do, even if the trail town does not have a library whose computers you can use. Don't forget headphones or chargers, extra SD cards, and any specialized camera equipment that you may want for certain scenic sections and not for others.

Different people, different packs

Chapter 6

+ GEAR

Finally! We're finally digging into that topic that everyone seems to obsess over: gear. It's really easy to get fanatical about gear and start believing that just because you don't have all the fanciest new equipment, it means you don't have what it takes to complete a hike. But, in truth, gear is less important than you think. When I hiked my first thru-hike of the Tahoe Rim Trail, I used only gear I'd found at the REI garage sale a few months before. I was not picky and was just looking for a good deal. I ended up with a zero-degree, 5-pound, synthetic sleeping bag for a July-August hike in California. It took up most of the room in my pack, and I sweated through every night. Even though I wasn't happy with my gear, I successfully completed that hike. And by the time I planned my next hike, I knew what I wanted to replace.

No matter what you start with, once you get on the trail, you will meet a lot of people who will tell you that you're carrying the wrong stuff. They'll say your stuff is too heavy or too light. But the most important thing is making smart gear decisions you can feel confident in. There is no one right answer with gear. It's really personal. I learned that for me (and for most people) a zero-degree bag for a July hike in California is only the right gear choice for those who enjoy sweat-fests. The more you hike, the more your system will evolve to suit you, your needs, and the climate and terrain.

I'm not going to tell you exactly what to buy. But I will help you avoid wasting a lot of money on gear you don't like or gear that causes you pain or discomfort. Even experienced hikers are constantly updating their gear lists, saving up for updated versions of their gear, or replacing

PHOTO CREDIT: JOHNNY CARR

Gear that works for one part of the trail may not work for a couple hundred miles farther north.

worn-out gear. Whether you're putting together a kit using budget, mid-grade, or premium items, this chapter will give you key tips and tricks for navigating the rabbit hole.

ASK THE RIGHT QUESTIONS

The best gear is what works for you, not what the reviews say or what a celebrity hiker endorses. In addition, what works for you on one trail and in one climate may not work for you elsewhere. But don't despair. There are some basic gear rules and principles that can help you make wise choices. It all starts with asking yourself the following key questions.

Just like you would never take a whole backpacking set up on a day hike, there's no reason for you to carry a camping set while you are on a day hike.

QUESTION 1: WHAT WILL I SPEND MY TIME DOING?

Whatever gear you choose for a particular trip should make you the most comfortable for what you are doing the majority of the time. If most days you plan to hang out in camp, hike a few miles, set up camp, and hang out some more, you are emphasizing camping over hiking. If you plan to spend most of the day actively moving, then quickly set up camp and go to sleep, you are emphasizing hiking over camping. Reflecting back on the "why" of your hike (see the "Introduction") can help clarify this for you. Is relaxing in camp important to you? Or pushing your body to go far every day?

Choose the gear that will keep you comfortable for this trip. If you are mostly camping, having a big, comfy camp chair is important—even if hiking with it will be annoying because it is heavy. If you are mostly hiking, having light gear is important—even if you are a bit cold when you aren't moving and not in your sleeping bag.

Most thru-hikers veer more toward the hiking side of the spectrum, so they don't carry extra clothes, for example. They stay warm by either moving or being in their sleeping bag. That also means that their packs and shoes are important pieces of gear to get right.

Water will be your first concern when planning the part of your hike that goes through desert.

QUESTION 2: WHAT WILL CONDITIONS BE LIKE?

Of course you can't predict everything, but trying to be prepared for literally any condition at any time is a good way to make sure your pack is totally unwieldy. Instead, do your best to research likely weather and terrain for your trip, and plan accordingly.

- How much and how long does it rain?
- What are typical high and low temperatures that time of year and at that elevation?
- How much snowpack do you anticipate and what is typically the quality of the snow?
- How exposed (sun or wind) is your route?

QUESTION 3: WHAT TRADE-OFFS AM I WILLING TO MAKE?

Gear is really all about trade-offs and balances. If something weighs less, it probably costs more. If it's more durable, it's probably bulkier or heavier. What's your most important priority? Is it getting the cheapest kit you can, like I did for

Setting up a Cuben Fiber tarp takes some practice, but it is one of the lightest shelter set-ups out there.

my Tahoe Rim Trail hike? You might end up with extra weight and bulk, as I did, but that was the trade-off I made, and it worked okay. Is it having the absolute lightest kit? It's likely to be pricey and potentially not super durable, depending on the exact products you choose. These days I tend to prioritize having the lightest kit I can over having the most comfortable kit, but sometimes I'll choose something heavier if it's more versatile or more durable.

An important note: You can often trade weight (or pricey gear) for skills. For example, many campers like a fully enclosed double-walled tent with bathtub floor and its own set of poles. Weight-conscious hikers instead may opt for a cheap tarp that can be set up with hiking poles and a well-thought out camp location. Both the double-walled tent and the tarp set up in the right camp spot will protect you from the elements. The big difference is the price, durability, and knowledge required. A tarp requires knowing how to set it up in different configurations, knots to keep the tarp in place, and the experience to discern a protected campsite from a future puddle. The more you know, the lighter and sometimes the cheaper the gear you can succeed with. You gain skills with practice. Practice at home before you go and practice on overnight trips with hikers more experienced than you.

QUESTION 4: WHAT DO I ALREADY HAVE?

Starting from scratch is one thing, but if you've been backpacking or otherwise recreating outdoors for a while, it's possible that some of the gear you already have will work just fine for a thru-hike. Make sure to take stock of what's already available to you so you can prioritize what's most important to buy or replace. A cool tool for keeping track is weighmygear.com.

LIGHTEN UP WITHOUT BREAKING THE BANK

I'm a big proponent of backpacking with ultralight gear—and here's why. Over the years, I've found that my body is happiest when my pack is the lightest. Even when a good pack bears a heavy weight well, you're still getting that impact in your feet, knees, and joints. Foot, knee, and joint issues are among the most common problems that take people off the trail. Ultralight gear really makes it

PHOTO CREDIT: LIZ THOMAS

Never just one job. On a cold morning on the Sierra High Route, Felicia "Princess of Darkness" Hermosillo and Whitney "Allgood" LaRuffa wear their rain gear to stay warm.

THE CASE FOR GOING LIGHT

PHOTO CREDIT: WHITNEY LARUFFA

Don't just take my word for it. Here's my friend Whitney "Allgood" LaRuffa on why a light pack is worth it.

In 1996 I set forth on my first thru-hike: the Appalachian Trail. I started off from Amicalola State Park with a Dana Designs backpack so big that it didn't just have one external frame to support it, but two. The pack weighed a whopping 85 pounds. It was a chore to get on and off, let alone hike under. Along the hike, I figured out things to change and what I could live without. I finished the AT with a pack weight around 35 pounds. That Christmas, I got a copy of Ray Jardine's classic *PCT Hiker's Handbook*, and that was the beginning of my ultralight (UL) ways. Over the next two years, I worked as a ridge runner—kind of like a ranger—for the Appalachian Trail Conference (later renamed the Appalachian Trail Conservancy). It was then that I experimented with lightening up by forgoing my tent for a tarp and trading out gear for multiuse items. By the end of the second summer, I had my pack base weight down to 15 pounds, which in 1998 was a pretty big feat. Fast forward twenty years. Now I'm a working stiff who still gets out a few weekends per month and gets to hike one major 200- to 300-mile trip per year. Ultralighting makes my weekends and vacations doable. By carrying an 8-pound pack of UL gear, I can go from cubicle to trail and push 25- to 30-mile days without any issue. Having a light pack makes the transition to trail easy, as I'm not concerned about the weight on my back as I labor uphill. Ultralight gear also eases the strain on my joints, like my knees and shoulder, both of which suffer from a lifetime of sports and injuries. I also find that, because of my light pack, I'm able to push farther each day than I thought possible. And I can lift my head up and enjoy the scenery all day long instead of looking at my feet, hunched over from a heavy pack. I cannot encourage people enough to lighten their load so that they, too, can walk comfortably among nature.

—Whitney "Allgood" LaRuffa

My comfort with minimalist cooking means I can get away with a very small stove made from a beer can.

possible for older people to get back on the trail, and it makes it easier to travel farther and faster—away from the crowds and deeper into the backcountry. In an emergency, with an ultralight pack, you can move more quickly towards help or more graciously offer to take on an injured partner's pack weight. Whether you already own most of your gear or are building your kit from scratch, here are a few tips inspired by ultralight gear guru Ray Jardine on how to lighten any pack for a thru-hike.

☐ **Tip 1: Think about versatility.** Your gear should function as a system. Ideally, each item works with the other items so that no matter what the conditions, you can be relatively safe and comfortable. Take clothing, for example. I normally wear a (non-cotton) T-shirt when I hike. If the wind picks up or the sun gets intense, I add a wind shirt. If it gets very cold, I put on my insulating layer. Because I'm already wearing a wind shirt under it, my insulating later doesn't need to be very heavy.

My rain gear system works the same way. If it's a light, warm rain, I just use my umbrella. An umbrella is arguably the most breathable piece of rain gear ever (plus I can also use it to block the sun). If it starts raining harder or gets colder, I add my wind shirt. If it starts raining even harder, I add my rain jacket. This system allows me to customize how much gear I need depending on the conditions. It also allows me to have the most breathable rain system at the start, and then trade off breathability for better coverage as conditions worsen.

Another way to think about this idea of versatility is to find multiple uses for one piece of gear. I use my cookpot as a mug, cup for cold drinks, bowl, plate—and cookpot. A bandana can be used as a towel or washcloth, to keep sun off your neck, as a pre-filter for water, and as a safety signal. A little creativity can go a long way to lightening your load.

☐ **Tip 2: Trade weight for skills.** I mentioned this already, but it bears repeating. A big part of a lightweight gear system includes bulking up on your backcountry skills. You can get away with having a lighter sleeping bag if you know that you're going to be wearing lots of clothes to bed every night and you're not afraid of being a little chilly. You can carry a tarp if you know how to pick a camp spot sheltered from the elements (more on picking sites in chapter 7). Many outdoors courses teach you to how to fashion splints or other pieces of medical gear from gear you carry in your pack or find along the trail (rather than carrying specific medical supplies). In his *PCT Handbook*, ultralight guru Ray Jardine discusses many tricks and skills ultralight hikers use to stretch the multiple uses of the gear.

☐ **Tip 3: Modify to make it work for you.** Jardine's book inspired me to experiment with gear modification—chopping off unnecessary straps, toggles, doodads, and tassels—to make gear lighter. Don't be afraid to modify gear to make it fit you better. But remember that anything you do modify can't be returned, and most things you cut off can't be sewn back on. I accidentally chopped an ice axe loop off a pack once, which made that pack unusable in high mountain sections.

☐ **Tip 4: Get creative with trash.** It sounds silly, but you can lighten your pack a lot by trading out heavy gear for garbage. Most thru-hikers use old Gatorade or Smartwater bottles as their water bottles. Trash compactor bags make great pack liners—and even rain gear in a pinch. Some of the lightest stoves out there can be made from old cat food or beer cans.

☐ **Tip 5: Don't bring everything all the time.** Just because it will be cold in the Sierra doesn't mean you have to start the PCT with your super-warm sleeping bag. You probably will not need to carry your ice axe in the desert. (I know many people who have, and the workers at the post office 100 miles from the Mexican border gets a kick out of making fun of hikers for it.)

Regardless of the season/weather in which you start, you'll hike through different weather. Buy or send yourself gear as the weather changes.

You don't need 4 pounds of sunscreen to last you from Georgia to Maine. For consumables like sunscreen, pack small amounts into 1-ounce bottles that you mail to yourself in your resupplies or bounce box. Or buy travel sizes along the way as needed. The same goes for fuel, bug spray, or even olive oil.

If I already own an item I know I will want for a certain section (like a pair of snowshoes in the San Juans of Colorado), I tell my resupply person to send it up the trail, perhaps to the trail town right before the section where I will need the gear. Likewise, PCT hikers send their bear canister, ice axes, and warm clothes to Kennedy Meadows, the last town before you enter the Sierra.

Many long trails have gear stores along the way that cater to long-distance hikers, including Mountain Crossings at Neels Gap (about 30 miles into the AT) or Laguna Mountain Sports and Supply (42 miles into the PCT). You can often find replacement gear for items that have worn out or gear that is better suited to the local conditions and regulations.

If I don't own the item already, I either buy it locally at a gear store or I find it online and have it sent to a resupply spot about two weeks ahead (so I won't

HIKE YOUR OWN HIKE

HOW I LIGHTENED MY PACK

PHOTO CREDIT: JOHNNY CARR

Over time most thru-hikers learn how to do more with less. For Johnny Carr, a little peer pressure didn't hurt either.

I successfully thru-hiked the PCT in 2014 and hiked most of the CDT in 2015, leaving only the last 800 miles to look forward to in another year. There is a lot of light gear out there, but if it all ends up in your pack, it will weigh you down. It is just as important to know what to leave out of your pack as it is to choose the correct gear. When you just start out backpacking, you can't typically get away with minimal-style backcountry travel—but experienced hikers can. When you start, you will definitely start heavier. As your experience builds, your pack weight can be lessened comfortably. My pack weight got lighter all the way from the Mexican border to the Sierras on the PCT by swapping out gear I had for lighter versions or simply sending unneeded gear home and tossing out what I didn't need when I got to town. I thought I was doing a pretty good job until I met Charlie Day hiker. This guy carries a ridiculously small pack and gets by because of his experience in the backcountry. We shared a hotel room in a trail town, and he made me empty everything out of my pack and justify why I had it—in a room full of other hikers. It made it very easy for me to get rid of weight—with some help from my friends. I ended up sending home another 2.5 pounds of gear that afternoon.

—Johnny "Bigfoot" Carr

get to the resupply town before my gear). Amazon Prime or V.I.P. Zappos items can be shipped in two days (or slightly longer to rural trail towns). Remember: If you order gear on the Internet, UPS and FedEx items cannot be sent General Delivery. The post office won't hold items sent by other carriers.

When I finally get my new gear, I send my old gear home using insurance and tracking.

Don't be afraid to change your gear with the conditions. Even if you love a piece of gear, it's quite possible that it may not work as well when the weather changes or you enter new ecosystems on your hike.

☐ **Tip 6: Be ruthless about what's in your pack.** Weigh all your gear and think really hard about what you will use on the trail. Most people bring too much clothing and food—stuff that stays at the bottom of their pack for the whole trip. Honestly, most thru-hikers wear the same shirt and same pants every day. If they want to look nice in town, they wear their sleep clothes.

And remember, practice makes lighter. Take your pack on a trip and weigh it right before you leave the car at the trailhead—that way, you won't try to sneak in a few last-minute items from your glovebox. Each time you go out, strive to get your pack a little bit lighter. Practice with an experienced hiker who you know has a lighter pack than you (and uses that light pack safely and comfortably). He or she may know tips and tricks to help you lighten your load.

WHAT TO EXPECT REGARDING DURABILITY AND GUARANTEES

If the manufacturer of your gear or the retailer has a generous return or guarantee policy, it can be tempting to use this benefit as a way to save money. But if you put in a fair amount of miles on your gear and have really worn it in, please do not call the company asking for a replacement unless their guarantee covers normal wear (very few companies do). Some thru-hikers have called shoe companies, for example, after putting in 1,000 miles on a single pair of trail running shoes that should only have a life of 300 to 500 miles. The end result is that thru-hikers look bad, and it's harder for those who really need replacements for faulty gear to get what they need. Be thoughtful about when you'll truly need to replace gear and work that into your budget.

Here's how long lightweight gear tends to last:

- Sleeping bags: More than 10,000 miles
- Shelters: 5,000 miles
- Packs: 2,500–3,000 miles
- Shirts and shorts: 1,000–3,000 miles
- Shoes: 300–500 miles
- Socks: 100–500 miles

This means that if you are going on a 2,000-plus-mile hike, you should expect to need at least four pairs of shoes, many pairs of socks, two pairs of shorts, two shirts, one pack, one sleeping bag, and one shelter. Of course, you can often extend the life of your gear by keeping it clean and doing all you can to minimize abrasion or punctures (more info on that later in this chapter), and you

Don't expect lightweight shoes to last forever. Plan to get new ones multiple times on your trip.

can save money by opting to repair instead of replace gear when possible. But don't expect gear companies or stores to foot the bill when you've used a piece of gear beyond its natural lifespan.

WHERE TO SPEND YOUR TIME AND MONEY

The most important gear decisions you will make are choosing your heaviest and most expensive items: sleeping bag, shelter, pack, and footwear. Read gear reviews, ask experienced thru-hikers, and try to borrow any item you're considering before committing. Consider shopping somewhere with a generous return policy, so if you discover after one test trip that you made a mistake, you aren't stuck with something that's not going to work for you. Remember that a test trip is the best way to know before you go.

PHOTO CREDIT: LIZ THOMAS

After 30 miles hiking the AT with nothing but a fleece blanket nabbed from the flight I took out to Atlanta, I knew I needed a proper sleeping bag. Here I am with my the bag I had just purchased at Neels Gap, which I then used on the AT, PCT, and CDT.

SLEEPING BAG

If you invest in just one high-quality item, let it be your sleeping bag or sleeping quilt. You will spend at least 8 hours a day in it, and your bag is a safety device as your last line of defense against hypothermia. This is not a spot to scrimp. A pricier bag can last decades and is usually lighter, which allows for less bulk so it compresses better. It oftentimes has better design features (like draft tubes), which keep you warmer, and has better loft, which also keeps you warmer.

Companies that make pricier bags tend to have excellent customer service, so if anything ever were to happen to your bag (e.g., holes, lost feathers, needs re-lofting), they are usually willing to help.

On the last day of my PCT thru-hike, I woke to feathers everywhere. There was a huge hole in my sleeping bag's footbox. (I blame a marmot.) I duct taped it up, finished the trail, washed the bag, and sent it to Western Mountaineering. They replaced the footbox panel and added new feathers. The footbox looked brand new, and they only charged me $30 and shipping.

Believe it or not, there is such a thing as a too-warm sleeping bag. A zero-degree bag may keep you warm—but usually is too much for three-season hiking. Why?

- You'll get hot and sweaty in your bag, making you uncomfortable.
- Your body will sweat trying to cool you off, giving you the sensation that you're actually too cold in your bag.
- It's heavier than a 20-degree bag (a more reasonable temperature rating for three-season hiking).
- It costs more than a 20-degree bag.

Instead, to stay warm, wear socks and a hat to bed, along with clean sleep clothes. Bathe or wipe salt off your body before going to bed, as salt crystals produce a cooling sensation on your skin, making you feel colder. Make sure you eat enough calories and go to bed warm in the first place (try moving around and warming up if you're not). Use your sleeping bag in conjunction with a sleeping bag liner or bivy, and use a good sleeping pad. Finally, use a tent or other shelter, especially if it's windy.

Bags come in different sizes (short/women's, regular, and long), and it's worth it to get a bag sized right for you. It's obvious that one that's too small won't work, but a too-big bag is also problematic: At night, you'll have extra space to warm up, meaning it will feel colder, and during the day, you'll carry useless extra weight. As a general rule, buy the snuggest bag that doesn't make you feel claustrophobic. Don't forget to leave room for your feet—especially if they are big. You don't want your feet pressing against the end of the footbox, as that will compress the insulation there, which can make your feet cold.

SLEEPING PADS

Sleeping pads aren't just about getting a comfy night's rest. Their main function is insulating you from the cold ground. R-value is a term used to measure the insulating factor of a sleeping pad. The higher the R-value, the warmer the pad. For three-season camping, I recommend a pad with an R-value of at least 2, higher if you tend to get cold at night. Most thru-hikers like an R-value of 2 to 3.5. Over a thru-hike, the R-value of a foam pad will decrease. Inflatable pads' R-value will generally stay the same over time, but inflatable pads can get holes.

PHOTO CREDIT: DEAN KRAKEL

Protect your inflateable sleeping pad by placing a groundcloth underneath.

If you carry one, be sure you also have a patch system and know how to repair your pad, and always have at least a groundcloth between your pad and the ground to protect it from spiky plants. Some hikers save weight by using a torso- or three-quarter-length pad instead of a full pad, or by trimming their sleeping pad to the outline of their body. Many hikers with shorter pads use their empty pack as the last quarter of their sleeping pad. While ⅜-inch torso pads may save you weight, find a different pad if you can't sleep more than 5 hours.

SHELTER

You don't need the most expensive shelter, but you should get a nice one. After all, it will be your home for months. If you think about it that way, even a $600 tent used over six months comes out to just $100 a month. You can't find that kind of rent pricing anywhere. Even if you're hiking a trail that has permanent shelters every 10 miles (the AT) or hiking through the desert of Southern California, you will need a shelter. Storms can happen anywhere, any time of year. And all it takes is one Boy Scout troop to fill up the trail shelter for the night. Tents and other portable shelters aren't just for rain protection, but also for wind protection

PHOTO CREDIT: LIZ THOMAS

My Mountain Laurel Designs Solomid and Felicia "Princess of Darkness" Hermosillo's Z-Packs Duplex on the Sierra High Route after a rainstorm.

and to generate a cell of warmth.

You'll live in your shelter for a few months. Make your palace as nice as possible. When shopping around for shelters, ask yourself:

Is there room to protect me and my stuff? A vestibule can be used to protect some items as well.

Will I rub against the walls of the shelter if I move around too much? Condensation collects on the side walls of a shelter and can get you wet. If you choose a smaller shelter where this is likely, think about getting a protective bivy for your sleeping bag to prevent it from getting wet.

Will I want to sit up in my shelter? Or can I live without that feature? Check out the headroom of your tent.

The shelter you get depends on your skills at campsite selection. A heavier tent can be set up just about anywhere and will be relatively comfortable. An ultralight tarp will not be comfortable in all conditions, but can be very comfortable if set up in protected areas. If you are willing to invest some time each night finding a protected campsite, you can get away with having a lighter shelter. (Learn more about picking a good campsite in chapter 7.) If you're new to camping and backpacking, you're more likely to do better with a more substantial option.

The footprint—how much ground space—your shelter needs will dictate the type of places you camp. Shelters with small footprints can fit into smaller places. This gives you more options when camping spots are limited—or if you are hiking with many other hikers with tents. Most thru-hikers go with shelters that require staking down. These tend to be lighter and provide more flexibility to pitch your shelter in multiple ways (e.g., storm mode versus lots of ventilation). However, they can be more difficult to set up than free standing shelters in certain areas with rocky soil or slab rock.

Many backpacking tents have built-in bug protection, but not all ultralight thru-hiking shelters do. Most thru-hikers don't want to carry bug netting for their shelter unless they really need to (after all, it's extra weight). Some opt to carry head nets or bivys with bug protection. Others use bug net inserts that fit inside the tent and only carry the inserts during the buggiest sections of trail. That said, if you really don't like bugs (or scorpions or snakes), you may enjoy a permanent bug net.

Zippers are often failure points—especially on a thru-hike where they are being used often and dirt can easily get lodged in the grooves of the teeth. This causes the teeth to stretch enough that they no longer lock together. Beefier zippers weigh more, but are less prone to failure. Some shelters don't use zippers—that's one less thing that can fail. To keep costs down, many ultralight companies may not seam-seal their shelters—a process that prevents water from leaking through the holes in the stitching used to sew the tent together. Instead, you're expected to do this yourself. Make sure you do this at home before you go, if needed.

HAMMOCK SHELTERS

PHOTO CREDIT: WILLIAM MURPHY

My friend, William "Pi" Murphy, uses a hammock as his shelter.

I've hiked over 3,000 miles on the AT and PCT with my preferred shelter: a hammock. I've also hiked several thousand miles as a ground dweller. Perhaps the biggest reason I prefer a hammock is the quality of the sleep. Once I adjusted to a hammock over the first few nights, it was very comfortable and gave me a deep and restful sleep. I've heard some people never adjust to the gentle sway, but I find it very peaceful. With my hammock, I'm not packing up a muddy or pine-tarred sticky tent. My shelter goes up and comes down cleanly. There's almost no impact or trace left of my campsite. Mice and ants are not issues—they're below you. I often have a wider selection of campsites with the hammock. Uneven ground and even hillsides are sound. Wet ground is fine.

Because hammocks are the less used option, there's less competition for prime sites with great views. I've camped on ridgelines and overlooks, over steep and rocky ground, above thorn bushes and once even above a tiny stream. Both broader site availability and faster setup and takedown help me spend less time making and breaking camp when I use my hammock. A hammock also seems to be more stealthy when you want to camp unnoticed. Finally, a hammock makes an outstanding chair as well as a bed, and few ground dwelling systems include a comparable chair.

A hammock does bring some additional challenges. There's a learning curve, which includes understanding the knots or other hanging mechanisms. It's important to avoid dangerous camp situations, from dead trees and precarious dead branches (aka widowmakers) to improper hang angles. Sometimes there is a lack of trees, such as in the desert or when hiking above treeline. To arrange arriving in a forested area to camp may require modifications to your hiking location or route. Staying warm in a hammock is half about staying warm on top and half about staying warm on the bottom. With a ground-based camp system, staying warm on the bottom is less of an issue in the summer. A hammock may be a slightly heavier system than a ground-based system, but it is close enough that one must consider all the components with care for either system to notice the difference at all. Many ground systems—even ultralight ones—are heavier than a well-chosen hammock setup. Overall, the combination of wider campsite selections and a better night's rest make hammocks a key component to my preferred shelter system.

—William "Pi" Murphy

Your pack may become a part of your body. Even during breaks you may forget to take it off, as Andrea "Breeze" Jordan does at this AT overlook.

PACKS

Wayne Gregory, founder of Gregory Backpacks and one of the fathers of back-packing, was among the first to say that you "wear"—not "carry"—a backpack. Your pack needs to fit as well as a piece of clothing. Actually, it needs to fit better than your clothes. At the end of a long hike, most thru-hikers feel as if their pack has become a part of them—another body part. In fact, I feel pretty naked without one on. When I don't have a pack on, I get "phantom pack syndrome"—the sensation that I'm missing a body part. So investing in a good pack is really worthwhile.

Buy all your other gear first and your pack last. That way, you won't accidentally get a pack too small to fit your stuff, or one way too big and bulky. No matter what the capacity of your pack, you will fill it. So it's better to go with a smaller-capacity pack for a thru-hike so you won't be tempted to fill it with unnecessary stuff. But remember that you will need room for food. Most thru-hikers use packs between 50 and 70 liters (this includes capacity in side and mesh pockets). If part of your trail goes through an area that requires bear canisters, make sure that your pack can fit the bear canister you intend to use or that you will send yourself a pack that can.

Most backpack companies tell you what the expected weight load should be. This will differ depending on whether your pack is frameless, internally framed, or externally framed. If you overload your pack, you could blow the stitching. There's little that sucks more than being 80 miles from your next resupply town with a one-strapped backpack—I've seen it. Again, weigh all your gear and add whatever you think your food and water on a normal carry will be. If it is below the maximum carry limit on the pack, you're good to go.

You want your pack to carry all your gear comfortably, but you also want to be able to get to that gear easily. Nice features to have in a pack include hipbelt pockets for storing snacks or a camera where you can reach them as you hike, one or more mesh stuff-it pockets on the outside, and easy access to water bottles with the pack on (less key if you use a hydration bladder).

Several hikers I know opt to use packs with fewer access points (such as hipbelt pockets) and use a fanny pack instead. Look for a pack with a removable hipbelt if you expect to lose weight on your trip. You'll have to buy a new hipbelt later, but it's less expensive than getting a brand-new pack.

The comfort of any pack—especially ultralight models—depends strongly on your ability to load it well. Many experienced backpackers (even experienced thru-hikers) pack their packs poorly (sometimes even myself included). On a shorter hike and when you carry lighter gear, you can get away with a lumpy pack. But on a long hike, a pack that does not distribute weight well—especially a heavily loaded pack—can lead to injuries and pain.

I suggest contacting the manufacturer of your pack to see if they have developed a video or instructions on how they suggest packing your pack. Here are the steps I use to pack my frameless backpack, based on tips from my friend Cam "Swami" Honan from thehikinglife.com:

Gossamer Gear packs used by my hiking team on the Sierra High Route. Some have light internal frames and some are frameless.

Fold your foam sleeping pad and insert it into the sleeve meant to hold the sleeping pad in place as a frame. Again, this is only for frameless packs. If your pack has no sleeve, put the folded pad inside the pack against your back. Put in the pack liner: Open up the pack and add a trash compactor bag to use as a waterproof liner. I prefer this system over a pack cover because it is less likely to leak.

Add stuff you won't use during the day to the bottom, like your shelter or camping equipment. Heaviest items should be in the mid to upper back areas to help keep your center of gravity towards the middle and aid in stability (although for many thru-hikers, water and food are heavier than their shelter). Note that women have lower centers of gravity than men.

If you are carrying a hydration bladder for water, insert it into your pack's sleeve, or otherwise aim to get it toward the middle of the pack near your back. The goal is to have the heaviest stuff close to your back area around the mid to upper area of your back, near your center of gravity, so that the weight is less likely to throw you off balance.

Add your food bag (likely your weightest item besides water) on top toward the middle (remember to take out enough snacks for the day).

Fill in the dead space in your pack by stuffing your sleeping bag—not in a stuff sack—into the nooks and crannies between the stuff already in your pack. It sounds crazy letting your sleeping bag be free in your backpack, but this helps its longevity by preventing compression of the down filling. It also makes a noticeable difference in equalizing the weight of the pack so you feel more stable carrying it. You can always put it in a waterproof stuff sack when the weather changes.

Top off your pack with stuff you will likely use during the day, such as snacks, extra layers, or rain gear. Twist the pack liner or fold it redundantly to prevent water from getting in should it rain.

Put any stuff that really needs to be accessible—like your most recent map, phone/camera, lip balm, sunscreen, or bug spray—into mesh side pockets or hipbelt pockets. Place water bottles into side pockets.

Avoid attaching anything with carabiners or webbing (with the exception of a sleeping pad, an ice axe, or snow shoes). Dangling parcels can throw off your balance and get caught (and subsequently lost) in vegetation. If it doesn't fit in the pack, you probably don't need it anyway. And it just looks sloppy.

FOOTWEAR

During your hike, you will be on your feet for most of the day. Shoes that fit you well thus become extremely important. Up your chances of finding a good shoe by shopping at a dedicated outdoor store or a store that deals with trail running. So what do you look for in a shoe? A trail-appropriate shoe will have tread with adequate traction, be constructed of good materials with quality stitching, have very good flex, and fit well. Most thru-hikers use trail runners for three-season conditions. Trail runners work well if you have a lighter pack. If your pack is heavier, you will need extra support for your feet, so stick with boots. Start by sizing up—many thru-hikers enjoy wearing their shoes loosely. Alternatively, find shoes with a wide toe box, like my personal favorite (and sponsor) Altra. Remember, your feet will swell and expand over the course of the hike. If you are buying all the shoes you need for the trip ahead of time (and you are headed on a 2,000-plus-mile hike), make sure to get some shoes that are one to two sizes bigger for the end of your trip.

While buying shoes, also think about getting replacement insoles. The factory insoles are usually cardboard-thin, a problem because such thin insoles

Choose a shoe with enough support for your pack weight. If your pack is light or ultralight, you can use trail runners. Those with heavier packs may want boots.

do not offer much support and cushioning versus aftermarket insoles. The lack of cushioning and support in factory insoles may lead to sore knees, aching arches, and possibly even plantar fasciitis.

Thru-hikers generally do not go with waterproof shoes for three-season hiking, opting instead for shoes that dry quickly and breathe better. The reason? Most thru-hikers will go through fords (river crossings) and puddles without taking off their shoes, so having quick-drying shoes is important for comfort and also to minimize the chances of blisters or trench foot forming. Mesh, non-waterproof shoes breathe better and keep your feet from overheating or sweating too much in hotter, desert climates, reducing your chances of blisters. The one exception is for snowy sections of trail. Waterproof shoes tend to keep your feet warmer in sub-40-degree conditions. Your feet may sweat a lot and get swampy, but at least they won't go numb from cold as easily.

As of publication (according to my unscientific sampling), the most popular shoes among thru-hikers on the PCT and CDT are the Altra Lone Peak or Olympus models, Brooks Cascadia, Salomon Speedcross or X-Ultra, or La Sportiva Bushido. With minimalist, barefoot, or zero-drop shoes like the Altras, be sure to train in the shoes before starting your thru-hike and to ramp up your

HIKE YOUR OWN HIKE

MY OWN GEAR JOURNEY

PHOTO CREDIT: DEAN KRAKEL

Dean Krakel, the 63-year-old photojournalist, shares some of the lessons he learned gearing up for his first thru-hike on the Colorado Trail.

When I'd been off the trail a few days, I went to an outdoor shop to replace the trail running shoes that I'd been wearing on the Colorado Trail (Durango to Denver). When the clerk heard I wanted something to hike in, he pulled down this pair of heavy boots and said, "This is what I'm going to wear on the CT when I hike it next year." I said, "Well, I just got off the trail, and I did it in these tennis shoes." We talked about equipment a little bit, but his mind was pretty set, and I couldn't say much. We've all got to hike our own hike, but he reminded me a little bit of myself when I decided to hike the CT. I bought gear first and then researched it, which is exactly backwards. There are so many blogs and so many people to talk to. I could have settled on my gear in a final way before the trip. Once I got the gear, my needs changed, and I found myself wanting something lighter or better or stronger or more versatile—which is how I ended up with three sleeping bags, three backpacks, three headlamps, two sets of hiking poles, three sets of fleece jackets, two down sweaters, and an ice axe. Gear really comes down to defining the difference between what you want and what you really need. I bought three fleece jackets, but I didn't wear them on the trip. I ended up with a lot of extra gear, but that's cool with me. I like gear.

—Dean "Ghost" Krakel

mileage in the shoes slowly. These shoes were designed to use different muscles in your feet than "traditional" shoes, so follow the various brands' instructions on how to transition before you go and train in your shoes before you go.

Most thru-hikers get 300 to 500 miles out of a pair of shoes, depending on the trail conditions, moisture, pack and hiker weight, and gait of the hiker. Careful hikers can get 700–1000 miles on one pair.

OTHER KEY GEAR DECISIONS

While your pack, shelter, sleeping bag, and shoes are the most important items to research and invest in, you'll also make decisions about the rest of the items in your kit. Some of these items—like stoves or trekking poles—you could live without and are subject to personal preference. Other items—like extra clothes—fall under the Ten Essentials. Your decision includes how much clothing to bring, what specific items (e.g., a wind shirt, fleece, both, or none), and what models. Over the years, I've tried going with and without some of these items and have used all sorts of different models of each item. Here's my best thru-hiker-specific advice on what to consider for those other essentials.

- Navigational tools: map and compass, databook, guidebook, phone navigation app, GPS
- Sun protection: sunglasses, sunscreen, lip balm, hat, sun protective clothing
- Extra clothing: rain jacket, insulating layer, hat, gloves, socks
- Illumination: headlamp, flashlight, extra batteries
- First aid supplies and bugspray
- Fire: matches, lighter, firestarter
- Repair kit and tools: duct tape, knife, needle/thread
- Extra food and hydration
- Water purifier
- Shelter

STOVES

Your biggest decision in picking a stove is what type of fuel to use. While most backpackers only seriously consider isobutane canisters or liquid white

Ten Essentials

The term Ten Essentials was first coined in 1974 in *Freedom of the Hills*, a classic mountaineers' and outdoorsperson's handbook. It's changed a lot today, and ultralight guru Ray Jardine says in *Beyond Backpacking* that opting not to take them all can be an acceptable risk fast and light hikers may take. To update the list, many outdoor organizations instead discuss the Ten Essential Groups, which allows adapting to location, climate, season, and geography. The following text is a kind of hybrid that fits well for thru-hikers. While not all thru-hikers carry every item listed here, almost all thru-hikers carry at least one item from each group.

This pot was made from an old beer can. It is held up by a Caldera Cone windscreen-potstand.

gas, the sheer length of a big thru-hike means that other fuel options start to look appealing due to efficiency considerations and ease of acquiring them. Your trail-specific guidebook should have information about fuel availability in your resupply towns.

Alcohol:
- Pros: Stoves can be very light and cheap (DIY from a soda can). Fuel is generally easy to find, even at gas stations and internationally.
- Cons: Fuel is less powerful so boiling times are slower. DIY stoves are harder to control and prohibited in some areas due to fire hazard.

Isobutane canisters:
- Pros: Stoves tend to be very easy to use, powerful, and have good flame control.
- Cons: Heavy and bulky, especially because you have to carry empty canisters and decide what to do about half-empty ones. Generally poor performance in subfreezing weather. Canisters are only available from specialized outdoor shops and slow to mail (they must be declared and shipped ground).

Esbit:

- Pros: Very efficient over the long term. Easier to mail than other fuels. Never spills in your pack. Can be used even if you lose your stove. Burns even when wet.
- Cons: Patience required, as fuel is less powerful. Can smell like dead fish. Difficult to find at local gear stores.

Wood burning:

- Pros: Fuel is typically free and plentiful, no need to carry it with you. Using a stove that burns wood is more efficient than cooking over a wood fire. Can provide a form of entertainment on long nights.
- Cons: Fuel can be unreliable or wet, depending on your terrain. Takes constant attention. May be against certain Forest Service fire regulations. Can be messy.

White gas:

- Pros: Powerful. Works well in cold weather. Can be easier to find than canister fuel.
- Cons: Stoves tend to be bulky, heavy, and require priming.

When buying stoves, you must also consider speed. Stoves vary widely in cook times depending on the fuel used and the design. Once you start using a faster stove, though, it will be hard to go back to a slower stove. Slower stoves tend to be lighter. Faster stoves tend to be heavier. Think about permits and regulations. Some Forest Service ranger districts restrict certain types of stoves, and some ranger districts require a fire permit in order to use any kind of stove. Check local regulations before you go.

You can also learn to make your own stove out of garbage at Zenstoves.net.

Whatever stove you choose, make sure to practice with it at home before you go, so you're comfortable lighting it, cooking on it, protecting it from the wind, and performing any kind of field maintenance that might be required.

With stoves, it is very important that you read the directions thoroughly before use. This is especially true for do-it-yourself stoves and all alcohol stoves. Every year, experienced thru-hikers burn themselves, destroy their gear, and sometimes even start forest fires from incorrect stove use. If you use an alcohol stove, never move or add more alcohol to a stove that is still burning. No matter what stove you use, set it up away from anything flammable or move flammable materials away. Keep extra water on hand to put out a fire if you've started one. Remember stop, drop, and roll if you catch yourself on fire.

Whatever stove you bring, remember to include a pot stand and windscreen (built into some stoves). Some ultralight hikers use their tent stakes as a pot stand. Other thru-hikers (myself included) use a combination windscreen/pot stand called a Caldera Cone. Other thru-hikers use aluminum or titanium foil as a windscreen. Find what works for you, your budget, and your weight restrictions, and remember always to set your stove up out of the wind.

WATER TREATMENT

You'll drink water from all kinds of sources along your hike, and it's a wise idea to treat said water to kill any microorganisms that may be lurking there. Since these guys are microscopic, even clean-looking water can be suspect. I tend to a have

PHOTO CREDIT: JOHNNY CARR

CDT thru-hikers quickly learn that cattle troughs are among the few sources of water in the New Mexico desert. These are supplied by windmill powered wells, so a windmill is a welcome sight on the horizon to thirsty hikers. But, because the troughs are frequented by cows, treat the water.

Using an inline filter to purify water from a cow trough, Wasatch Traverse, Utah.

a strong stomach, but many of my good hiker friends are especially susceptible to developing waterborne stomach issues on the trail. Waterborne illness are not only unpleasant (diarrhea and vomiting) but can also lead to severe dehydration, blood in urine, and hospitalization. Here are the main types of treatment options that thru-hikers should consider.

Most filters use microscopic pores (0.2 microns or less) to snag bacteria and protozoa while allowing water to flow through. They come in many shapes and sizes, including gravity filters (best for groups), squeeze filters (like the Sawyer Squeeze or MINI, my options of choice), and pump filters (not many thru-hikers use these, but they can be useful in desert areas where you may be filtering out of puddles or deep, hard-to-reach wells).

Physical filter:

- Pros: Water drinkable right away, doesn't leave a taste. Makes it easy to "camel" up and drink a lot at desert sources. Some filters can last for 100,000 gallons. Removes gunk, including the bacteria and protozoa cells.
- Cons: Requires maintenance, can be slower especially in silty conditions, most hollow-fiber filters become unusable if frozen.

CDT thru-hikers collecting water from potholes and mud puddles.

One of the advantages of a pump filter is that it lets you suck water out of shallow pools or low-flowing sources. But most thru-hikers instead carry an extra cup or use their cookpot to scoop water where it may be difficult to fill a water bottle.

I used to be pretty paranoid about keeping that cup clean, but have since read from medical expert Buck Tilton that if contaminated water scoopers are exposed to the sun's UV (ultraviolet) radiation as they dry, most waterborne germs are killed. If you let the cup dry and wipe off any excess dirt, you are probably safe from giardia.

Drinking from a cattle trough, Maah Daah Hey Trail, North Dakota, 2012

Chemical:

- Pros: Light, generally easy to use, some eliminate viruses
- Cons: Takes 30 minutes for water to be drinkable, leaves a taste, takes 4 hours to kill cryptosporidium spores, requires replenishing (either sending to yourself or buying locally), your brand of choice may not be available at all outfitters or in all states

Several chemical options are available, including chlorine dioxide drops (like AquaMira) or tabs (like MSR Aqua Tabs) or iodine tabs (like Potable Aqua or Polar Pure). Some hikers use bleach. To do this, they use regular, unscented bleach in a small dropper and use two drops per liter to treat their water. Do not use color safe bleach, bleaches with added cleaners, or bleach past its expiration date. Iodine

Waterborne Diseases and Illnesses

Although many water sources in the backcountry are safer than you may think, they can be sullied by pack animals, pets, wildlife, and the dirtiest culprit of all—humans. Other hikers with gross practices such as bathing in water sources, or even worse—going to the bathroom less than 200 feet from water—can ruin the water source for the next thirsty person. Below are a list of some waterborne diseases and illnesses. For more on avoiding illness and what to do if you think you've caught a bug, see chapter 9.

Cryptosporidium parvum (aka Crypto)

Ingesting this protozoa can lead to diarrhea, vomiting, and noticeable stomach issues. Hikers may develop illnesses as soon as two days after exposure. It can be resistant to chemical treatments, but because it's usually 4–6 microns in size, most filters are effective, as are UV radiation and boiling.

Giardia lamblia

This protozoa can also lead to diarrhea, vomiting, and often sulfurous-smelling gas. Hikers typically develop symptoms ten days or more after infection. Its size range is bigger than Crypto—1–20 microns with cysts sized 1–10 microns. Most filters can catch most giardia, as can chemical treatments, boiling, and UV radiation.

Bacteria

Escherichia coli (aka E. coli) and salmonella are the most common bacterial illnesses that thru-hikers develop. While bacterial illnesses vary widely, filters, UV radiation, chemicals, and boiling should kill the bad guys. These illnesses are related more to eating bad food in town than to bad water.

Viruses

On the trail, norovirus is the most common virus hikers get sick from. It also has symptoms of diarrhea and stomach pain. Viruses are very small—0.04–0.1 microns—meaning that most filters won't catch them. UV radiation, boiling, and chemicals will kill them, but norovirus is most commonly passed from human-to-human contact, not water.

Pesticides, Herbicides, Chemicals, Metals

Trails like the AT and CDT are routed through agricultural, ranching, and grazing areas where human-placed substances could impact the water. Filters remove some but not all of these substances. In areas where there historically has been mining (like much of Colorado), there is evidence that inorganic chemicals could be impacting even pristine-appearing springs. Luckily, some filters remove at least some of the elements, like arsenic and mercury.

tends to be quite cheap whereas chlorine dioxide tends to be pretty pricey. Note: According to the World Health Organization, iodine builds up in your thyroid and isn't a good choice to use regularly for longer than a few weeks at a time, especially for infants, children, and pregnant women, unless you include a post-disinfection iodine removal device, like activated carbon.

Ultraviolet:

- Pros: Takes less than a minute, doesn't leave a taste
- Cons: Requires batteries and relatively clear water. If it breaks or batteries die, you're out of luck.

An ultraviolet light purifier like the Steripen bombards water with UV rays, neutralizing bacteria, protozoa, and viruses (which can be a particular problem in developing countries). For more information, see the Center for Disease Control and Prevention guide to drinking water treatment and sanitation for backcountry and travel use.

TREKKING POLES

Thru-hikers are pretty split about whether trekking poles are useful, but the science is on the side of saying yes. Here's why:

- Fewer injuries. Poles reduce the risk of injury and tendonitis in knees, calves, thighs, and even hips, according to Michael Torry, PhD, director of biomechanics research at Steadman-Hawkins Sports Medicine Foundation in Colorado. Trekking poles also allow hikers to keep a more normal stride and a faster pace with less effort.
- Less pounding. Up to 4.4 percent of the force that reverberates through your body with each step is absorbed by the poles. After a long day and thousands of steps, that support adds up.
- Relief for ailing knees and joints. Dr. Torry says that angling the tips of your poles forward slightly can reduce the compression in your joints as you hike downhill. When hiking uphill, angle the poles backward for an extra boost and reduced ankle stress.
- Fewer face plants. While researchers didn't test stability, they agree with what many backpackers already know: Four legs are better than two on uneven terrain.
- Less fatigue. According to Christopher Knight, PhD, who led a 2001 study at the University of Massachusetts, properly used poles reduce the workload for lower-body muscles and joints by transferring some of the load from your legs to your arms. Subjects in Dr. Knight's study

Trekking poles can offer up relief while you're out on the trail.

(who hiked with loaded packs for an hour on a treadmill) said the trek felt easier with poles.

- Help set up ultralight shelters. Many tarps and other ultralight shelters rely on poles to hold them upright.
- Extra balance during river fords and on wet or icy terrain. When crossing swift-moving or deep water, having an extra "leg" to ground yourself can make the difference between staying upright or ending up downstream. While there is no substitute for crampons and an ice axe, poles can help you balance when terrain turns wet, slippery, or icy.

When walking on flat terrain, hold your poles so your arms are bent at about 90 degrees. Aim to have poles hit close to your feet angled down—not straight. Take time to readjust pole length when going uphill (shorten) or down-hill (lengthen) so you can maintain a comfortable grip and upright posture. Dr. Knight recommends using wrist straps and a light grip on the handles.

My friend and super experienced hiker Justin "Trauma" Lichter is a poling expert. He wrote a very detailed article that documents how he uses his experience

Nordic skiing and skate skiing to increase the efficiency of using hiking poles. I recommend reading his whole post and watching his videos at justinlichter.com.

When buying poles, consider three-section poles that collapse down nice and small, because odds are you'll stash them in your pack for certain sections, especially areas that may require some hand-over-hand scrambling. Non-collapsible poles are awkward to lash onto your pack. On the other hand, you can often find non-collapsible ski poles for cheap, so this could be a place to save money. Lighter poles mean lighter loads, but lighter poles also tend to be pricier. Skipping shock absorbers is an easy way to opt for lighter poles. Look for poles that adjust via flip-levers; these are much easier to maintain and fix than the (usually cheaper) kind that twist to adjust.

CLOTHES

What you wear is highly personal, but this is one place where even the least expensive gear can get the job done. Most hikers have one set of clothes that they wear day in, day out (with some extra layers to stay warm). Some hikers carry separate sleep clothes. Keeping that in mind, here's how to choose the clothes you will be living in for the next few months. Look for clothing that:

- Fits well. Is any movement restricted? Do you have your full range of movement? Does anything feel too tight? Well-fitting clothes allow enough looseness for movement but not so much that a lot of extra air needs to be warmed inside of the clothing. Can you lift your arms above your head without your lats feeling constricted? Would this be comfortable enough to sleep in? Remember: You are going to be living in these clothes on the trail.
- Is light and can be layered with other light layers when it gets colder.
- Stays up when you move (particularly important for elastic in pants).
- Won't be too bulky in your pack.
- Protects from exposure to the sun—you will be seeing a lot of sun on a thru-hike.
- Serves a function separate from the other gear in your clothing system (with the exception of socks—I always carry extra).
- Has at least some pockets to stash maps and lip balm. Harder to find in women's clothing.
- Dries quickly (no cotton).
- Wicks and breathes well. A synthetic or wool shirt works by wicking away sweat, allowing it to reach an increased surface area to evaporate quickly. It also breathes well, allowing a flow of air between your body and the outside of your shirt so that sweat does not accumulate to begin with.

If you expect to travel through mud and rain, consider carrying sleep clothes in addition to your everyday hiking clothes.

- Doesn't have any annoying seams. Most chafing happens to thru-hikers along the seams of their clothes. If you feel uncomfortable in the fitting room, chances are that feeling will turn into something worse later.
- Has some treatment (natural or otherwise) that keeps odors down. You won't be washing clothes often, so finding a fabric that minimizes smells (wool is better at this than synthetics and in my opinion is worth the price) is going to make you and your hiking partners happier.
- Is the right color. Some people prefer to wear natural colors that blend into the background to maintain the wilderness experience and be stealthier in camp. Others like bright colors that photograph well.
- Looks good. I know it sounds lame, but I'm one of those people who feel like I perform better if I am wearing clothes I know I look good in.

WHAT IS IN YOUR PACK?

Now that you know the basics behind why thru-hikers might have certain items in their packs, let's look inside the kits of five different thru-hikers who have successfully hiked many different trails.

LIZ THOMAS: THE PRO

We'll start with me, and by this point I hope you don't need an introduction. I think it's important to tell you up front that I'm sponsored by several of the companies whose gear I'm recommending here. I wouldn't use or recommend a product if I didn't love it—I spend too much time on the trail to settle for uncomfortable or underperforming gear—but you should know that I do also officially represent some companies and have gotten free gear from others.

My sponsors are Gossamer Gear, Mountain Laurel Designs, Montbell, Sawyer, Darn Tough, Katabatic Gear, and Altra. Other companies that have provided me with free gear include Purple Rain Adventure Skirts, Toaks, Qi Whiz, Trail Designs, and NW Alpine.

Here's an overview of what's in the kit I usually carry.

Liz's backpack, fully packed.

Liz's sleeping quilt, bivy, backpack, etc. for early fall conditions in the Pacific Northwest.

☐ Sleeping quilt (1)

A sleeping quilt is a great way to save some weight on a sleep system without sacrificing warmth. The Katabatic Flex 30°F Quilt is super warm, has great coverage, and is not drafty at all. Supposedly it is good to 30°F, but I've used it in much colder temperatures. It works really well for three-season hiking—especially for only being 17.5 ounces.

☐ Light gaiters (2)

I discovered Dirty Girl lightweight, breathable gaiters on the PCT after months of struggling with sand and pine needles in my shoes. I was tired of having to constantly stop to remove rocks from my shoes. These gaiters attach to any shoe (they come with two-way sticky Velcro that you put on your shoe. That way, your gaiter will stay attached to your shoe).

☐ Shelter (3)

My Mountain Laurel Designs SoloMid has been a trusty companion for three seasons. I set up the sleek, simple, and adjustable pyramid design with one or two trekking poles. I love it; it would be hard to find anything else that offers as much shelter, coverage, and protection for only 11 ounces.

☐ Snow gaiters (4)

I design my cold/wet/rain/snow clothing system to be very versatile and modular. For most three-season conditions, instead of rain pants, I wear a rain skirt and Mountain Laurel Designs Light Snow Gaiters. Using the two together allows me more breathability and mobility than rain pants. If I'm getting too cold or wet with just the rain skirt, I add the gaiters. If I get too hot with the gaiters on, I'll go back to just the rain skirt. I wear the gaiters over my tights and it helps keep them dry when I'm walking through deep snow. It also helps keep snow out of my shoes when postholing. At 2.3 ounces for the pair, they keep me warm for a ridiculously low weight penalty.

☐ Bivy (5)

The Mountain Laurel Designs Superlight Bivy plays many roles in my gear system. A bivy is like a rain shell for a sleeping bag, or a tent that just fits around a bag. First, it protects my sleeping bag from getting moist from condensation or splashes. Second, I can use it instead of a groundsheet, or as my only protection when cowboy camping (sleeping under the stars). This protects my bag from pine needles and rough surfaces. Third, I can stuff gear I don't want to be frozen (like my water filter or anything with a lithium battery) into my bivy but outside of my sleeping bag to keep it warm without taking up real estate inside my sleeping bag. Lastly, it adds between 5 to 10 degrees of warmth to my sleep system. Well worth the 7 ounces!

☐ Baselayer tights (6)

I love using Montbell Light Trail Tights instead of pants while hiking because they layer well with a skirt or shorts. They also can be used as sleepwear and dry much more quickly than pretty much any full-leg coverage garment. Since they're super stretchy, they provide enough flexibility and mobility for rock climbing and yoga moves. These tights are thicker, warmer, and more durable than any tights I've seen of comparable weight (only 3.4 ounces!).

☐ **Rain skirt/kilt (7)**

A male friend of mine turned me on to the rain skirt back in 2009, and I've never worn rain pants since. A rain skirt is easily pulled over my clothes without having to take my shoes off—providing near-instant rain protection at 2.3 ounces of weight for this design by Mountain Laurel Designs. It's also more breathable than rain pants, which means I won't sweat inside my rain gear. When it's super cold out, I sleep in my rain skirt—which is breathable enough that it adds warmth without causing me to sweat inside my sleeping bag. The simple and adjustable design allows me to open it up to turn it into a small groundsheet or silnylon tarp.

☐ Pack (8)

What I love about the Gossamer Gear Gorilla pack is that it can fit a bear canister big enough to carry seven days' worth of food, be dragged up and down granite cliffs, is super comfy, and still only weighs 1 pound. Packs are all about comfort and fit, and this one gets high marks from me on both.

☐ Puffy jacket (9)

You can often spot a thru-hiker in town because they're wearing a dirty, expensive-looking puffy layer. Pretty much every thru-hiker carries one. It keeps us warm in camp, when we're not moving, during breaks, and sometimes at night when we wear it in our sleeping bags. My Montbell EX Light is 900-fill down and weighs only 5.4 ounces. It provides a lot of warmth and wind protection for that weight and layers well with my wind shirt under it or my rain jacket over it.

☐ Wind shirt (10)

The Montbell Tachyon Anorak wins "Most Valuable Piece of Gear" for any trip. At less than 2 ounces, it keeps off wind and sun and works as a first layer of rain protection.

☐ Rain mitts (11)

The 1-ounce Mountain Laurel Designs eVent Rain Mitts provide a waterproof protective layer for my hands when it's super cold. Typically, I wear them over my PossumDown gloves (more on those later) to add quite a bit of warmth. I keep them in the pocket of my rain jacket—if it's cold enough for me to wear my rain jacket, my hands are already probably cold and I'll want my overmitts soon.

☐ Trekking Poles (12)

Carbon fiber trekking poles are not for everyone, but the Gossamer Gear LT4 poles have served me well over the years. I mostly use my trekking poles for setting up my shelter and helping on the downhills, so I want light poles that won't drag me down when I'm carrying them in my pack. These poles also condense down to a small size and attach easily to my pack (4.1-ounces per pole with .5-ounce strap).

☐ Bandana (13)

The ultimate multipurpose piece of gear: can be used to keep sun off my neck, wash myself down, pre-filter dirt out of water, wipe my nose, and so on.

☐ Hydration system (14)

I use my Sawyer MINI filter (pink, though it comes in every color imaginable) or a Sawyer Squeeze filter as an inline filter with my Platypus Hoser hydration reservoir. I cut the hose, insert my filter, and then attach the hose plus filter to my Platypus reservoir. Then I put "dirty" water into my reservoir, and when I suck on the Hoser's bite valve, I get clean water. At night I hang my reservoir and run the system as a gravity filter to deliver clean water right into my cooking pot.

☐ Umbrella (15)

The Montbell U.L. Trekking Umbrella is one of my favorite pieces of gear: It keeps me dry when it's raining and is the most breathable form of rain gear. When raining, an umbrella prevents heat loss due to convection, when cold water is against the skin (which can happen when rain gear wets out). It also keeps the sun off me when it's too sunny. It's super wind resistant (better than any other umbrella I've tried). When I'm not using it, the umbrella folds down to a small size that fits into my pack's water bottle pocket (even when there's a bottle in there) and weighs only 5.4 ounces.

☐ Cook system (16)

When local fire regulations allow it, I use the Trail Designs Caldera Keg-F System (using Esbit fuel), which is the lightest stove system I know of. It's super efficient and wind resistant and simple to set up. You can either make your own pot (from an old beer can—I did this for years) or buy one that has been reinforced from Trail Designs. The plastic clear thing is the protective case it comes in. You can also use the protective case as a mug/bowl. Since the case has a top and a bottom, you could use the system for up to three people (one person has the top, the other the bottom, and the third eats out of the pot/beer can). The stove itself is the small piece of metal on the bottom, which is a stand for a tab of Esbit, a solid fuel. The same system works with an alcohol stove. The stove is 2.7 ounces and the protective plastic case adds 3.6 ounces.

For years I used a short titanium spoon while backpacking. It was hard to get food out of freeze-dried food packets or tuna packets with a short spoon. I upgraded to a long spoon and am very happy for it. That clear bag pictured is a Loksak OPSAK, or odor-proof sack. I use that as my food bag, as it decreases the chances that critters will smell and be attracted to my food.

☐ Gloves (17)

Made of a merino wool and possum fur blend (really!) called PossumDown, these super-warm and soft gloves (about 1 ounce) work really well, even when wet. They provide enough insulation that I've also used them exclusively as potholders. The only downside is they aren't very durable.

☐ Fire-making (18)

I use a .4-ounce Mini BIC lighter. I don't typically carry a lot of back-up items, but I carry a 0.1-ounce matchbook that I picked up for free from a restaurant. Bonus is that it reminds me of a favorite restaurant at home when I'm on the trail. Note: You should carry a backup fire starter in a waterproof container.

☐ Headlight (19)

The Photon Micro-Light LED Keychain Flashlight turns into a headlamp with a clip that attaches to the brim of my visor. I can wear it as a necklace during the day or night so I always have it with me. After I removed the keychain ring, the whole setup is less than an ounce and provides the perfect amount of light to take care of camp chores. However, I use a real headlamp on trails where I will do a lot of night hiking, or when days are shorter.

☐ **Notebook and sharpie (20)**

The .6-ounce mini Rite in the Rain paper is waterproof and great for journaling. I like a .3-ounce double-ended Sharpie so that I can more easily write notes on waterproof map sets and know that my entries won't get destroyed if my journal gets wet.

☐ **Puffy hat (21)**

A hat (1.1-ounce) is one of the best ways to add warmth to your clothing and sleep system. It compresses down to the size of a silver dollar and fits easily into my hipbelt pocket. This way I don't have to stop to put it on, take it off, and put it back on again when lots of weather changes are occurring.

☐ **Compass (22)**

I don't carry a fancy or expensive compass. It doesn't need to have a mirror or even have the ability to change declination (although the latter especially is helpful on longer trips). Having a compass is essential for all trips for when the trail gets obscured and especially on all cross-country routes. And checking my direction on the compass is fun to do even when I'm on an established trail.

☐ Wallet and medicines (23)

My wallet (1.1-ounce) includes cash, driver's license/ID, credit card, ATM card, health insurance card, and important phone numbers. For meds, I carry over-the-counter ibuprofen, Benadryl, Tums, Gas-X, Naproxen, and Excedrin. Prescriptions are limited to anything my doctor prescribes me for giardia, Lyme disease, or heavier-duty pain killers.

☐ Toilet kit (24)

I used to not carry a potty trowel, and instead tried to dig catholes with rocks, my shoe, or a hiking pole. Inevitably, the holes ended up being shallow, narrow, and insufficient to do their job. Someone told me about the QiWhiz—a potty trowel that only weighs 0.4 ounce. I figured that for such a minor weight penalty, I could afford to make my catholes a lot better by carrying a trowel. It's changed my life and made going in the backcountry a lot less stressful. I use Bark Bags to pack out used toilet paper.

☐ Sunglasses and visor (25)

Sun protection is essential on almost any thru-hike.

☐ Menstrual Cup (26)

The Keeper menstrual cup is lightweight (.5 ounce) and less bulky than tampons, and doesn't require packing used hygiene items out.

☐ Mini-dice (27)

Miniature entertainment for when I have extra time in my tent to hang out with hiking partners while waiting out a storm.

☐ Camera (28)

Thru-hikers who want better quality photos than what they get on their phones opt for a point-and-shoot. Many thru-hikers like a camera that is shockproof, dustproof, and waterproof. A lot of my hiker friends who are great photographers bring heavier-duty cameras and lenses—occasionally a DSLR even. Just remember to protect your camera from rain and trail! I've learned that the hard way over a few trails and more than a few broken cameras. Bring an extra camera battery or external battery charge system (like a Anker), too.

☐ Socks (29)

I can't stand putting on wet socks, so I always bring a few spares. I like the Darn Tough Ultralight Merinos because the weave is denser than other socks, so they keep out dirt and trail grime better. A pair ends up being a little more than 1 ounce—so I don't feel guilty carrying a few pairs. Since they're so light, they also dry out quickly.

☐ Sleep socks (30)

When it's cold out, you're more likely to feel it in your feet, so I carry special socks that are warmer than my hiking socks (and are dedicated for sleeping). Like my gloves, my sleep socks (1.4 ounces) are the merino wool and possum fur blend from PossumDown.

☐ Small sundries (31)

These include sunscreen (1-ounce tube), Gear Aid repair patches (green round things), lip balm, hand sanitizer (clear bottle), Neosporin (circular container), toothpowder (in white dropper bottle), and toothbrush (not pictured).

☐ Rain jacket (32)

This 4.5-ounce cuben fiber NW Alpine Eyebright Jacket is no longer is made, but the Montbell Torin Flyer or Versalite are my other go-to rain jackets.

WHAT I WEAR

Here's what I actually would wear on my body on a trip with a kit like this:

- Shirt: Montbell Wickron Long Sleeve: Excellent sun protection with a cooling fabric. I can use the pockets to store my compass, or maps.
- Sports bra: After twenty thru-hikes, I still haven't found a model I like.
- Underwear: I've used Ex Officio Give and Go Sport Mesh, Uniqlo Airism, and SmartWool 150 weight and been happy with all of them.
- Socks: I love the Darn Tough merino quartersock light. It's thin and tightly woven—which helps prevent blisters. The merino has natural antibacterial properties that prevent the socks from smelling like garbage. I enjoy the quarter length because it provides my ankles with plenty of protection from the elements without being too much sock.
- Shoes: The Altra Lone Peaks are a treasured trail friend. Breathable and lightweight, they make me feel nimble across rocks. The toe-shaped footbox allows my feet to swell and get fat from walking all day every day without pinching toes or blackening toenails.
- Skirt: I never used to wear skirts before discovering the Purple Rain Adventure Skirt, which is flattering, dries quickly, provides plenty of ventilation, and (my favorite part) has a boatload of pockets to put small guidebooks or maps, lip balm, and my phone.

John "Cactus" McKinney on the Appalachian Trail

JOHN "CACTUS" MCKINNEY: THE LIFESTYLE HIKER

Cactus has hiked more than 9,000 miles along the AT, PCT, CDT, Colorado Trail (twice), San Diego Trans-County Trail, and the San Juan River Trail. I'd describe him as a "work-hard, play-hard" kind of hiker. He likes to hike fast for the first part of the day and then take long breaks. Here's what's in his typical pack (he doesn't have gear sponsorships). (All gear descriptions are in Cactus's words.)

☐ Pack (1)

I use a ZPacks ArcBlasts currently (21 ounces), but it was too badly damaged for the shoot so I included this Granite Gear Vapor Trail pack (discontinued) because I used it on the Colorado Trail in 2011. I prefer a pack without a frame, but the frame on this one is quite minimal, and the pack is under 2 pounds.

☐ Fleece (2)

I use the Melanzana Microgrid Hoodie (12.2 ounces for men's large). Since it is synthetic, it stays warm even when wet, including sweat When paired with my wind shirt, it's quite warm. I either carry this fleece with a wind shirt or a Western Mountaineering Flash down jacket without a wind shirt, depending on conditions and climate.

☐ Pack cover (3)

Sea To Summit Ultra-Sil Pack Cover (2 ounces)

Cactus's backpack

☐ Gloves (4)

Black Diamond PowerWeight Liner Gloves—I use these most often in the morning or when hiking above treeline (2.4 ounces).

☐ Rain gear (5)

The jacket is a GoLite Malapais (alas, GoLite is no longer in business—it's now MyTrail). The pants are the Sierra Designs Hurricane. I always carry full rain gear and wear it more often for warmth than for rain (jacket: 8 ounces; pants: 7 ounces).

☐ Sleeping pad (6)

Therm-a-Rest NeoAir X-Lite full-length inflatable pad (12 ounces).

☐ Headlamp (7)

Black Diamond Spot (3.3 ounces).

☐ Wind shirt (8)

The Montbell Tachyon Anorak weighs less than 2 ounces. I wear this quite often in the morning or evening and often when hiking above treeline. It provides a great barrier from the wind, and when layered over my fleece, the combo competes in warmth with a down jacket.

☐ Hats (9)

I have two hats, one thick for warmth, one super-thin for use while walking. Sometimes I just pack the thicker one for use in camp and while sleeping.

☐ Baselayer tights (10)

REI Midweight Base Layer Bottoms: With these and the rain pants, my legs can stand some pretty low temps.

☐ Sleeping bag (11)

The down Western Mountaineering SummerLite is a great two- or three-season bag: very light and extremely well made (19 ounces).

☐ Food bag (12)

This was custom-made for me by ZPacks out of their Cuben Hybrid material. I was shredding the normal Cuben Fiber food bags every 1,000 miles or so.

☐ Stakes (13)

MSR Groundhog (.5 ounces) and Hyperlite Titanium Shepherd Hooks (.3 ounces).

☐ Umbrella (14)

This is the GoLite umbrella (not for sale anymore). I use it more often than rain gear during rain, but I still carry rain gear and sometimes use both together.

☐ Inner tent (15)

Hyperlite Mountain Gear Echo II Insert (for keeping out mosquitoes and other bugs—8 ounces).

☐ Cook system (16)

I use a Snow Peak Trek 700 Titanium mug as my cookpot, a Snow Peak LiteMax Titanium canister stove (1.8 ounces), and a (.4 ounce) Sea To Summit Long Spoon (plus fuel and a lighter, of course).

☐ Water system (17)

I use a Platypus 2-liter Platy water bag, two 1-liter Smartwater bottles from the gas station (covered with stickers), a half bottle to use as a scoop (fits around a

Cactus's backpack, sleeping bag, clothing, etc.

PHOTO CREDIT: CAVEMAN COLLECTIVE

full bottle), the USB-rechargeable Steripen Freedom (discontinued, but the Ultra is similar), and Katadyn Micropur tablets as back-up.

☐ Tarp (tent fly) (18)

ZPacks 8.5x10-foot rectangular tarp, made from Cuben Fiber. It's a little larger than the tarp that Hyperlite includes with the Echo II shelter and therefore gives a small beak/overhang in the front to keep the rain out.

☐ Ditty bag (19)

The bag is made by Eagle Creek (.6 ounces). It holds first-aid supplies, Tenacious Tape (for gear repairs), sports tape, a Leatherman-style CS multitool, and other knickknacks.

WILLIAM "PI" MURPHY: THE GEARHEAD

My friend Pi has hiked the AT, PCT, the Hayduke Trail, the Colorado Trail, and 1,700 miles of the CDT. He loves talking about gear, so you're about to hear a lot about his kit (Pi doesn't have gear sponsorships). (All gear descriptions are in Pi's words.)

This kit is what I took for half of the Colorado Trail in the fall. The only trail circumstances I've been on where my choices were completely different was the Hayduke Trail with rock scrambling and 30-plus-mile water carries in summer desert heat. For anything else, my pack list looked much like this, sometimes with slightly warmer clothes, or sometimes with a slightly lighter and less warm sleeping bag in midsummer, when I know I can get away with it.

Pi's backpack

PHOTO CREDIT: CAVEMAN COLLECTIVE

Pi's sleeping bag, backpack, shelter, etc.

☐ Sleeping bag (1)
Enlightened Equipment Revelation 30°F quilt in orange and black (16.6 ounces).

☐ Water treatment (2)
Sawyer MINI water filter, backflush syringe, and extra capacity, plus a dropper bottle of bleach to be extra sure (yes, two water treatment systems). Bleach is on the yellow leash tied to my pack, in the contact-lens dropper-size bottle.

☐ Tarp (rain fly) (3)
Equinox Myotis Ultralite Tarp (14.5 ounces for 8x8-foot) and tarp lines with clips from Dutchware Gear.

☐ **Shelter (4)**

Hennessy Hammock Expedition Asym Zip (2 pounds, 2 ounces). I like sleeping in hammocks rather than grounddwelling.

☐ **Stakes (5)**

MSR Mini-Groundhog: I've tried the Hyperlite Titanium Shepherd Hooks, and they pull out like greased sticks whenever you camp on an exposed saddle and a hailstorm blows through, so now I bring proper tent stakes (.35 ounces per stake).

☐ **Pack (6)**

Mountain Laurel Designs Exodus, special order, no hipbelt (16 ounces).

☐ **Pad (7)**

Gossamer Gear Evazote ThinLight foam pad is good to sit on and makes sleeping in the hammock warmer. I use this to line and stiffen my pack as well (2.5 ounces).

☐ **Cooking system (8)**

BushBuddy Ultralight Woodstove, Snow Peak Trek 900 Titanium mug/cookpot, Toaks Titanium Short Handle Spoon on a line so I can find it in my food bag, lid is a cut-up Fosters beer can (careful, sharp), two lighters, sometimes tinder. The stove is more than a cooking system. I get infinite fuel for no added pack weight, cowboy TV, a hobby, and a chance to learn the skill of fire tending. It can be a fiddling extra thing to deal with at the end of a long day of hiking and is often banned in drought years, so it isn't the choice for everyone. It sure is the choice for me (stove: 6.4 ounces, pot: 6 ounces, spoons: .3 ounces).

☐ **Fleece (9)**

Brand doesn't much matter; differences are in cut and fit and personal preference.

☐ **Sleep shirt (10)**

Silk "tropical" shirt that I got at a thrift store. For sleeping and town days, or, in an emergency, it can be torn up for bandages or a sling.

☐ **Guidebook (11)**

I argue with it all the time (no matter the book), but I also carry it. And a fun book. I put them both in a Tyvek postal envelope, along with (not pictured) a pen and postcards to compose to friends back home.

☐ **Scarf/hat (12)**

The blue/black hat is from DutchWare Gear, which calls it a SCAT—part scarf, part hat.

PHOTO CREDIT: CAVEMAN COLLECTIVE

☐ Socks (13)

Two pairs "other" socks (besides the ones I'll be wearing hiking). One pair is never worn hiking, but rather kept nice for sleeping in. Dirty hiking socks never go into my sleeping bag!

☐ Compass (14)

The red line tied to my pack has a small compass, the Suunto Clipper. It's a bubble compass the size of a quarter.

☐ Wind pants (15)

Luke's Ultralite Argon Wind Pants (I also like Montbell's Dynamo Wind Pants). Either one is half the weight or less of track/wind pants you'd find at a sports store.

PHOTO CREDIT: STEVEN "TWINKLE" SHATTUCK

William "Pi" Murphy

☐ **Umbrella (16)**

The EuroSchirm Chrome-dome umbrella (now that GoLite is out of business). I end up bringing it, and about a third of the days I love it, feel like a genius to have brought it along. About a third of the days it indifferently rides in my pack. And a third of the days it seems like the dumbest thing I've got along besides the guidebook. Still, just like the lying guidebook, I seem to keep packing it before starting most any adventure.

☐ **Sun hat (17)**

Sunday Afternoons women's sun hat. Yes, as a 6-foot-tall, 200-pound guy, this is my hat. I found it in the Grand Canyon, but would happily pay my own money for another when it wears out.

☐ Rain jacket and rain skirt (18)

Luke's Ultralite Pertex SHIELD Rain Shell, American-made. Talk to Luke about anything you need and he'll get it done just for you. The coat isn't level-three bulletproof, but I'd rather use light stuff that works great with a little care than mediocre stuff that doesn't ever get lighter with care. DutchWare Gear makes a rain skirt; mine is ULA from years back.

☐ Ditty bag (19)

Toothbrush and mini tube of paste; knife (usually the smallest Swiss Army), Fenix LD01 flashlight with wrist string from a camera; Mini BIC lighter; Neosporin, good for cuts, scrapes, burns, and help with preventing minor infections; Aquaphor, good for blisters or hot spots too; a pill bottle wrapped in duct tape containing a few Imodium, Sudafed, ibuprofen, needle and thread, and safety pin. My doctor gave me a prescription for the pills for giardia, as well as a few Oxys in case I need to walk out on a twisted ankle. If desert hiking, I carry salt too.

☐ Food and bear bag and water system (20)

A very large waterproof Outdoor Research stuff sack with Lawson Glowire. Wide-mouth water bottles (Gatorade), 2– to 3–liter.

☐ TP kit (21)

A ziplock with toilet paper and hand sanitizer.

☐ Sunglasses (22)

I need a new pair every 1,000 miles or so due to breakage and loss, so I just buy cheap ones at the gas station.

HOW PI'S KIT MIGHT CHANGE

This would be my choice for a thru-hike on the AT with a late start and an early finish. If hiking in April or into September on the AT, I might add a Montbell Thermawrap jacket and beef the quilt up, say to a Western Mountaineering 20°F UltraLite sleeping bag. For the PCT or CDT, I'd hike with the added jacket and heavier (warmer) sleeping bag for sure, and possibly trade the hammock (keeping the tarp) for a groundcloth for the desert portion of the PCT. Also, the CDT was too windy in many parts for the umbrella, though I did bring it.

PHOTO CREDIT: AMANDA JAMESON

Amanda Jameson on the Colorado Trail in 2015.

AMANDA "ZUUL" JAMESON: THE NEWCOMER

My friend Amanda is relatively new to thru-hiking. She shared the kit she used on her first thru-hike, the Colorado Trail, from August to September 2015 and has

PHOTO CREDIT: COLLECTIVE CAVEMAN

Amanda's backpack, fully packed.

since gone on to hike the PCT as *BACKPACKER* Magazine's thru-hiking correspondent in 2016. While she may not have as much experience as some of the other folks, it's important to look at Amanda's CT kit—because it will likely look like your first kit. Since at this point she was still learning some backcountry skills, her gear tends to be easier to set up than some of the gearheads I interviewed. She also has more redundancy in case she lost something or it failed. She carried a few creature comforts and safety items that the other hikers did not—like bear spray, camp shoes, and laundry bags but still managed to keep her pack weight relatively low. I credit her skill in putting together such a good first pack on her research and the sage advice she gleaned from more experienced hikers. (Amanda had no gear sponsorships.) (All gear descriptions are in Amanda's words.)

Amanda's sleeping bag, shelter, backpack, clothing, etc.

☐ **Sleeping pad (1)**
Therm-a-Rest Z Lite Sol full-length sleeping pad

☐ **Compression socks (2)**
Generic brand, made for folks with diabetes. They encourage circulation to keep feet warm at night.

☐ **Puffy jacket (3)**
Rab Neutrino Endurance

☐ **Batteries and charger (4)**
Anker Astro E1 5200mAh Ultra Compact Portable Charger external battery plus wall plug; extra headlamp batteries

☐ **Laundry Ziploc (5)**

I used this gallon ziplock for trail laundry, usually of socks and underwear. I rinse first, put a little Dr. Bronner's in and vigorously shake, and then rinse again. I always dump my dirty water at least 200 feet from a water source. It's absolutely worth going brand name on Ziplocs, be it for food or something like this. It's worth it not to have them break down on you so quickly. And you can always reuse them.

☐ **Groundsheet (6)**

Tyvek groundsheet/tent footprint

☐ **Sleep leggings (7)**

Uniqlo HEATTECH Leggings (Liz's note: Uniqlo may be a fashion brand, but I've hiked (not just slept) thousands of miles in Uniqlo HEATTECH and think they are second to none for the money.)

☐ **Cooking kit (8)**

MSR Pocket Rocket stove (3 ounces)
Snow Peak Trek 900 mL Titanium mug/cookpot (6 ounces)
Innate Doppio Tumbler (soon to be sold by GSI) (3.7 ounces for 8-ounce tumbler)
2 Mini BIC lighters (.4 ounces)
Rubber band to hold pot lid and pot together, with mug and lighter inside

☐ **Camp shoes (9)**

Patagonia Men's Advocate Stitch camp shoes (discontinued)

☐ **Baselayer tights (10)**

Patagonia Capilene 3 (now called Midweight) bottoms (6.2 ounces)

☐ **Undies (11)**

Patagonia Women's Active Hipster Briefs (1.2 ounces)

☐ **Bear spray (12)**

I carried this for more for my parents than for myself. I never used it, and never had to think about using it, even though it was in easy reach the whole time. Colorado's not home to grizzlies, and the black bears that are around, in most cases are more scared of you than you are of them. If I hike the CDT one day, I'll probably carry it north of Colorado, but otherwise, I don't think it's for me (11 ounces).

☐ **Water bottles (13)**

Smartwater/Gatorade Bottles and Platypus 2L Bottle: 4-liter capacity total

☐ **Sleeping bag (14)**

Marmot Plasma 15 (1 pound 15 ounces for 6-foot length)

☐ **Wind shirt (15)**

Montbell Tachyon Anorak (1.9 ounces)

☐ **Gloves (16)**

Black Diamond WindWeight Liner Gloves (3.4 ounces per pair)

☐ **Pack (17)**

ULA Circuit (41 ounces)

☐ **Food and Bear Bag (18)**

I found this while I was in Hong Kong; it's loud and orange and roll-top and also has contour lines on it. I keep my stove, pot, cup, and a lighter, along with all my food, in here.

☐ **Notebook (19)**

Rite in the Rain notebook (.5 ounces)

☐ **Shelter (20)**

Tarptent Rainbow (36 ounces)

☐ **Socks (21)**

Injinji Trail Midweight Micro: These toe socks look and feel a little weird the first time you put them on, but I attribute my lack of a blister problem to them (2.16 ounces for medium).

☐ **Headlamp (22)**

Petzl ZIPKA (4.2 ounces with batteries)

☐ **Repair kit (23)**

Duct Tape. I recommend splurging on the brand name.

☐ **First aid (24)**

Bandaids and alcohol wipes were basically the extent of my first-aid kit—three of each, plus the needle and floss, sealant, and medical tape. Anything that these couldn't fix, I'd need proper medical attention for. I ended up using a couple for minor stuff, and was glad I had them on hand.

Medical tape
Sealant (works on gear and flesh wounds)
Needle plus floss (for draining blisters and fixing clothes)

☐ **Makeshift bidet (25)**
Human Gear GoToob (3 ounces): The last thing I want to do is pack out crappy toilet paper, so I don't even pack in toilet paper. Instead, I use spurts of water from a GoToob and my hand to clean myself, and actually get clean instead of smearing things around. (Toilet paper is fine when you have access to a shower every day or so, but when you don't—ew.) Clearly, this method is paired with hand sanitizer (then, sometimes, soap and water) and even more hand sanitizer, but I find I'm left even more clean after.

   A note for the ladies: Using a bidet is awesome when you're on your menses—there's none of that terrible, horrible squick that can happen when you're both exerting and on your cycle. I also highly recommend using a menstrual cup when hiking, because again, the last thing I want to do is pack out used pads or tampons. I used a MeLuna cup (.5 ounces), but use the Internet to find one that works for you.

☐ **Quicklace replacement kit (26)**
I hiked in Salomon shoes, which have quicklaces rather than normal shoelaces; I carried a replacement in case one broke.

☐ **Back-up water treatment (27)**
Iodine by Potable Aqua and Taste Neutralizer tablets (primary treatment: Aqua-Mira drops)

☐ **Bug spray (28)**
Repel Lemon Eucalyptus

AMANDA'S LESSONS LEARNED

I took this kit on my Colorado Trail thru-hike, but I definitely did things differently on my PCT thru-hike. I never carried a full bottle of bug spray. I carried a larger external battery (to make sure my phone and other electronics were always charged). I ditched the bear spray, and I had AquaMira for my entire trek. On the PCT, I was stoveless for 1700 miles—though I ended up having my stove for the last 900 miles, with no regrets—and I think I'd go stoveless again on a shorter trek. I'm still considering some changes: getting a half-length inflatable sleeping pad and using a tarp for a shelter. There's always room for improvement in a kit, and you have to learn what works for you.

PAUL "PMAGS" MAGNANTI: THE BUDGET KIT

My buddy PMags runs a popular hiking website, Pmags.com, and has tons of experience thru-hiking, inventing his own routes, and backcountry exploring. I asked him to put together a gear kit using budget items that are approachable for the average person. (Paul has no gear sponsorships.) (All gear descriptions are in Paul's words.)

This gear could best be described as the "dirt bagger deluxe" kit. It meets the following conditions:

- Good for thru-hiking an established trail in three-season conditions
- Is not ultra-minimalist
- Will not break the budget

This kit would be suited for something such as the Colorado Trail, the CDT, or any trail in the cool, but mainly dry, conditions of the Rockies.

Pmags's backpack, fully packed.

The core items (sleeping system, pack, shelter system) are good quality. They may not be top-end items or the lightest, but they work well and are very reasonably priced. The other items are a mix of thrift store, military surplus, discount store, and other odds and ends. While I use or have used all the items in the pack, some of the items have been repurposed as spare/loaner gear or for different types of trips (off-trail, deep shoulder season, or even dispersed camping) versus solo backpacking trips on an established trail in three-season conditions. I made notes of what I currently use in those cases.

☐ **Sleeping pad (1)**
Therm-a-Rest Z Lite Sol (three-quarter length): Less expensive than an inflatable pad, better than the minimalist choice of the "blue foam pad," the Z Lite is a classic, durable, and reasonably comfortable pad with good R-value for three-season use.

☐ **Hydration kit (2)**
1 quart Gatorade bottle: The Gatorade bottle is light and cheap. Comes with a drink!

1-liter Platypus SoftBottle: For when I don't need the extra water, the Platy stashes nicely.

Nalgene Cantene 96: For larger water carries, I've been using this piece of gear for years. The wide mouth makes it very easy to use, too.

☐ **Baselayers (3)**
Paradox thermal bottoms (top not shown): A Costco special; I think this set cost $30 or so total. Costco sells an even less expensive non-zip thermal shirt.

☐ **Socks (4)**
Target's C9 Running Socks: Big fan of these running socks. Durable, light, and cost effective.

Merino wool socks: My "snivel gear." A warm pair of dry socks, only worn to bed, is heaven. From Costco.

☐ **Sleeping bag (5)**
GoLite Andrenaline 20 (discontinued): A good-quality bag is ideal. I added this older bag, as a similar down bag may be bought used for perhaps $150 or so. Costco also sells Klymit down bags for $140 that are good budget bags.

☐ **Water treatment (6)**
Aquamira drops are an effective and inexpensive water treatment.

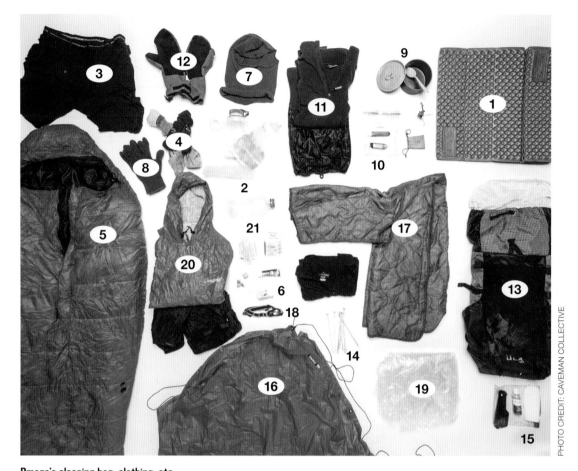

Pmags's sleeping bag, clothing, etc.

☐ **Balaclava (7)**

Polypro balaclava: A longtime favorite of mine that is worn in all four seasons. Very versatile and inexpensive. This one is fifteen years old!

☐ **Wool liner gloves (8)**

Another four-season mainstay, coupled with the shell mitts, a versatile system for all conditions.

☐ **Cooking kit (9)**

Ubens BRS Ultralight gas stove: A sub-1-ounce, less than $20 canister stove suitable for solo hiking. Alcohol stoves are coming under increased scrutiny in the increasingly fire-prone American West (because it's hard to control them).

Open Country 3 Cup Hard Anodized Aluminum pot (3.8 ounces): Light, cheap and effective. Use your bandana for a pot grip. Standard Lexan spoon.

☐ Toothbrush with duct tape (10)

Duct tape does everything. To quote the author Andy Weir: "Duct tape is magic and should be worshipped."

I've also got my toothbrush and dental floss here, because I store them in a Silnylon food bag (Silnylon is no longer an exotic fabric and is reasonable in price).

☐ Fleece (11)

100-weight fleece: One of my most versatile pieces of clothing. I wear it in all four seasons. This one cost $10 at Sports Authority.

☐ Shell mittens (12)

Outdoor Research Shell Mitts: These are no longer made. But similar eVent mittens may be purchased for less than $40 (about 3 ounces).

☐ Pack (13)

Ultralight Adventure Equipment (ULA, CD7 model): At $145, roughly 50 liters, and under 19 ounces stripped down, it is a good overall lightweight pack for most uses. I line it with a trash compactor bag to protect gear from getting wet.

☐ Stakes (14)

Gutter nails are light, good, cheap, and available at the hardware store.

☐ Toilet kit (15)

Tent Lab's Deuce of Spades trowel, toilet paper, hand sanitizer. LNT means leave no #2 and TP lying around!

☐ Tarp (16)

8x10-foot Campmor Ultralight Tarp: At 13 ounces and $100, this tarp is a nice compromise between the affordability of a traditional tarp and the very light, but very expensive, Cuben Fiber tarp. I'm using bank line to tie it, which is just fantastic, because it's lighter than paracord and cheaper than accessory cord. Originally used for fishing, it is tarred so it is abrasion-resistant

☐ Jacket (17)

M-65 Field Jacket Liner: Warm (wear it under a rain jacket), light, compressible, and perhaps $10 to $15 at online surplus stores. I used a liner on my late winter Benton McKaye Trail thru-hike (10 ounces).

Paul "Mags" Magnanti loves being outdoors as much as possible and unlike many three-season thru-hikers, doesn't let winter stop him.

☐ **Headlamp (18)**

Fine for three-season use when days are long.

☐ **Groundsheet (19)**

This is window shrink wrap from the hardware store. Similar to polycryo sold elsewhere, but cheaper. Cut to size. (1.6 ounces for 40x86 foot groundsheet)

☐ **Wind and rain gear (20)**

Frog Toggs Ultralite 2 Jacket: Good for on the trail. Works surprisingly well. Generic wind pants: My legs pump out a lot of heat, so I don't like real rain pants (6 ounces). Wind pants work well for me. Plus, being breathable, they work in a wide range of conditions.

☐ **First-aid/repair kit (21)**

WHAT PMAGS WEARS

Here's what Paul actually would wear on his body on a trip with a kit like this:

- Poly-cotton blend button-up shirt: I actually like the ventilation of a poly-cotton blend shirt. Mine is a repurposed "casual dress" shirt from Target.
- Nylon shorts: Generic hiking shorts from a discount store
- C9 Running Socks from Target
- Bandana: Multipurpose. Helps keep me cool.
- Tru-Spec Military Boonie hat: Well-worn and loved.
- Timex Indiglo watch: For dead reckoning.
- Keychain Lite Swiss Army Knife Classic: A basic, versatile tool kit for everyday life and the outdoors.
- GI Type P-51 Can Opener (to use as a multi-tool)
- Safety sunglasses: Light, durable and inexpensive. Found at hardware supply stores.
- Silva Starter 1-2-3 compass
- Cascade Mountain Tech Carbon Fiber Trekking Poles: Light and inexpensive, often available at Costco. Work very well.
- Brooks Cascadia: Light, but stiffer sole compared to many trail runners. I do enough off-trail hiking where it fits my needs more so than more minimalist footwear.

LIFE ON THE TRAIL

Chris "Atlas" Laster revels in the beauty of the CDT.

Chapter 7

WHAT TO EXPECT FROM LIFE ON THE TRAIL

Compared to the weeks and months leading up to a thru-hike, I find life on the trail to be calm, refreshing, and a serious amount of fun. There is a simple peace to putting one foot in front of the other. I also find joy and security in knowing that for the next few months, my goal is singular and simple: safely get to Canada or Mexico or Mount Katahdin or wherever by the power of my own feet. Every fiber of my being is dedicated to this cause.

There's an honesty and authenticity that comes from putting my body and mind toward that goal and being in tune with the natural environment around me: a mind, body, place connection that gives me flashbacks to moments on the trail even when I'm at home. On the trail I am free to be me.

But that doesn't mean that the day-to-day routine of a hike is a cakewalk either. Weather, injury, and mental challenges all adversely affect the hiker. In fact, although I've completed twenty long trails, I have quit three. I've had a lot of time to decompress and reflect on why that was. It's one of the reasons I wrote this chapter—to prepare you for the on-trail challenges that no one talks about, and to give you all the tools I can to keep you on track to reach your goals.

When people quit trails, there's usually not just one reason. The first time I hiked the AT, I thought about quitting, and it was for a combination of several smaller reasons—each fairly minor—including chafing on my feet and an awkward social situation. Each additional unpleasant thing—a wet campsite, dehydration, an unpleasant hitchhike—could've been the straw that broke this thru-hiker's back. My biggest defense was a series of daily routines and rituals to keep my spirits and morale up.

By thinking through some worst-case scenarios from the comfort of your home now, you can prevent common thru-hiker errors and make your hike more fun. Learning about this ahead of time can make a huge difference in your success. In this chapter, we'll learn about those day-to-day routines, how to stay motivated, and basic safety and medical care.

EATING AND DRINKING

Food and water are the gas in the tank of your thru-hiking machine—they're the foundation of powering a hike. We eat and drink every day of our lives, so it should be simple, right? But it's funny how the simplest things have the power to derail us if they get out of balance. Life on the trail requires keeping the gas tank full. While we covered a lot of nutrition information in chapter 5, here are some more practical tips for staying fueled during your long days on the trail.

AVOID HITTING THE WALL

The body can only digest roughly 300 calories and a liter of water per hour. So giving your body fuel frequently helps keep you from hitting the wall when

The Danger of Hanger

Hanger: Anger caused or exacerbated by hunger.

Hanger makes you take a minor annoyance and turn it into an on-trail tantrum. Hanger breaks up relationships on the trail. Hanger plus exhaustion turns any mishap into a confrontation. Hanger destroys friendships. Hanger leads to poor decision making. Hanger causes fights between hikers and local businesses, ruining the trail for everyone else. So here's the bottom line: Eat often. Eat regularly. Monitor your blood sugar. Avoid hanger.

Eat often. Eat regularly. Avoid hanger.

A cold soaked rehydrated lunch is a satisfying meal. The long spoon keeps my hands clean while eating. Lunchtime is always map reading time.

you're hiking. Most hikers like to eat something—an energy bar, a candy bar, or a calorie-containing drink—every 2 to 3 hours (or more often!) to prevent bonking. Once my hiker hunger gets going on a thru-hike, I eat three bars (at least 600 calories) every 2 to 3 hours.

It seems like it shouldn't be hard to eat frequently, but you'd be surprised at how difficult it can be in practice. Maybe you're trying to get through a hard section in the rain and don't want to stop to eat. Or maybe being at altitude or intense exercise decreases your appetite. Or maybe you plan to stop to camp in 20 minutes, so you decide not to eat.

Delaying eating works fine if you really will stop in 20 minutes, or if the hard section will be over in a few minutes. But if the trail stays tough, that's a bad time to forget to eat. You need the food to fuel your body and mind to make good decisions. Or if the place you intended to camp is full or doesn't have good places to set up, you're going to have an even harder time choosing a campsite on an empty stomach. Being hungry can make you less attentive to obstacles and dangers and make your footwork sloppy.

PHOTO CREDIT: WHITNEY "ALLGOOD" LARUFFA

Using my inline filter as a gravity filter to make myself a drink mix on the Sierra High Route.

I've been in both these situations many times. One way I combat this prob-lem is to stop, even if it doesn't seem like a great time, and eat a very small (100 calories or less) snack to push me over until camp time or a good break spot. That way I can continue making good decisions.

STAYING HYDRATED

Staying well hydrated is another of the most important things you need to do every day to keep yourself healthy and strong. Dehydration is just as dangerous as hanger—worse, actually, because it's a health risk. Here are my best tips for staying hydrated on a long hike.

Naomi "The Punisher" Hudetz and I camped near this this spring on the Great Divide Trail. Since springs tend to be relatively clean water, we felt comfortable not treating our water—saving us a step in the morning and at night.

☐ **Tip 1: Make water easily accessible and potable.** I drink filtered water from a Platypus Hoser with an inline Sawyer Squeeze filter while I'm walking. If you don't like to use a hydration reservoir, make sure you can reach your water-bottle side pockets easily without taking off your pack. Make sure that the water in those pockets is something you know is drinkable. "I don't want to have to stop or take my pack off for water" and "I don't want to stop to filter or treat my water" are both big reasons people end up dehydrated.

☐ **Tip 2: Time your breaks.** If you're in the desert or a dry area, take your break near a water source. Use this break to drink a few liters (also known as "cameling up"). Don't overdo it—that can cause some really uncomfortable sloshing in your belly—but drink plenty. (It'll take some trial and error to figure out how much you can comfortably chug.) Leave the water source feeling completely hydrated. That way you can avoid touching the water in your bottles for the next few miles.

☐ **Tip 3: Use drink mixes.** A pleasant taste helps you drink more. In addition, drinking a mix with salt helps you get enough of this essential mineral. Salt helps you retain the water you do drink instead of peeing it all out or getting water bloated. Find drink mixes with salt (plain old Gatorade mixed with some added salt works well enough for me). Otherwise, eat salty foods.

PHOTO CREDIT: KATE HOCH

On the Low to High Route across Death Valley, Naomi "The Punisher" Hudetz and I carried extra water capacity and hung our empty jugs off our packs.

☐ **Tip 4: Camp near water—and use it.** If possible, camp near water sources (but not too near—more on that later). That way you can make sure you are plenty hydrated at night, and also plenty hydrated in the morning.

☐ **Tip 5: Be hydrated at night.** Night is when your body recovers and rebuilds itself, and those processes need water to work. Yes, peeing at night while you're camping can be unpleasant, but getting dehydrated is worse in the long term. And you don't need to go overboard; if you are hydrated enough to pee before going to sleep and need to pee when you wake up, you should still be getting some recovery benefits.

☐ **Tip 6: Always carry extra water capacity.** You might only have a liter or two full at any given time, but even if you are hiking somewhere with plenty of water, you should have the option to tote more. I usually carry an extra Sawyer or Platypus bag because they weigh very little and can be condensed down to a small size. Sure, they ride in my pack empty most of the time, but this extra capacity gives me the flexibility to carry more water if there are fewer water sources than I had expected (e.g., many springs and streams have dried up for the season).

SIGNS OF DEHYDRATION

There's a saying out there: "A happy hiker pees clear." And it's true; monitoring your urine is a great way to make sure you're getting enough water. Your pee doesn't need to be perfectly clear, but it should be pale yellow rather than the dark shade of apple juice. I also use the rule of thumb that I should pee at minimum four times a day, or at least once every 3 hours.

On the other hand, if you experience any of the following symptoms, you might not be getting enough to drink:

- Headache
- Loss of appetite
- Thirst
- Dry mouth
- Irritability
- Dizziness
- Loss of energy

If you think you might be dehydrated, increase your water intake and consider taking a break to mix up a drink mix.

Do be aware that there's such a thing as being too hydrated. Or to be accurate, drinking too much water without getting enough salt can cause a condition called hyponatremia, where the level of salt in your blood gets dangerously low. If you've been drinking and peeing a ton and experience any of those dehydration symptoms (besides thirst), make sure to eat a salty snack and see if it resolves.

My ultramarathoning friends tipped me off to salt pills, which are for sale at running stores and REI. These provide a huge dose of salt. I think they improve my performance and focus when I feel like I've hit a wall, so I always keep a few in my med kit. Salt tabs are pricey, though. I've found a salt packet from a fast food joint seems to work almost as well.

MAKING CAMP

Making camp is another key everyday part of a hike. Luckily, making camp on a thru-hike isn't much different from making camp on a shorter backpacking trip. You may be using lighter shelters than you're used to, however, which requires more careful site selection.

PHOTO CREDIT: JOHNNY CARR

A hydrated hiker is a happy hiker.

Yes, this tarn in the Wind River Range, Wyoming, is beautiful. But there are a bunch of reasons why you shouldn't camp here.

Remember to plan your campsites ahead, not just during the route-planning phase but also while on the trail. The AT often goes straight up and down mountains, so there are limited flat spots. The PCT is designed to have many ridge walks, which means it also has limited flat spots at times. Each day (preferably in the morning), look at your maps and databook and plan where you hope to stay so that you don't end up with a precarious camp on the edge of a cliff.

LOOK FOR SITES AWAY FROM WATER

Despite what every tent ad shows, camping right near water is a bad idea. Why? Well, for one, it's against the Leave No Trace principles we'll go over in chapter 8. But even more than that, lakes and rivers are usually in the low points of an area. Cold air settles to the lowest spot. That means you'll be colder camping near the water than choosing a spot a bit higher. Also, moist air near water sources

PHOTO CREDIT: LIZ THOMAS

A beautiful snow-free camp in the San Juans on the CDT set up on rock and dirt.

can lead to condensation in and around your tent. That makes you wet—which makes you colder.

Find a spot at least 200 feet from water—that way wildlife will have plenty of room to get a drink without getting scared by you (or you getting scared by them!) and you'll avoid the wet, cold terrain trap that water usually creates. The best campsite may be a dry camp. Eat near water, hike on a little bit, and sleep away from water.

PICK A DURABLE SURFACE

Pick a surface like sand, pine needle duff, or slickrock that won't look any different after you camp on it. Not only can your tent cause damage to meadows, plants, and grass-like vegetation, but the plants lead to condensation. You and your gear get wet because plants undergo a water vapor exchange (aka "breathe"). Some plants can also cause damage to your tent or other gear: Think of pine needles puncturing holes into an almost see-through tarp, for example.

Beetles are killing many trees in the American West, which have been made more susceptible to pests due to drought. Some ecosystems like chapparal on the PCT, have evolved to burn periodically. All thru-hikers will walk through burnt forests. It is incredibly likely you will experience at least one trail detour due to forest fires.

As grand as the views are from an alpine campsite, camps below treeline are more protected from the elements. If you camp under a tree, the tree acts like another roof over your head—keeping out water, blocking wind, and also keeping you slightly warmer. Caveat: Especially out West, be careful to look around and make sure the trees you're camping under are all alive. Dead standing trees are called "widowmakers" for a reason.

STAY AWAY FROM TRAILS AND ROADS

There are two reasons I recommend this. First, it's polite. We hike to get a wilderness experience, and seeing tents up and down the trail does not contribute to that. Camp out of sight from the trail to maintain that protected view for other hikers. Second, it's arguably safer. If the first is not enough incentive, camp away from the trail for protection from wildlife and humans. Wildlife, including bears and big cats, use the trail at night because it is easier than walking off-trail.

Long trails are sometimes routed on roads, like this part of the CDT near the Gila Wilderness in New Mexico. But that doesn't mean you need to camp right next to one.

That's one reason why it's common to see scat from large wildlife on the trail. Second, if anyone were to mess with you and your camp, they would likely find and access your camp from the trail. By camping away from the trail, you'll be harder to find. And the farther you are from a road, the fewer random trouble-makers are likely to happen upon you. (That's my theory, at least.) To avoid this issue, especially when I am solo, I camp at least a mile away from the road and plan my days to end so I am not near trailheads.

Cowboy Camp

Cowboy camp: To camp under the stars without a shelter.

Cowboy camping is the fastest way to set up and break down camp, which is why it's a thru-hiker favorite. It's not for everyone—especially for those who don't like bugs—but it can be a liberating way to enjoy the wilderness.

TRY COWBOY CAMPING

Many hikers, especially on trails in the American West, opt not to use their shelter on dry nights and instead cowboy camp. If you are cowboy camping, pay extra attention to picking a good site as just described. You'll have no protection from wind or condensation, so good campsite selection is even more important. Check the sky or forecast (if you can) before you decide to cowboy camp, and be prepared to set up your shelter if you start feeling raindrops. Cowboy campers are especially vulnerable to getting condensation on their sleeping bags, so tree coverage is key (unless you're in the desert). Always use a groundsheet to give your sleeping bag and pad some protection from plants, rocks, and sand that could moisten or abrade your gear. Pick a site free of ant hills and watch for mosquitoes. Cowboy camping isn't for everyone.

HOW TO STORE YOUR FOOD AT NIGHT

One of the biggest questions I get from potential hikers is what to do with your food when you're at camp for the night. Let's go over the options. Some sections of trail, like the PCT in the Sierra, require bear canisters. If so, then it's simple to know what to do with your food. Land managers will even tell you which models are approved. But if a bear canister is not required, most hikers don't carry them, because they're heavy and bulky.

If your trail does require canisters, you'll probably need to buy your own, unless you're hiking a short-enough section that renting one from a gear store or ranger station makes sense logistically and economically. Several companies, like Wild Ideas Bearikade, offer canister rentals and will mail to your home or the trail town before you enter bear country.

Bear canisters aren't very big, so pick calorie-dense food and food without a lot of dead space to maximize the room in your can. Remember to put all items

Bear cans can protect your food from animals.

with scent into your bear can, such as bug spray, sunscreen, lip balm, and of course, food. At night, put your bear can 100 feet from your camp. Choose a spot somewhere visible from your tent and where it can't roll away or go down-river if a bear messes with it. Bright tape on your can makes it easier to find.

Besides a bear canister, the other main way to protect your food from bears is by hanging it in a bear bag. Hanging a bear bag is an involved process. In practice, most thru-hikers are selective about when to hang their food. They'll carry bear canisters or hang where they are legally required to do so, or when they're in grizzly habitat or areas with known bear activity. Otherwise, for better or worse, they usually don't bother.

To bear bag, you'll need 50 to 100 feet of rope, a stuff sack for your food, and a few carabiners. A smaller stuff sack and a rock are optional. (Note: Some companies like Mountain Laurel Designs sell ultralight bear bag setups that include all the parts you need.) Find a tree 100 feet from your camp, or up to 300 feet from camp in grizzly country. Make sure that tree has a branch that allows you to get your bag 12 feet off the ground, 6 feet from the trunk, and 6 feet below the branch. Here's how to do a simple single-branch bear hang:

Put a rock or sand into a small stuff sack and attach it to one end of your rope. Attach the food stuff sack to the other end of the rope. Remember to put all items with scent into your bear bag. Throw the small stuff sack over your selected branch. Make sure your friends are out of the way when you throw in case your aim is off. Pull the rope to raise the food stuff sack to the appropriate height/distance from the tree.

To make your life easier, throw your rock stuff sack and get your rope up before dark. You can always attach your food bag and lift it after dark, but aiming and throwing at night is a pain.

The Ursack is a chew-proof bag made of material that is very hard for bears (or humans) to tear, chew, pierce, or cut. Ursacks save hikers from the pain of having to throw a rock over a tree branch while providing a bear-proof option that weighs less than half of the lightest weight bear canister. It also works in alpine areas where trees are too small to develop significant branching. There are a few downsides, though. The Ursack has not been approved for use in some areas, most notably Yosemite National Park and parts of the Sierra. It also requires special care to make sure you use it correctly, though I personally find it much easier to use correctly than it is to bear bag correctly. Some users are skeptical of the Ursack because bears can still crush your food, even if they won't be able to steal it. Nonetheless, I personally find the Ursack to be one of hiking's greatest inventions. Its light weight, lack of bulkiness, and ease of use make it ideal for thru-hikers when regulations allow for them.

To use the Ursack, put all your odorous and edible items into an odor-proof bag (more on that later). Place the odor-proof bag inside the Ursack. Tie the Ursack's cord with a double overhand knot. Make sure not to overstuff your bag and to close off the bag completely so there is no opening. Then, use a strong knot like a figure 8 to attach the Ursack to a fixed object like a tree, preferably at least 100 feet from your tent. You can also hang your Ursack from a branch using the methods described in the previous section.

Even where bear canisters or hanging aren't required, you still need to make sure you're protecting your food from smaller critters. Mice, squirrels, chipmunks, and marmots are responsible for far more food and pack damage than bears. These animals love salt, so they'll chew up your clothes, boots, even a hiking pole handle! Here's how to protect your gear and food when you're not in bear country.

Nightly Camp Chores Checklist

On the trail we have ultimate freedom to do what we want, when we want. With freedom comes responsibility for our bodies, the natural environment, the communities we walk through, and how we interact with others. Having a routine on the trail can take some of the guesswork out of "what to do next" and help you automate essential tasks. Here you'll find my nightly camp chores checklist, which I developed so that I don't forget any of the crucial tasks that make my hike more pleasant.

Personal clean-up:
- ☐ Get water
- ☐ Bathe
- ☐ Change into dry clothes

Camp setup:
- ☐ Clean camp
- ☐ Set up shelter
- ☐ Put down groundcloth
- ☐ Set down sleeping bag and fluff

Dinner:
- ☐ Cook
- ☐ Eat
- ☐ Wash pot
- ☐ Brush teeth
- ☐ Remove scented items from pack, including pockets
- ☐ If necessary: tie up Ursack, stow bear canister, or hang bear bag

Foot care/gear prep:
- ☐ Laundry (especially socks)
- ☐ Remove insoles
- ☐ Hang up wet clothes
- ☐ Foot care/blister care
- ☐ Journal
- ☐ Sleep

If it will get below freezing at night:
- ☐ Bring water bottles inside and flip them on their side so ice won't prevent you from drinking in the morning
- ☐ Put electronics inside sleeping bag or bivy
- ☐ If carrying a water filter, put it inside a Ziploc bag and put inside sleeping bag or bivy
- ☐ Put shoes and insoles inside a plastic bag and place inside sleeping bag or bivy
- ☐ Take any wet clothes, especially socks, and put under sleeping pad but above groundsheet

I carry a Loksak OPSAK odor-proof sack as my food bag. These plastic bags look like oversize Ziplocs and, when used correctly, have been shown in studies to be able to prevent bears and other wildlife from finding food.

When regulations do not specify what to do with your food, besides hanging a bear bag or using a bear canister, here are your choices:

- Option 1: Leave it outside. Leaving food outside your tent increases the chances your food may get taken. You can hang your food bag from a low branch that you can reach easily, so at least it's off the ground a little.
- Option 2: Keep your food inside your shelter. In the unlikely scenario that an animal wants your food enough to mess with you and come into your tent, then you'll have to interact with the animal.

It's ultimately a benefit-cost-risk analysis decision for each hiker to make. If you know you won't be able to sleep at night having food in your tent and are worried about it, then by all means—hang your food. Remember your food storage decisions not only impact you but also the life of an animal.

DAILY ROUTINES

You can get a good overview of life on the trail just by learning what a typical daily routine looks like. Daily routines will change depending on sunrise/sunset, temperatures and climate, terrain including water and campsite availability, and your physical condition, skills, and personal preferences. Since there can be some major differences in routines, I'm sharing both mine and my friend Amanda "Zuul" Jameson's.

This was my schedule for the Wasatch Range Traverse I did in September 2015. As I was solo and on a tight schedule, there wasn't a lot of hanging-out time. This trail didn't have a ton of water, so I stopped at almost every water source and drank and refilled bottles. A typical day on the trail obviously varies, but this is a good model for how I spend some of my more aggressive days on the trail:

Night before

If not in bear country, prepare a breakfast drink mix to be ready to down in the morning. If in bear country, prep a bottle of clean water ready to have drink mix added to it.

5:30 a.m. (sunrise)

Get up and start packing.

5:45 a.m.

Finish packing and down a drink mix plus water. Put a few energy bars or gels in my pocket and start walking.

6:30 a.m.

Start eating other parts of my breakfast (what's in my pocket) as I'm walking.

7:00 a.m.

Short break to shed some layers, maybe poop.

7:30 a.m.

Start putting on sunscreen while walking.

8:00 a.m.

Eat another bar while walking.

10:00 a.m.

Eat another bar.

12:00 p.m. or whenever I reach a good spot or water source

Sit, take off shoes and socks, and remove shoe inserts from my shoes. Take out my shelter and sleeping bag and hang them somewhere where they won't snag so the condensation from the night before can dry out. Drink a ton of water and drink mixes. Stretch, and wipe off sweat and dirt. Maybe make a cold meal. Eat. Pack back up and refill water bottles. Reapply sunscreen.

1:15 p.m.

Back on the trail.

3:15 p.m.

Eat another bar.

5:15 p.m.

Eat another bar.

Start soaking a dinner (I was stoveless on this trip.)

7:30 p.m.

Start looking for a campsite.

7:45 p.m. (sunset)

Hopefully have found something. Set up sleeping bag, shelter if needed, and get all my stuff organized.

8:00 p.m.

Get in my sleeping bag and start eating my soaked dinner and other bars.

8:10 p.m.

Prep my breakfast for the morning.

8:20 p.m.

Look at maps and prepare for the next morning.

8:45 p.m.

Go to sleep.

AMANDA'S DAILY SCHEDULE

Amanda's first thru-hike was the Colorado Trail, which she walked from August to September 2015. While temperatures were cooler, she had great weather, which allowed her to be less strict with her schedule than she would have been with worse weather. Even though Amanda had done a ton of research and got advice from loads of experienced hikers, as it was her first long hike, and she was figuring many things out about herself and her hiking style. She discovered one big problem: She has a hard time eating on the trail.

6:30 a.m.

Alarm goes off for the first time. Evaluate the day in my head, see if I can sleep in a little longer.

6:45 a.m.

Alarm goes off for the second time. Start to gather the things I keep in my sleeping bag—external battery, cell phone, headlamp, SPOT device, hiking shorts, warm leggings. Start the morning dance of getting dressed in my sleeping bag.

6:50 a.m.

Trade top of sleeping bag for puffy, finally sit up. Inhale energy gummies (preferably with caffeine included). Pour drink mix plus dried fruit plus chia seeds into water bottle to mix for walking breakfast. Check maps for the last time this morning.

7:00 a.m.

Emerge from sleeping bag and tent; start packing. Pull out snacks—toaster pastries, energy bars, more gummies—and put in hipbelt pocket. Feel guilty for not eating much, so end up munching while packing.

7:15 a.m.

One last idiot check of the campsite to make sure I haven't left anything. Bathroom break before walking.

7:20 a.m.

Start walking.

7:45 a.m.

Brief break to adjust layers, force more food/drink mix down my throat. Continue walking.

9:00 a.m. or on any big uphill

Start sucking on energy gummies for energy and to take my mind off the climb. Continue to shovel in food in between gummies and during short breaks to catch my breath.

11:00 a.m. or at a water source

Take wet stuff out of pack to dry and lay/hang out, if applicable. Prep whatever purification method I'm using. Finish drink mix and whichever water bottle is most empty; grab water to purify. Take off shoes and remove socks and inserts while purifying water. Get thoroughly disgusted thinking about eating; cook lunch anyway. Look over maps and elevation profiles while mindlessly chewing and swallowing; adjust day's goals based on how I've been hiking and how I'm feeling. Prep more snacks in hipbelt pocket. Laze about until pot is clean or stuff is dry, whichever comes first.

12:10 p.m.

Start walking again.

2:00 p.m.

Dread eating something. Do so anyway.

4:30 p.m.

20-minute break. Shoes and socks off, inserts out. Grab another handful of something to eat, but only because calories are necessary for hiking. Do one last main check on day's goals—decide to push or play it safe based on the miles I've already made, my target campsite/town day, and how worn out I'm feeling.

6:00 p.m. or last water source

10-minute break for water purification (I drink a lot of water) and more snacking.

7:00 p.m.

Start looking for camp. If I've done my planning right, I should reach a campsite noted on the maps around 7:30.

7:30 p.m.

After a little trouble actually finding the camp my maps were referring to, start settling in as it gets dark.

7:40 p.m.

Stare balefully at food. Eat probably less than I should, empty bladder, and retreat into tent when I can't stand the cold anymore.

8:00 p.m.

Look over maps and such, recalibrate my projected days into town based on the miles I've made, mentally prepare myself for tomorrow. Take notes for the day's blog, or actually blog if I've got enough battery between my phone and external battery.

9:00 p.m.

Stare at the tent ceiling thinking that, between my aching muscles and my mind racing ahead to tomorrow, I'll never actually sleep.

9:15 p.m.

Eventually sleep.

Small actions, like taking care of your feet, can ensure you are a happy camper in the long run, as Hannah Williams learned on the PNT.

TRICKS FOR THE LONG HAUL

Staying comfortable on the trail isn't about avoiding everything that can make your trip hard. It will rain. It will get dark. You will get hungry. And you will make mistakes. But the key to succeeding as a thru-hiker is realizing that you have less room for error built in to your life on the trail than you do back home, or even on a shorter trip. Because of that, it takes vigilance and discipline to keep your margin of error as wide as possible and make sure that one mistake or hardship doesn't snowball out of control.

What if it's raining on your way to your city office? No big deal, let your pants get wet, even cotton ones. They'll dry at your desk by lunchtime. Rain on a day hike? You're fine letting yourself get soaked on the way to the car, then cranking the heater. Even on a shorter backpacking trip, you'll probably recover from a night or two with a wet sleeping bag; you'll have a bed, roof, and dryer soon enough. On a thru-hike though? Do all you can to keep your nighttime clothing and sleeping bag dry, because they're the only things that stand between you and hypothermia. There's not nearly as much room to screw up on a thru-hike, so it's up to you to guard and maintain the buffers that stand between you and a dangerous situation.

As a thru-hiker, you need to stay vigilant, even though you may feel too tired to do things the "right way." Take care of problems now, before that blister becomes infected or that scrape on your pack becomes a hole. Keep your key gear dry. Pack up carefully so you don't lose anything. Store your food properly so critters don't run away with it. If you're feeling bad, sit down, take a break, eat and drink something. And every time you make a decision, keep that margin in mind, and make the choice that keeps it wide. You're not out there to prove anything. You're out there to have fun and be safe.

PACE YOURSELF

The most obvious unique feature of a long hike is that you'll be hiking, well, a long time. Everything you do on any given day impacts what can happen the next day, the next week, and maybe even the next month. We've already discussed pacing in the fitness and route-planning chapters, but it's so important, I want to talk about it again here.

The pace you choose each day should be a pace you can sustain for the length of the trip. If it is unsustainable, you can expect to take some zero days or deal with some painful consequences. I advise people to start their hikes at half to two-thirds of their physical ability. If you can day hike 20 miles, start your trip at 10 miles per day. Go at that pace for a week, and then ramp it up to 15. If you're out for a six-month trip, your first two to three weeks are your training weeks. They help you get your "trail legs."

Your physical capability isn't just a matter of how many miles your muscles can go, but also how many miles your joints, ligaments, and tendons can take. Thru-hiking is not just about having chiseled thighs or ripped calves. It's how strong your far-less-sexy and less noticeable foot and ankle muscles are. Foot and ankle injuries, more than any others, are the ones that take people off the trail. And injuries don't just happen to your body; they affect your morale and psyche, too. Review how to train for a thru-hike (see chapter 2) for ways to strengthen your feet ahead of time.

If you're only using half to two-thirds of your physical strength per day on the trail, you have a good margin of error if something unexpected happens. You have enough strength to bail out a buddy. You have enough strength to push it to town to avoid a big storm. You have enough strength to make good decisions in crises.

PHOTO CREDIT: JOHNNY CARR

Choose a reasonable pace and realize it will change depending on climate, terrain, weather, and your body.

Take Amanda's advice from the previous section: during breaktimes, evaluate whether you are on track to meet your day's goals based on how you are feeling, the progress you've made so far, the weather, and the terrain ahead. Thru-hiking is about pushing yourself, but also knowing your limits. Finding the balance between the two is an art that takes a lifetime to master.

Staying within your limits doesn't just mean keeping your daily mileage within reason. It also means keeping your overall mileage in reason. Some people find that their body holds up well on thru-hikes of 500 miles, but starts falling apart around 1,000 miles. Section hiking is the smart thing for many hikers' bodies and minds (not to mention their jobs, relationships, and finances).

Pushing yourself past your limits—or close to the limit of your physical ability for many days—is one of the main reasons people quit their long trail. Why?

- **No fun.** Going past your limits sucks the joy out of a hike. It's fun at first to see how much you can push, but after a few days, it quickly turns into a death march.

- **Overuse injuries.** Just a day or even a few hours of going past where your body is comfortable is enough to cause the kind of damage that will take you off the trail for a few weeks.
- **Minor injuries.** Pushing past your limits makes you more susceptible to blisters or other foot wounds. These can make your hike less comfortable (making your hike less fun). In extreme cases, these minor injuries can get infected, which will also take you off the trail.
- **No energy to take care of yourself.** I've met many hikers who push so hard they're too tired to eat dinner at night. If you don't eat, then you don't get the benefit of recovery that food can provide (not to mention the morale boost food provides).
- **No energy to make other smart decisions.** If you're exhausted, it's going to be a lot harder to navigate. It's going to be a lot harder to set up your shelter. Everything just becomes a lot more difficult when you are tired.

HIKE YOUR OWN HIKE

DON'T COMPARE YOUR PACE TO ANYONE ELSE'S

PHOTO CREDIT: AMANDA JAMESON

Here's Amanda "Zuul" Jameson, who thru-hiked the Colorado Trail 2015 as her first thru-hike and the PCT in 2016.

As a newbie thru-hiker, I wish I had known not to compare myself to others on the trail. At the beginning of my CT thru-hike, I was doing 12 to 18 miles per day, but I was getting passed a fair bit, especially on the uphills. In towns, I heard from others that "normal" thru-hikers did 20 miles in a day—or more. I just wasn't there. I kept mentally punishing myself for "not being good enough." It took me about 340 miles on a 486-mile trail to realize that, even though I was walking fewer miles per day than others, I was still getting it done. That was an amazing accomplishment. I ended up cutting myself some slack. And to my amazement, I averaged 20-mile days for the last six days of my hike. It's your hike. Don't let comparisons diminish this awesome thing you've set out to achieve.

—Amanda "Zuul" Jameson

HOW MY PACE FOUND ME

Here's Dean Krakel, the 63-year-old photojournalist from Denver, Colorado, who hiked the Colorado Trail in 2015 as his first thru-hike.

About halfway through my CT trip, I was looking back across the mountain, and I saw these two figures moving incredibly fast—faster than any people I've ever seen walk with a pack. They just floated over the landscape. They passed everyone else on the trail and would have passed me, except I was standing there waiting for them—I wanted to see who they were. They were a pair of women who did ultra-running but were backpacking, and they had light packs and were killing 30-mile days. They were knocking it out. They'd cover in a day what it would take me several days to cover.

I hung with them for about 5 miles and then said I needed to take a nap. We said goodbye, and I never saw them again, but I did talk with them after the trip. They said they had actually decided to slow down after they met me and, eventually, they quit the trail at the midpoint. I finished.

I admire people who can consistently walk 20-mile days. That was my goal when I started the CT. I trained hard. I cut my pack weight down to 24 pounds so I could knock out 20-mile days. But, as it turned out, I didn't define the pace. The pace found me.

Every day on the trail was different. My mileage varied. But I turned out to be a pretty solid 10- to 12-mile-per-day guy. For me, the pace worked. I was able to study elk tracks and take pictures and journal and take naps. I found that the slower pace let me live the Colorado Trail instead of just move along it. To set pace, you need to figure out what the intent of your trip is. Is it something you are checking off the list? A physical challenge? What is it? For me, the entire trip was a journey. I even started enjoying hitching into town to get resupplies. Previously, I had considered it an obstacle to my time and mileage, but the towns became a part of my trip, as did everything. Take time to smell the flowers, study the tracks, drink from the springs, feel the environment around you, listen to the wind, and look at the clouds. Somebody's got to do it.

—Dean "Ghost" Krakel

Remember: As a hiker, making miles is not your only job. Taking care of yourself is your job too. Scaling back to half the mileage you know you can do may seem drastic, but I've seen skilled and super-fit ultramarathoners and military professionals get off the trail from overuse. Those guys let their ego get in the way of making their goal, for a number of reasons:

- Needing to prove to themselves and others that they can do a particular task or pace.
- Trying to stay with a particular hiking group or partner who is faster than them.
- Setting an unreasonable deadline to finish the hike.

A thru-hike is a marathon, not a sprint. Even if you start out slow, you should not judge yourself. You will get faster and be able to hike more miles. But that's only if you manage to stay on the trail that long.

CARE FOR YOUR GEAR ON THE TRAIL

Just like your body, your gear needs special love and attention to make it through a long hike. You need to take care of it to make it last. First, don't ever throw your pack down. Most ultralight gear—heck, most gear—needs to be babied to survive a thru-hike. Don't sit on your pack. Don't throw it on the ground. Don't set it on sharp rocks. Don't drag it across rough surfaces. Take care when walking through brush.

Gear doesn't last forever. Be prepared to replace some items at least once during your trip.

Dry your gear out every day. All shelters and sleeping bags will get a little condensation (dew) at night. Inside your shelter, your breath condenses and forms droplets on the walls. Don't worry—your tent isn't leaking (probably). It's just condensation. Moisture can lead to mold and other wear on your shelter. It can also decrease the loft (puffiness) of your sleeping bag, which makes the bag less warm.

That's actually how I got my trail name, "Snorkel." During my first AT thru-hike, my down bag wasn't as warm as I thought it should be. A guy at a gear store figured out it was because I was keeping my head in it every night and my breath was getting trapped in the down, decreasing the loft. "You need a snorkel," he told me.

Bottom line: Get rid of that moisture! Thru-hikers need to be diligent about drying their gear at every opportunity. I dry my gear during lunch breaks. This is easier to do on a drier trail like the PCT. On a wetter trail, like the AT, I would plan my lunch around breaks in the clouds and rain.

Having dedicated sleeping clothes protects your sleeping bag from grit and dirt, which cause wear. It also reduces the amount of body oil and sweat that end up in your bag. Oil and sweat are associated with smelliness and reduced loft. Many hikers wear their mostly clean night clothes while they are in town resupplying. This makes them look more respectable when hitchhiking (easier to get a ride) and less offensive during the ride (not as smelly).

Consider a sleeping bag protector. You can protect the outside of your sleeping bag with a breathable bivy bag or sleeping bag cover—essentially, an extra layer of sleeping bag liner fabric that keeps condensation and dirt off your bag. You can protect the inside of your bag from the dirt on your body by using a liner bag. Both add additional warmth to your sleep system and extend the life of your bag.

Remember to wash your sleeping bag. I usually wash my bag at least once during a 2,000-plus-mile trip. I will take a zero (rest) day and either use a laundromat or hand wash it. Washing my sleeping bag at home after a long trail is a favorite end-of-hiking season ritual.

Use breaks wisely. How often you take breaks and how long those breaks are really depends on how you would like your day to go. It also depends on how long you can stand to be on your feet without needing to take the pressure off them. As you get stronger and more skilled in your hiking, you may find you need fewer breaks. Or you may find that becoming a stronger or faster hiker means that you can afford to take more breaks. Regardless, it's good to maximize your time on a break. While there is no one right way to take breaks, I make sure I maximize my time off my feet by doing a few "chores" that help me care for myself and my gear.

I always tank up on water during breaks (like here on Mt. Lafayette in the White Mountains of New Hampshire).

Here's my typical lunch break routine:
- Find a nice spot, preferably out of sight from the trail, near water, and protected from wind.
- Get water (if it's nearby).
- Put on another layer and hat immediately if it is cooler, to trap the heat from exercising before my body temp starts dropping.
- Hang up or lay out my sleeping bag, tent, and other gear to dry (if needed).
- Take off shoes and socks, take insoles out of shoes, and let them all dry (if it's not too cold).
- Foot care (check for blisters, care for them, massage feet, elevate or cool feet down).
- Eat.
- Hydrate (may as well make up a drink mix here).
- Reapply sunscreen, bug spray, etc.

· Check maps, evaluate progress, identify important intersections or navigational challenges ahead, determine options for camping that night.

USE BREAKS TO DEAL WITH EXTREME CONDITIONS

Breaks aren't just a good time to take care of yourself and your gear. Used wisely, they can actually help you be a smarter hiker. When and how you take your breaks will depend on weather conditions, climate, and your physical fitness and skill level. But when it comes to breaks, everyone can benefit from them.

Posthole

Posthole: Sinking straight down into snow with each footstep, like a fence post into dirt.

Postholing can happen even when the snow you're encountering seems solid enough to hold your weight. Snow freezes and melts and refreezes, causing multiple layers to form. When you take a step on the surface, sometimes the layers under the crust are not as compact or solid as the top layer. Thus you posthole into the snow, sometimes up to your waist. This situation is even more common in areas with talus (large rocks), where holes can form between rocks and collect snow. You can minimize postholing by hiking early, when the snow is still frozen.

PHOTO CREDIT: LIZ THOMAS

During early summer, snow conditions often cause hikers to posthole.

View from Camel's Hump, a highlight of the Long Trail in Vermont

Many thru-hikers find that hiking during the heat of the day through desert sections isn't the most productive use of their energy. To avoid heatstroke, sunburn, and dehydration, hikers wake up early and hike during the first light of the day. Then they take a nap in the shade during the hottest hours. Finally, they continue hiking as it becomes cooler toward evening.

Postholing in snow means that hiking takes more time, energy, and therefore food than normal—sometimes even twice as much for a given distance. To avoid the posthole slog, hikers often start early in the day—like midnight—and hike while the snow's layers are still frozen. Then they'll take a break in the middle of the day or end very early as the snow starts softening.

If it's raining, don't be afraid to set up your shelter and take a nap while you're waiting for the storm to roll over. Some trails, most notably the Appalachian Trail, have three-sided shelters positioned on average every 10 miles along the trail. I've taken many lunch breaks out of the rain in these shelters.

If you see a storm rolling in and know you are headed above treeline, take your break below treeline and wait for the thunder and lightning to pass. If you can find a windbreak, shelter yourself from the elements and give your mind and nerves some time to settle before heading back into it.

A note about breaks: Many hikers find that when they take breaks longer than 15 minutes or so, their bodies become stiff from cooling down. You'll have to warm up again, so you may notice a slight shuffle in your walk as you get up from your break. Don't worry. The iconic "hiker hobble" is normal and usually goes away after 10 minutes of walking.

The Wind River Range in Wyoming, a highlight of the CDT

Chapter 8

SAFETY, ETIQUETTE, AND SPECIAL CONCERNS

After slogging through miles of soft snow—sometimes falling in up to my waist—I reached a dry patch of grass at the end of a steep cliff looking down on a valley. I was in the South San Juan Wilderness, hiking at the end of May—a less than ideal season to be above 12,000 feet on the CDT. Three of my friends joined me in the respite from the snow: two Germans and a Spaniard.

"Can you believe it?" they asked each other, in English. Yes, it was beautiful, but there were other places like this. It wasn't extraordinary. Yet the Europeans' eyes were sparkling with an intense look usually reserved for a romantic meal in Paris.

"There's no cell towers. No roads. No houses or lights," the Spaniard explained to me. How foolish I was to take the view for granted. We Americans are so spoiled to have large swaths of landscapes and views that are wild.

When I'm hiking a long trail and haven't seen another person for a while, sometimes I look around and pretend I'm an explorer seeing these great lands for the first time. Of course, this is silly—to begin with, someone built the trail I'm walking on. But that's the magic of a long trail: to be able to walk relatively easily into a wild place and see landscapes that—aside from the trail—don't have obvious signs of a human's touch.

But even in these places—even in designated wildernesses—humans can impact the land. And sadly, the humans that do this are sometimes our fellow hikers. Graffiti, trash, and human waste on the trail immediately take the magic away from what is otherwise an enchanting place. And as hiker numbers go up, these occurrences are becoming more common.

Equally harmful is the impact of humans on the small communities near the trail. For many, the greatest healing power of hiking is walking into a trail town, meeting different people, and learning to accept the kindness of strangers. For those who have been neglected, abused, or otherwise hurt by others, it is healing and empowering to receive hospitality from those who seemingly have no reason to be kind. Yet as hiker numbers increase, a class of so-called entitled hikers are disrespecting local people, trashing up these treasured communities, and giving hikers a bad name.

Every long trail's future depends on your actions—toward both the natural environment and other people. Those who work to build and maintain trails and protect our natural areas need to know that hikers are on their side. Good stewardship sends a clear message to land managers and communities that long-distance hikers are using the trails and our lands responsibly (and I can only hope they will see this and decide to give us more). This chapter is about how to become the best trail citizen you can be—perhaps the most important lesson in the whole book.

TRAIL ETIQUETTE

I don't want to seem like Miss Manners or your nagging parent, but it's important to remember that, even though we're off in the wilderness, we're still part of a community. And just as the world is a kinder, better place when we all follow etiquette rules in our normal lives (like not cutting in line at the bank), understanding the rules of behavior for the wilderness means you're ready to be a positive citizen out there as well. I truly think that most of the time when someone acts improperly in the wilderness, it's because they just don't know any better. So it's with complete faith in your courtesy and compassion that I dedicate this part of the book to what being a good trail citizen means. Please do take the time to reflect on these topics and take this stuff seriously—it impacts not just hikers now, but the future of hiking itself.

PHOTO CREDIT: DEAN KRAKEL

Generally, downhill hikers yield to uphill hikers. Hikers yield to horses. Bikers yield to hikers. And hikers with dogs should yield to other hikers.

LEAVE NO TRACE BASICS

Leaving the woods a better place than you found them is always important, but even more so on a long-distance hike, especially on trails that see lots of hiker traffic, like the AT and PCT. That's where following the principles of "Leave No Trace" travel are especially important. Thru-hikers have a responsibility to know, practice, and promote Leave No Trace principles. Set a good example by studying up at Int.org and taking a Leave No Trace awareness workshop. For more details on each principle, visit www.lnt.org. Leave No Trace also offers Awareness Workshops across the United States.

Leave No Trace is all about preserving beautiful places like this for future generations . . . and for ourselves when we hike this same trail again in a few years.

SEVEN KEY RULES OF LEAVE NO TRACE (LNT)

Here are the seven key guidelines of LNT as they apply to thru-hikers, with comments from Ben Lawhon, education director for the Leave No Trace Center for Outdoor Ethics, a nonprofit group dedicated to reducing recreational impact on the wilderness.

1. Plan Ahead and Prepare

"An unprepared hiker creates a higher risk for impact," explains Lawhon. "If you didn't know you needed gaiters, you might trample vegetation to keep your boots dry instead of hiking through the puddles." Call a ranger to learn about terrain, weather, and regulations.

Know the regulations and special concerns for the area you'll visit.

Prepare for extreme weather, hazards, and emergencies.

Schedule your trip to avoid times of high use.

Don't hike with all your friends in a line. Split larger parties into groups of four to six and camp apart.

Repackage food to minimize waste that can fall out of your pack or get taken off by the wind.

PHOTO CREDIT: DEAN KRAKEL

Use a map and compass to eliminate the use of marking paint, rock cairns, or flagging.

2. Travel and Camp on Durable Surfaces

"Durable surfaces rebound better than delicate ones," says Lawhon. Hike on rock, sand, gravel, and established trails; avoid stream banks, cryptobiotic soil, and alpine plants.

Durable surfaces include established trails and campsites, rock, gravel, dry grasses, and snow.

Protect riparian areas by camping at least 200 feet from lakes and streams.

Good campsites are found, not made. Altering a site is not necessary.

In popular areas:

Concentrate use on existing trails and campsites.

Walk single file in the middle of the trail, even when wet or muddy.

Keep campsites small. Focus activity in areas where vegetation is absent.

In pristine areas:

Disperse use to prevent the creation of campsites and trails.

Avoid places where impacts are just beginning.

Because you are out for so long, thru-hiking teaches you to appreciate what nature has to offer without feeling like you need to take it home with you.

3. Dispose of Waste Properly

Pack it in, pack it out. This phrase is used often in the outdoor world and means that any item you bring into the woods—from candy wrappers to toilet paper to that annoying tag on your hat—needs to go back to civilization with you.

Inspect your campsite and rest areas for trash or spilled foods. Pack out all trash—both yours and trash you discover—and leftover food. To wash yourself or your dishes, carry water 200 feet away from streams or lakes and use small amounts of biodegradable soap. Scatter strained dishwater. Deposit solid human waste in catholes dug 6 to 8 inches deep at least 200 feet from water, camp, and trails. Cover and disguise the cathole when finished. Pack out toilet paper and hygiene products. (We'll talk more about those last two shortly.)

4. Leave What You Find

"Hikers can spread nonnative species, which is a huge cause of habitat destruction," explains Lawhon. "By not taking plants or animals, and cleaning your boots before you leave the trailhead, you can make a difference."

Preserve the past: examine, but do not touch, cultural or historic structures and artifacts. Leave rocks, plants, and other natural objects as you find them. Avoid introducing or transporting nonnative species. Do not build structures or furniture, or dig trenches.

5. Minimize Campfire Impacts

Most thru-hikers rarely use fires. Failing to extinguish campfires properly can lead to forest fires. Don't be that guy. "If fires are legal, use established rings, a mound, or a fire pan and gather only dead wood no thicker than your wrist," says Lawhon. Campfires can cause lasting impacts to the backcountry. Instead, use a lightweight stove for cooking and enjoy a candle lantern for light. Where fires are permitted, use established fire rings, fire pans, or mound fires. Keep fires small. Only use sticks from the ground that can be broken by hand. Burn all wood and coals to ash, put out campfires completely, then scatter cool ashes.

6. Respect Wildlife

"This is a safety issue," says Lawhon. "Once a squirrel or a bear gets a taste for human foods, it actively seeks them out, which can lead to dangerous behavior."

Observe wildlife from a distance. Do not follow or approach them. Never feed animals. Feeding wildlife damages their health, alters natural behaviors, and exposes them to predators and other dangers. Protect wildlife and your food by storing rations and trash securely. Control pets at all times, or—better yet—leave them at home. Avoid wildlife during sensitive times: mating, nesting, raising young, or in winter.

7. Be Considerate of Other Visitors

"This is the do-unto-others rule—yield to fellow hikers, keep noise levels down, and camp away from the trail," says Lawhon. "Remember, we're all trying to enjoy a finite resource."

Respect other visitors and protect the quality of their experience.

Be courteous. Yield to other users on the trail. Those going uphill have right of way (the rationale is that it is harder to get your momentum back if you stop on the uphill).

Step to the downhill side of the trail when encountering pack stock. Take breaks and camp away from trails and other visitors. Let nature's sounds prevail. Avoid loud voices and noises. If you listen to music, podcasts, or books (and most thru-hikers do at some point), use headphones instead of your phone's speakers or portable speakers.

If you must make a phone call, step away from the trail and keep your conversation short and quiet. Try texting whoever is calling you instead.

Use an ultralight trowel to dig a cathole 6–8 inches deep.

THE SCOOP ON POOP

Yes, we just covered this in the "dispose of waste properly" LNT principle, but it deserves a special paragraph or two of its own. For many years, thru-hikers, especially those with an ultralight philosophy (myself included), did not carry potty trowels. The rationale was that you could dig a decent hole using gear you already were carrying. Recently, the potty trowel technology has gotten good enough that you can carry a trowel that weighs 0.4 ounce. (That's what my trowel weighs.) Now many experienced thru-hikers are carrying trowels because it makes their lives easier. There is nothing worse than digging a bad hole when it's already almost too late—except trying to dig that hole with a less-than-optimal tool.

Poorly buried poop has become a huge problem on the PCT now—especially in areas of the desert where a lot of people camp near water sources. It was a huge problem on the AT until the ATC installed privies. Don't be part of the problem. Bury your poop well and carry out your toilet paper.

Wiping method and technique is a favorite topic of discussion for bored thru-hikers. I go into this thoroughly in the Peeing on Trail section (most women have to wipe twice as much as guys so that seemed like a good place to put it). For this section, though, I want to discuss packing out toilet paper. In many climates, especially the American West, TP doesn't biodegrade quickly enough to simply bury it. There are just too many hikers for the ecosystem to sustain all that TP, and hikers keep pooping in the same places (usually near campsites near water), concentrating the used TP situation even more. Animals are digging up old catholes, further spreading used TP about. It's just gross—and can easily be solved by packing it out.

Packing out toilet paper initially sounds disgusting, but becomes routine over time. I've found the easiest way to do it is by bringing Bark Bags, which are designed for dog owners to pick up their pet's poop at parks. People are totally comfortable using the bags to pick up actual dog poop—so using them to pick up poopy toilet paper is even easier. I bring a new bag for each time I poop, collect the toilet paper, and tie off the bag letting out all the air. Then I put the tied off bag in my usual trash bag. The color of the bag keeps me from having to see the used toilet paper and it keeps my used toilet paper separate from my other trash (in case I discover I accidentally threw out something that I needed, like a map). This method is clean, quick, and sure beats trying to nudge used toilet paper into a trash bag with a stick like I had done for years before. The same Bark Bag method can be utilized for used tampons and pads. Many hikers find that paying for an extra trash bag in the form of Bark Bags is a waste of money (after all, technically any old bag will work), but, regardless of what bag you use, this system makes it easier to do the right thing.

BACKCOUNTRY CELL PHONE AND ELECTRONICS ETIQUETTE

There's another area of LNT I want to expand on: the "be considerate of other visitors" principle and how it relates to cell phones. We go to the trail seeking remote wildness. Yet these days thru-hikers end up getting reception for hundreds of miles. Cell phones are great for safety, and it's cool that we can live-blog and update our Instagram with photos from the trail. But using electronics (like phones) in the woods is a stark reminder that we increasingly have lost our truly wild places.

If you choose to use a cell phone—whether it's to check your email, coordinate a ride from the trailhead, or update your blog—avoid doing so at places and times that will impact others. Consider keeping your phone on silent and opting for texting or silent app-based forms of communications over phone calls whenever possible.

Here's one idea: Treat using the phone like taking a poop. Go away from the trail to do your electronic business. Be courteous to other hikers and keep your voice down.

HIKER ENTITLEMENT

When you're on a long hike, you can derive such great pleasure from the simplest things: a can of soda, a warm shower, and a mattress in a bunk room. Long-distance hikers are so blessed to have friendly locals and businesses in many of our resupply towns who want to support hikers and provide those comforts.

But these locals and businesses have to cover their expenses to survive. Trail towns are usually located in less economically well-off areas where folks really can't afford to be losing money. So it's really important to remember that any kindness that comes your way—whether it's a can of soda or a discount—is just that, a piece of kindness. It's really easy for hikers to feel that just because they've accomplished something amazing, they deserve a special treat or reward. But the services and kindnesses we receive as hikers are not a right, they are a privilege that can be revoked. Every year, a hostel closes or a trail angel decides to stop hosting hikers—all because of entitled behavior from a few bad apples. According to the Appalachian Long Distance Hiking Association, bad hiker behavior closed four hostels on the AT just in 2015. This should be obvious, but as ALDHA says, just because you live in the woods doesn't mean you need to act like an animal.

So how should a hiker act in town? A lot of this is common courtesy—say please and thank you and clean up any messes you create, even if they're at hotels. Don't sneak extra hikers into your hotel room—and don't trash those rooms. Tip your servers 20 percent or more; after all, they had to put up with your smell and multiple orders of French fries for the past hour.

If you're staying in the home of a trail angel—whether that person is listed in your guidebook or not—always leave a $20 donation to cover their water, laundry, electricity, gas, phone, and food bill. Offer to help with chores and always ask before smoking, drinking, or bringing your hiking dog in their home. Ask before doing things like drying your gear, throwing out trash, or charging electronics—different businesses and trail angels have different rules. Just because one trail angel let you do something does not mean another one will. Trail angels are doing you a favor, so fit yourself into their schedule—not the other way around. If you can afford a beer, you can afford to pay for the services these kind strangers are providing.

Lastly, if you see another hiker who is out of line, approach them and discuss how one person having a bad mouth and bad attitude can ruin the trail for other hikers for years. When we're out there, we are all ambassadors of the hiking community, so please do your part to keep town services alive and well for years to come.

If you travel on exposed ridgelines when the weather looks nasty, be prepared to bail to lower elevations. Felicia "Princess of Darkness" Hermosillo and Whitney "Allgood" LaRuffa are on the Sierra High Route.

SAFETY BASICS

We're not going to cover here every survival trick or outdoor skill you might possibly need in the outdoors. But there are some special considerations for thru-hikers you should definitely know and understand, and we'll also point you to resources for learning more. And there's good news: The trails most appropriate for beginning thru-hikers also tend to have lots of safety fallbacks, such as frequent bailout points and plenty of helpful, kind people going by. That doesn't mean you shouldn't take responsibility for your own safety, but rest assured, on a popular long trail you're hardly out there "alone."

BAD WEATHER

Remember: On a thru-hike you have to live with wet gear and your cold self a lot longer than you would on a short hike, so it's worth thinking about your rainy-time strategy with some foresight. On the AT, for example, it could rain every day for weeks. Depending on your hiking style, your tolerance for cold and being wet, your schedule, and the climate and local geography, you may expect to hike a lot in the rain or you may not have to hike in the rain at all. Here are some guidelines for deciding if you should power through or sit this storm out:

Temperature. If it's 90°F out and raining, the water from the sky may be a welcome respite from the heat. I'm much more likely to hike in the rain if I'm feeling plenty warm.

Forecast. Is it supposed to rain for the next week, or will tomorrow be hot and sunny? If tomorrow's weather looks good, you can walk through the rain and dry your gear tomorrow. Just remember to keep your sleeping system dry.

Proximity to town. If you were planning to head into town that day and are an hour or so away, go ahead and walk through the rain. Soon enough, you'll be in a warm room with the heater cranked up.

Skill level, gear, and hiking companions. If you have proper gear, walking in even frozen rain is doable. You also need to have the proper skills and experience to know if you are becoming hypothermic. It helps to have another person with you in case something were to go wrong.

WHAT TO DO WHEN IT STARTS TO RAIN

Stop and make sure your sleep system (sleeping clothes and bag) is dry and well protected, ideally in two ways (with a pack liner and maybe even a stuff sack if the weather looks nasty). It's crucial that this gear stay dry no matter what. Make sure any other sensitive gear is protected from water. Put on rain gear and use an umbrella, if necessary. Keep your core warm and dry. If it is really bad and you are getting cold, consider these options.

Stop. Put up your shelter immediately, change into dry clothes, eat something (preferably hot and with a high fat content), and get in your sleeping bag. Getting in a few extra miles is not worth getting all your gear soaked and putting yourself in danger of hypothermia.

Find shelter. Put on your rain gear and keep hiking in the rain until you reach a shelter with a roof, a pit toilet, a picnic bench, or a tree with good branch coverage.

Book it to town. You may need to take a side trail. This is especially worthwhile if your gear (especially your sleeping bag) is already wet.

Make a fire. Most thru hikers don't make fires very often. But when things are really bad, that would be the time to responsibly make a fire and dry out your gear.

If you're in your sleeping bag and still cold:

Move around. Do sit-ups or push-ups in your sleeping bag.

Pee. Your body wastes a lot of energy trying to keep urine warm. You'll feel warmer after peeing, even if it means stepping outside of the tent for a minute.

Your hiking style and priorities change when it is cold and wet.

HOW TO DEAL WITH LIGHTNING

Lightning is a real and scary risk in the backcountry, especially when you're out in the open above treeline. It's a particular concern on the Colorado Trail and the CDT. There's nowhere truly safe to escape a lightning storm in the backcountry, merely better and worse options. Your best bet is to be in a uniform forest of tall trees. Your worst bet is to be high up in an unprotected area. On trails that cross large stretches of unprotected high country, like the AT in the White Mountains or the CDT and CT, you should be aware of weather patterns and plan your day as best as possible to avoid lightning. In Colorado in the summer, it's good practice to start very early so that you can cross high country stretches or passes before the storms roll through, typically in the early afternoon.

If you do get caught in a lightning storm, here are some tips on how to minimize the possibility of a strike. Avoid stormy weather if you can: Check the weather forecast and get an idea of local weather patterns (e.g., does a storm always roll in at 4 p.m. here during the summer?). Plan your trip around the weather—especially if you know you will be going above treeline. This may involve waking up especially early to get up and over exposed areas before noon. It may also involve taking a zero (rest) day in town when the weather forecast in the mountains looks dangerous.

Keep alert: Check your maps early for bailout points—trails that will get you off exposed ridges if a weather storm were to come in. Be aware of signs that the weather is changing, such as when your arm hair stands up from static electricity in the air. Even when forecasters claim the weather will be good, systems are often unpredictable in the mountains. It's better to use your senses than to rely on technology.

When to abandon ship and get out: When you see lightning, count the seconds until you hear thunder. Light travels faster than sound, which is why you can use this as a measurement to determine how far the strike is from you. If you count a number less than 30, get low and off the ridge immediately—even if you need to get off the trail and go cross-country to do so. Pay special note where you came from though. At 30 seconds, lightning is 6 miles away. But because weather can move quickly, it behooves you to head lower right away. When the weather improves, you don't want to get lost returning to the trail.

How to bail: Get below treeline, but find an area that does not have lone trees, such as areas with low bushes. Lightning generally strikes the highest object in an area (think of weathervanes on houses designed to prevent lightning strikes on roofs). To avoid a strike, get as low on the mountain as you can, and as low to the ground as you can reasonably get in lightning position (more on this below). If you are hiking with others, space yourselves at least 100 feet apart to avoid lightning arcing from one person to another.

Get into lightning position: Crouch and minimize the amount of surface area of your body touching the ground. Ball yourself up and keep your feet together. This reduces the negative effects of ground current. Wrap your arms around your legs to allow electrons to flow from the ground through your arms instead of your torso, keeping you safer if a strike were to occur. This also helps you stay in a crouch longer. If you're getting too tired to squat, though, it's better to sit than lie flat on the ground. While scientists agree that lightning position reduces the potential bad effects of a strike, they still argue whether it will actually reduce your chance of being struck.

Avoid natural features that attract lightning: Unfortunately, often the lowest point in an area is near water—which conducts electricity and can harm you during a strike. Keep a distance of at least 100 feet from lakes, puddles, and ponds. Before you are tempted to take refuge in a cave or rock outcropping, you should know that lightning can also create an electric arc that bridges gaps. You should avoid the temptation to take shelter under boulders and rock formations—or in sheds or under picnic tables. Should you be lucky enough to make it below treeline, avoid taking shelter under the biggest trees, too.

Ditch your metal gear: Metal conducts electricity. Place your metal gear 100 feet away from you. Metal gear includes framed packs, jewelry, belts, ice axes, cooking gear, etc. Remove crampons and place then away from you if doing so will not jeopardize your stability on the terrain.

Wait it out and resume hiking 30 minutes after the last lightning strike you've heard or seen, as electrical charges can linger in clouds after storms.

For more information on lightning, read NOAA's Lightning Safety website or the NOLS Backcountry Lightning Safety Guidelines.

HITCHHIKING

As we discussed in the route planning and resupply sections (see chapters 4 and 5), there are often times on a thru-hike where hitchhiking is your best option for getting to a town. Check local regulations before hitchhiking—in some states, hitchhiking is illegal. Hitchhiking may be illegal on certain types of roads or inside certain town limits.

It's understandable to have some hesitation about hitchhiking—even in places where it's legal. A thru-hike might very well be the first time you've ever even considered such a thing. If you feel unsafe hitchhiking, it can be avoided, but it's logistically difficult, as you'll have to arrange rides in remote areas at unpredictable times. If you choose to try it, rest assured that it's scarier in theory than in practice.

Thru-hikers have endless discussions about the best tips for hitchhiking. Here are a few that work for me:

- Never hitchhike in states or in areas where it is illegal. Check local regulations before you head off. This is no joke. I know personally multiple hikers who have been harassed by the local cops.

HIKE YOUR OWN HIKE

HOW I EMBRACED HITCHHIKING

PHOTO CREDIT: KATE HOCH

Kate "Drop 'N Roll" Hoch, who hiked the PCT in 2011 and CDT in 2013, explains how her views of hitchhiking evolved.

I grew up as a goody two-shoes who did everything to please her parents. Hitchhiking was not really on my radar as a possibility. The summer before hiking the PCT, I hiked a short section on the AT with a friend who had hiked the entire AT a few years earlier. Rather than set up a car shuttle, she insisted that we'd be just fine hitchhiking back to our car. I trusted her judgment, and I was actually excited about it. We very quickly got picked up by a woman in a pickup truck with a dog. She dropped us off in town, no problem. We got some ice cream, stuck out our thumbs, and again got picked up, this time by an older couple who were vacationing in the area. Both of the rides that we got were from the type of people I didn't envision picking up hitchhikers. They were normal people. They didn't have shotguns in their backseats. It was just totally fine. They were just interested in what we were doing. That experience gave me a lot of confidence to hitchhike in the future. I still try to avoid hitchhiking alone, but I have hitchhiked alone, and it's been fine. Being a woman just makes it easier to get picked up.

—Kate "Drop 'N Roll" Hoch

- If you get cell reception, try calling local hostels or hotels and seeing if you can pay for pick-up instead of hitchhiking. Patronize their business afterwards to show thanks.
- If you get cell reception, let family or friends know where you are and where you are headed. Turn on satellite trackers so they can follow your safe progress to town. Check in after you make it to town to let them know you have made it safely.

- If I am at a trailhead, I will ask people parked there (especially if they look like they have been day hiking) about where they are going and whether they could give me a ride. I always offer to pay them.
- Be a woman or hitchhike with one—people are more likely to pick up female hitchhikers.
- Hitchhike with another person. This may slightly decrease your chances of getting a ride, but it makes you both safer.
- Hitchhike in a place with a lot of visibility (so drivers have time to react).
- Leave your driver room to pull over.
- Wear bright clothes so drivers can see you.
- Don't wear sunglasses or a hat when hitching, so that drivers can see your eyes.
- Try to make yourself look nice: Wash your face, run your hands through your hair, put on your town/sleep clothes or a puffy jacket or rain jacket.
- Make yourself smell nice: Give yourself a sponge bath or put on sunscreen to try to mask your hiker scent.
- Have your pack and gear ready to go—drivers don't want to wait for you to pack up your gear.
- Observe the driver and passengers and make sure you feel safe before you enter the car. Trust your gut and don't feel bad about turning down a ride after you've seen the driver. Never get in a car with a driver who appears intoxicated or under the influence.

Once you do get a ride:

- Be respectful of the driver.
- Always offer to help out by covering gas costs.
- If your driver wants to discuss religion, politics, or any other awkward subject, humor them (at least if the conversation feels harmless). Who knows? I've learned some of the most fascinating things about our country and its people from my hitchhikes.

BEAR COUNTRY

Hikers are more often concerned about being mauled by bears than they are of the real danger—that bears will be accustomed to hikers' food and as a result, be killed. Safe travel and food storage is as much about keeping bears safe as it is about you, and with some common sense, advanced preparation, and knowledge about the area you're in, you'll be a lot safer traveling through these areas. To prevent an encounter:

Grizzlies and black bears have different temperments, so how you react to them will be different.

Don't hike alone through serious grizzly country. Bears are less likely to attack groups than individuals. Parks Canada suggests that in peak grizzly season and dense habitat, groups should include 4 people minimum (and in some extreme cases, 6 people).

Make noise. For real. Bells are a nice thought, but loud conversation or singing will better alert bears to your presence. Given the opportunity, most bears will avoid a human encounter.

Carry pepper spray in grizzly territory. Keep it handy and know how to use it. Wait until a charging bear is within 60 feet, then sweep the spray to create a cloud at ground level. Bear spray is like pepper spray except with width and power more attuned to a fire extinguisher. Depending on the brand you use, it can shoot 25–40 feet. According to the Interagency Grizzly Bear Committee

(IGBC) it should last for at least 6 seconds. Studies have shown that bear spray is significantly more effective in reducing rates of injuries from charging bears that carrying a gun (depending on the study, bear spray success is 90 percent versus firearm—only success is 50 percent of the time).

Be scent-smart. Store food in bear canisters, an Ursack, or hang it properly. Avoid fragrance-heavy shampoos and hygiene products; they smell just like food. Never, ever preemptively fire pepper spray around your tent; it's like marinating your campsite. Do not spray it onto another human's body. This does not work like insect repellent.

Stay vigilant. Paying attention to terrain features can give you an advantage: If you come to a section of trail with recent evidence of bears (such as scat or overturned stumps), make extra noise. Give bears a chance to hear you and flee before their protective instincts kick in.

If you encounter a bear:

- Make yourself known. Be loud. Yell, clap your hands, even throw things. Making yourself really big by waving your arms works too. You want to scare the bear away and show it that you aren't afraid of it.
- Don't run. Bears are fast. A black bear can run up to 35 miles per hour. Grizzlies can reach up to 30 mph. The fastest human speed ever? About 27.44 miles per hour by Olympic sprinter Usain Bolt.
- Don't climb. Climbing a tree is a poor idea. Bears love to climb, and they are good at it. At the very least, they are better at it than you. Basically, running or climbing shows weakness and fear, something a bear will literally feed off of.
- Use bear spray. Bear spray is like a combination of mace on steroids and a fire extinguisher. As mentioned earlier it's been proven to be more effective against grizzly bears than using a gun. Follow the directions on your bear spray to determine distance and where you should aim it. And avoid getting any of the bear spray on yourself or other people—it burns.

If you are attacked by a bear:

- Play dead. Lie face down with your pack on, spread your legs (so it can't roll you), and protect your neck and head with your hands.
- Fight. If a grizzly starts to feed or you're attacked by a black bear, you have to fight. Go for the nose, eyes, and ears. Give it your all.

PHOTO CREDIT: LIZ THOMAS

Really, it's safe out there for women. Go out there and do it.

SPECIAL CONCERNS FOR WOMEN

Being female on the trail isn't really that different—except for when it is. Some of this advice—especially the safety advice—is important for all hikers. No matter what gender you identify with, I suggest at least skimming this section.

I've hiked thousands of miles as a solo woman. It's really okay for women to hike alone (well, as okay as it is for any gender). The chances of getting attacked in the wilderness are much lower than the chances of being attacked in civilization. That said, there are still some smart precautions you can take to help stay safe and healthy.

Naomi "The Punisher" Hudetz checks her DeLorme during a snow storm on Lineham Ridge on the Great Divide Trail. She used it later that night to let folks at home know where we were camping and later in the trip to coordinate our pick up from the trail's end.

COMMUNICATE WITH FOLKS BACK HOME

Regardless of your gender, you need to let folks at home know that you are okay—especially if they have been instructed to call search and rescue if you don't communicate for a while. Remember that someone at home should have your itinerary and be expecting you to check in. On most major trails, a cell phone can be used to communicate with the outside world about every five to seven days. If that isn't often enough, or you or a loved one is very worried, consider getting a satellite communicator, like a SPOT or DeLorme (now Garmin) InReach. These devices give you a way to communicate with the folks back home every night and tell them you are okay. All models have an emergency button that should contact search and rescue from any location. Some models will allow people at home to track where you are on a map on their computer. With the DeLorme, you can even text the outside world from the middle of nowhere.

Sometimes the hardest part about being a woman on the trail is how much friends and family back home will be worrying about you (unfairly—I suspect that many people would worry less about a man doing the same trip).

Don't camp near roads. I avoid staying at campsites or shelters within 1 mile of a road. I don't have a ton of evidence on this, but my logic is that if someone's going to cause trouble, they're likely not going to bother hiking too far to do it.

Keep your location private. Delay your social media updates and resist the temptation to real-time update your location or sweet campsite to the world.

Hit roads in daylight. Avoid parts of a trail or route that involve road-walking during the night.

Use your trail community. Other people on the trail become your family and will go to extreme lengths to help you if you go missing or if someone is giving you a hard time.

Learn the facts. Realize that while safety from human predators might feel like a big priority, it's really not a primary concern on most trails in the United States.

HYGIENE

In many of the clinics I teach, women take me aside and meekly ask, "Can you tell me about women's hygiene?" It seems like these issues are often treated like something to be discussed in backrooms and in whispers instead of in print in a book—maybe because so many books are written by men. But we're addressing this issue head-on here.

DEALING WITH YOUR PERIOD

Many women find that their period stops or becomes less heavy or doesn't last as long during a thru-hike. For some women, it can also become less predictable on a thru-hike—so be prepared, even when you don't think you have anything to worry about. If you're using a menstrual cup, you should shop around for one that is the right fit for you. Most companies offer "before you've given birth" and "after you've given birth" options, and even then, depending on your anatomy, some cups may work better for you than others. Test out your cup for at least one cycle before your trip to get the hang of how to use it and how to get it in and out of your body (believe me, you don't want to figure that out on the trail). Follow directions on the box, especially regarding keeping it clean. Definitely don't use a cup if it is painful. Do your research in advance, because only a few companies allow you to return a used one if you are dissatisfied.

Hygiene Rules

Follow these women's backcountry hygiene rules from a wilderness doctor to stay clean and healthy on your next backpacking trip.

The Expert: Luanne Freer, MD, is the founder and director of Everest ER, a nonprofit medical clinic at Mount Everest Base Camp.

Let it flow. Holding your pee could cause a urinary tract infection. Make sure you go whenever you feel the urge. Also not okay: drinking less water in order to avoid peeing.

Change into dry clothes. You might not mind lingering after hiking in the rain, but your body does. Damp or wet clothes can lead to a yeast infection.

Wipe smart. If you're using natural wiping materials, try using two, one for the back and one for the front, to make sure that you don't get fecal matter where it shouldn't be.

Wear wool undies. Wool is naturally odor-resistant and pulls moisture away from your skin. It's ideal to have fresh underwear every day. Dr. Freer recommends choosing one of the following: bringing one pair and washing them daily, bringing a pair for every day you are out, or somewhere in between—it depends on how you feel about backcountry laundry. In 2015, *BACKPACKER* ran a survey where very few of the respondents reported that they'd carry a fresh pair of undies every day for a seven-day trip. Most female thru-hikers carry extra pairs.

Never use antibacterial soap on your body. This kills both the good and bad bacteria, which makes it difficult to fight infections. For backcountry bathing, try biodegradable wipes.

Prevent chafing. Moisture plus friction leads to painful, abraded skin. Thru-hikers use lubricants like Body Glide, Gold Bond, Anti-Monkey Butt Powder, and Vagisil in problem areas.

Some women opt to use tampons or sanitary pads in the backcountry. If you go this route, you need to pack out all your used hygiene products. If you don't want to see them in your clear trash bag, you can always wrap them in a ramen or granola bar wrapper first. I'd recommend the same Bark Bag method for packing out used toilet paper described in the Scoop on Poop section. Just like at home, clean your hands (ideally with treated water and biodegradable soap, but hand sanitizer or wet wipes will work in a pinch) before and after switching out your cup, tampon, or pad. If you're wondering, research has shown that being on your period in the woods does *not* attract bears or lions.

PEEING ON TRAIL

A lot of women ask me questions in clinics I teach about how to pee in the woods (or more specifically, how to wipe after peeing). The more I have discussions with other women, the more I realize there is no one right way to do it. Here are a few methods that work for me or for other female thru-hikers I know:

Air Dry: This is the method I use and find many experienced female thru-hikers use. It involves crouching and wiggling to drip dry and break some surface tension. It involves the least gear and works well for ultralight hikers, though it can lead to a scent and residue and is definitely not for everyone.

Pee rag: It's exactly what it sounds like: a bandana or other lightweight cloth to use in lieu of toilet paper after peeing. We know, sounds gross. But it won't smell, and if you tie it to the outside of your pack, it'll be dry by the next time nature calls. "Many viruses and bacteria [on the rag] can be inactivated by exposure to heat and by drying," explains Paul Auerbach, MD, author of Wilderness Medicine. Wash the rag every few days—but always at least 200 feet from a water source and never directly in a water source. Pee is sterile and UV from the sun can help disinfect. Choose a pee rag with different colors on each side so that you always grab from the "clean" side and always wipe from the "dirty" side. Whatever you do, only use this for number 1, not number 2.

Natural Wiping Material: Use wide, soft leaves as you would for wiping after number 2 (watch out for poison ivy). Sticks (the long way) and smooth stones are great for breaking surface tension. Snow is . . . refreshing. It's also a great way to clean yourself.

Backcountry Bidet: Amanda discusses this method in her gear list, but we will summarize it here. Fill a small (1–2 ounces) goo tube with clean water (some add a drop of two of biodegradeable soap—any scent but Peppermint). Squeeze onto yourself to clean. Use your non-dominant hand for extra cleaning (soap and hand sanitizer will help keep your hand clean afterwards). Blot with a pee rag or air dry.

Toilet paper: In a recent *BACKPACKER* survey of more than 1,000 female hikers and backpackers, more than half said they use toilet paper when peeing in the woods. That number shocked us, because frankly, we can't quite figure out why. Toilet paper should not be buried because it takes a heck of a lot of time to decompose (especially in dry areas). Plus if you're just peeing, you're not going to dig a hole, right? And it's definitely not OK to just leave toilet paper in the woods (and TP used for pee is far more common to find on the trail than TP used for poo). That leaves packing it out, which for weight-conscious backpackers, seems like a totally unnecessary pain in the behind. Still, I have at least one very experienced partner who swears by TP. She's very prone to UTIs and says wiping with clean TP is the only way she has found to prevent infection. To expedite packing it out, she uses the Bark Bag method to pack out used toilet paper (described in the Scoop on Poop section on page 250).

Wet Wipe/Shop Cloth: Far more common for use on cleaning up after pooping than peeing, this heavy duty wiping material will definitely need to be packed out but can feel refreshing and gets the job done with less material. Some people dehydrate their Wet Wipes or use pre-dehydrated Wysi Wipes instead.

Female Urination Device: How about not needing to wipe at all—or even drop trou? Enter FUDs, which are anatomically designed funnels that let women pee standing up almost as easily as a guy can. There are about a dozen brands out there. Look for a design that has no parts to lose and has boil-proof plastic. Find a FUD that sits securely against your body and gives confidence you've got it positioned correctly. For any FUD, make sure to practice at home in the shower, and know it might take a while to get used to going this way. Unlike outdoor activities with limited drop-your-pants mobility like bigwall rock climbing or mountaineering, I personally don't understand why a woman would need one of these devices and have never used one. Nonetheless, a small but dedicated group of long distance hiking ladies swear by them.

GROOMING AND LONG HAIR

Some long-haired folk bring a comb, while others leave their hair in braids for days. I usually throw my hair in a topknot and ignore it—only dealing with it when I'm in town. What you do with your hair—and your face—depends a lot on how much you care about looking and feeling good in the woods. Many hikers (male and female) will give themselves a sponge bath every night (remember: never dip your sponge directly in a water source and wash up at least 200 feet from water). Others wipe themselves—or at least their faces—down with wet wipes every night. Some people can't live without their moisturizer or mascara. Whatever you take to clean and groom, if that will make or break your hike, then by all means, bring some with you (ideally, in a small container). Like almost any item you may want to bring on the trail—if you're not going to be happy without it, you should bring it so you can more fully enjoy the outdoors. Just make sure you follow Leave No Trace rules (including keeping soap out of water sources).

For me, the best thing about being outdoors is not having to care. I just embrace being dirty. It may not give me the most attractive Instagram photos, but I'm not out there to show others what I'm doing. I'm out there to live my hike.

PHOTO CREDIT: DEAN KRAKEL

Before leaving for the Colorado Trail, Dean Krakel did a lot of research about nutrition and diet for hikers.

SPECIAL CONCERNS FOR OLDER HIKERS

While the majority of thru-hikers are in their 20s and 30s, the second most common group is hikers living their post-retirement dream. The freedom that comes with retirement means that plenty of folks over 50 attempt—and complete—long hikes as well. Compared to young people, retirees may find that their muscles take longer to build or heal after injury. It's worth paying special attention to make sure you don't get injured in the first place. Older bodies have a different metabolism than young folks. Here's some special advice for hikers over 50 that will help get your body performing decades younger.

EATING AND DRINKING

Starting at age 50 age-related muscle loss sarcoponia starts ocurring. But exercise and training can almost give you younger muscle mass, especially with vitamin K and calcium-rich food. On the trail, all hikers' bodies tend to need more vitamins and minerals than they would otherwise need in a sedentary life. If there are supplements that you take in real life (or should be taking), be sure to take them on the trail as well. By age 70, total body water decreases by about 8 percent, which increases the risk of dehydration, heatstroke, and hypothermia. The fix: On trail days, drink, at minimum, your body weight in ounces (150 pounds = 150 ounces), even more on hot days. Average thru-hikers easily go through 6 quarts a day.

GEAR

When it comes to gear, going light is always important, but that's even truer for less resilient older bodies. Pay special attention to trimming your load. Older hikers tend to have lower metabolisms so get cold more easily. Be sure to bring adequate layers and a warm sleeping system. As you age, you lose fat in the one place you want it: your feet. Make up for lost cushion and increase comfort with extra-padded socks and aftermarket insoles. When it comes to specialized gear for older hikers, I have two words for you: hiking poles. They're proven to help reduce impact on your ankles, knees, and hips.

HEALTH

Older bodies can't repair injuries as well as younger ones. The best solution is to avoid getting injured in the first place by pacing yourself well and listening to your body. Much like in "real life," older hikers are more susceptible to heart attacks, including on thru-hikes. Hikers like to say, "It'd happen if he were sitting in an office, too. At least he went doing what he loved." You should still know the signs of heart attacks before you go, though, and have a plan for what to do in case of emergencies (including discussing medication with your doctor, having a will in place). Skin thins with age, and your ability to heal wounds decreases. That makes open cuts more susceptible to infection, especially in the backcountry. If you do get a cut, flush, clean, and treat the wound promptly and thoroughly. And make sure to slather on the SPF 40 sunscreen, especially at altitude.

REGENERATION TIME

Two of my older clients shared advice they got from their doctor before starting their first thru-hike. Because older bodies take longer to repair, these hikers take two to three days off in each town to let their bodies recuperate, regenerate, and heal. While it ends up making the hike a lot longer (they are section hikers who cherry-pick the best seasons for walking), this tends not to be a problem for them. This couple also sleeps 10 hours per night to give their body maximum time to heal between days of doing nothing but walking. Their trick seems to

work. They say they never feel tired or injured on the trail (despite doing this for years). Maybe this is great advice for hikers of all ages.

COMMUNICATION

Remember to call home. Older hikers tend not to update on social media as much as younger hikers, and family members get worried. If family members are skeptical about you going out, consider carrying a SPOT or DeLorme InReach satellite messenger, so you can communicate with the folks back home every night and tell them you are okay. These devices track your GPS location on a map and send that information via satellite to the Internet. Your movement and position are shown on a map to those who want to follow your progress. You can set a password so only your loved ones can find where you are, or make it public so all your fans can follow along on your trip from their desk. You can decide how often you want to send out your location, updating every minute or just updating when you want others to know where you are, like at your campsite each night.

With the Delorme InReach, for a subscription fee, you can even two-way text message with loved ones from the middle of nowhere. If the folks at home are super concerned, this is way cheaper and lighter than a satellite phone. Before you go: Make sure you know how to use it and your family members know how to check up on you.

If you do have family that is concerned, invite them for some training hikes or encourage them to visit you on the trail. Share your itinerary with them and get them excited about your trip. Show them before you leave how physically and logistically prepared you are for your adventure.

Highline Trail in Glacier National Park

Dean Krakel walked the last half of the CT with a dislocated shoulder. Here are some tricks to avoid injury, and to deal with it if it happens.

Chapter 9

 # TROUBLESHOOTING INJURY, DISEASE, AND FIRST-AID

As a 22-year-old who had managed to go through life without a broken bone, I started my first big thru-hike with a level of hubris and naïveté that injury could never happen to me. One thousand miles in, I found myself with a peculiar problem: It was painful to walk. Sometimes it seemed like my feet actually felt more comfortable if I hobbled along with no shoes at all. I would hike 100 yards barefoot only to find new pain from pine needle pricks and sharp rocks.

The problem persisted on my next thru-hike of the PCT. In Ashland, Oregon, I finally saw a doctor about my issue. He told me I had plantar fasciitis—a common ailment among thru-hikers. He suggested new shoes, new insoles, and a series of exercises. I am so fortunate that the pain cleared and that in subsequent hikes I found tricks that helped me avoid further pain (mainly, switching out my shoes every 300–400 miles and using zero-drop shoes). But the lesson stuck: On the trail, physical injury and illness can happen to anyone.

Peruse this list and make sure you know the signs, symptoms, and on-trail fixes for these common hiker ailments. And even if you never get an injury on the trail, chances are your friends and people you meet along the way may need your help and advice.

PHYSICAL PROBLEMS

If you think you can do a thru-hike without getting blisters, cuts, bruises, or scapes, you're wrong. Every hiker falls now and then, and minor boo-boos are almost unavoidable. Below are some simple issues you're likely to encounter during your hike and the problems that are most specific to thru-hikers. Consider taking a Wilderness First Aid class of some kind if you're planning to do lots of adventuring in your life. Check your local gear stores, as many offer classes or will know where to find a provider.

BLISTERS

Ah, the dreaded blister. How can such a small thing cause such big problems? If you're hiking for months, odds are you'll have to deal with a few blisters here and there. Before your trip, purchase shoes that fit you well, where you can't feel any of the sides rubbing against your feet—including your toes. Most shoe stores have an incline board where you can determine whether your toes will hit the end of the shoe when you are going downhill. Remember that your feet will likely swell after hiking on them all day, so it's often better to size up. I prefer breathable (aka not waterproof) shoes for most three-season hiking because they cause less foot sweat—moisture is a major contributor to getting blisters. I also look for lightweight shoes that will cause less rubbing on my feet. Test your shoes out on hikes. Breaking them in can only help. Cut your toenails short before your hike and when you resupply in town.

While hiking, listen to your feet. As soon as you notice a hot spot (any sort of rubbing), stop, take off your shoes, clean the spot, and dry it. Depending on your gait, shoe fit, and body chemistry, some blister methods may work better than others. At night, I will clean the blister and pop it with a sterile safety pin, let it dry as I sleep, and cover with Leukotape (a sports tape without stretch that has some major stickiness from a zinc oxide adhesive). Some hikers will treat clean, dry hot spots with tincture of benzoin, derived from a Styrax genus of plants. It can help Leukotape (or moleskin or any blister care item) stick to you better. It can also work alone as a second skin on hot spots to prevent them from developing into blisters. Leukotape is easy to find online but can be hard to find in stores. Tincture of benzoin can be found in drug stores in small bottles or in thru-hiker friendly single-use capsules.

Even the most careful and prepared hiker can slip in a creek, stumble on a rock, or get scraped up on a blowdown tree.

During breaks, take your shoes and socks off and let your feet dry out. Remove any grime from between your toes. Use a sock with a tight knit weave that can keep trail dirt out. Gaiters are another great defense against trail grime. Make sure they are lightweight, though, as bulky gaiters can sometimes heat your feet up, causing more foot sweat and moisture.

At night, dry your feet out and wear clean (or at least dry) socks to bed. Wash your socks out with water (no soap) to get rid of any dirt that could increase friction and rubbing—the cause of blisters. Alternatively, use a clean pair of socks each day.

CHAFING

Chafing is a result of salt rubbing against your skin. Sometimes it starts as "pack-ne" ("acne" created by your pack) and turns into chafe. It can happen to any active person, but is most likely to happen to thru-hikers because of the length of time they are doing their activity and lack of access to showers. Chafing can lead to scarring (I have some on my neck from a hike four years ago). Chafing can be so painful that it makes people quit the trail for good. Some places hikers chafe include:

- Along the seams in your clothes, especially your bottoms.
- Between your upper thighs.
- Where your pack rubs along your shoulders and lats.
- Between your butt cheeks (yes, really).
- On your low back (from your pack).
- Under arms, lats, and armpits from your pack. This often happens from wearing tank tops or no shirt during backpacking. Your pack can get so saturated by sweat that even if it fits perfectly, chafing happens.

Prevention is the best medicine: If you feel your skin starting to get irritated, stop and deal with it right away by applying a lubricant of some kind. Here are some chafing tips from the hikers featured in this book (I won't mention names to protect the innocent):

During the day, use a lubricant like Body Glide, 2Toms SportShield, or Bag Balm. I clean up with water, a wet wipe, and then hand sanitizer. I powder at night with Gold Bond, as long as there are no open wounds. At night I clean up with water, a wet wipe, and then hand sanitizer. Then Gold Bond it. The Gold Bond is a great preventive measure as it stops sweat at night. It's useful as a preventive measure or for very minor chafing.

Bicycle spandex is the only thing that stops chafe for me. I wear knee-length. The spandex is miserable in the heat and everything gets crunched up, but it's worth it because I don't get chafing.

At night, I get nude in my sleeping bag to keep the chafe I already have from scabbing over or callousing, and so all the potential areas for chafe dry up. I like to put my soft, clean, cotton town clothes on my chafe at night. That prevents me from being so sweaty or getting dirt into the chafe at night.

For open wounds when you should have stopped and taken care of it, but didn't, use Vagisil Anti-Itch cream (conveniently sold in 1-ounce containers). It helps with fungal and bacterial infections, and the Vaseline base helps against rubbing. Others have had success with a triple antibiotic ointment instead.

Avoid getting pee or sweat on your chafe. The high salt content makes the chafe burn.

If you notice chafe, stop and clean up with a wet wipe immediately. The alcohol in hand sanitizer dries stuff fast. Add a thin layer of Vagisil. Keep low-back chafe very clean, as it could get infected easily because your pack is dirty. My thighs are very sensitive to seams. They chafe and scar, so I often wear my baselayer inside out.

INJURIES

There's a distinctive movement thru-hikers make after waking up in the morning. Instead of walking normally, hikers teeter from foot to foot, gingerly loosening their muscles in a walk-like motion commonly called "hiker hobble." Watching hikers move after their muscles stiffen up may be good for laughs, but it also shows that soreness is a very common occurrence for long-distance walkers. After walking all day, back to back days, feeling sore is normal.

Those of us who played sports in high school or college may remember our coach's advice—that we need to push hard through the pain. But how can a hiker tell the difference between when they are feeling sore and when they are truly injured? What is the difference? Two experts offer their two cents on how to tell the difference between soreness and injury.

The first step to diagnosing pain is mentally retracing your steps, says NOLS Wilderness Medicine Institute instructor Chris Brauneis. If you can think back through the past day or so and point to a time when you tripped on uneven terrain, rolled your ankle, or slipped in a boulder field, odds are you've tweaked something and are looking at an injury. If you know what caused the pain, you can often track whether or not it is an injury.

Brauneis also associates pinpoint pains with injury rather than soreness. If you can describe the pain and pinpoint it to a very specific spot (as compared to hurting all over), it may be a sign that something is injured.

In the case of the hiker hobble described above, after some movement and warm-up, many hikers find their soreness goes away. James Fisher, an Arizona-based personal trainer of adventure athletes, says if you wake up with debilitating stiffness but feel your pain diminishes as you warm up, you're probably just sore.

Is there swelling?

"You can tear muscle, and if that's the case you'll usually get swelling. That's a really good indication that something is wrong," says Fisher. If your skin looks like it's bubbling up or feels hot to the touch, you've probably hurt yourself beyond the standard collection of overuse micro-tears. Usability of the muscle after a tear depends entirely on how bad it is.

What if it's an injury?

Telling the difference between soreness and injury is just the first step. Injuries can be further divided into two categories: muscular and skeletal. The distinction is critical. According to Fisher, muscle tends to strengthen about ten times faster than tendons and ligaments, which attach to bones and therefore fall into the skeletal category. Slow-to-repair skeletal injuries are a far greater cause for concern than damaged muscle.

HOW TO TELL MUSCULAR FROM SKELETAL PAIN

If you can increase the pain by pressing the spot with your hand, it's probably muscular. If it's a deep pain that probing can't reach, it's more likely to be within a joint or bone. This is a good rule of thumb if you have a slow-growing pain and suspect an overuse injury like a stress fracture. "Those are the tricky ones," says Brauneis.

Often the only way to diagnose a stress fracture is with an X-ray, though Brauneis still relies on the usability test—examining a patient's range of motion and ability to bear weight—to determine how bad things are. If your leg is in unbearable pain or buckling under you, it's time to see a doctor. If not, carry on but keep an eye on it. Get it checked out if it worsens.

New and interesting noises can also be a bad sign. Two bone ends grinding against one another will make a sound called crepitus, and a tendon swollen in its sheath can squeak during movement. If your pain comes with its own orchestra, it's time to back off for a few days and go see a doctor if rest doesn't fix the problem.

DOES AN INJURY MEAN IT'S TIME TO GO HOME?

Injury doesn't always mean you have to pack up and go home. "If you determine the injury is still usable, you can still treat it in the field," says Brauneis. Again, the NOLS WMI team generally employs the usability test. If you can distribute your pack weight among your companions and keep going at a slow pace, it's possible that the injury will start to heal without taking time off—but be considerate about how that will affect your companions. Brauneis says he's had patients carry on with a sprained ankle, going slow, soaking in icy streams, and improving without having to stop altogether.

"Another thing we rely on is the fun factor," Brauneis says. "Even though a person might not have a broken bone, what's their experience going to be?" If forging ahead means misery, it might be worth getting off the trail and resting a few days.

Fisher emphasizes prevention and preparation—for both injury and soreness— to keep you on your feet.

"You're going to be sore the first week of your thru-hike. You have to plan for that and be flexible on your mileage," he says. Maintaining a conversational pace and avoiding lactic acid buildup can also fend off soreness. Fisher recommends extra rest on big downhill days—the eccentric contraction of your muscles fighting against gravity is more likely to make you sore than the concentric contraction of going uphill.

"Don't bite off more than you can chew mileage-wise, elevation-wise, or pack weight-wise." Fisher says he's fixed more of his clients' problems than he can count by cutting unnecessary pack weight. Backpackers should also stretch regularly; tight muscles, especially the hip flexors, can lead to lower back problems. Talk with your doctor about taking medications to reduce everyday aches and pains.

It's hard to train for 20-mile days, and "training on the trail" needs to be treated as such: rest and recuperation are part of the process. The best way to stay on the trail is to avoid the soreness versus injury dilemma in the first place. Underestimate your abilities and take it easy. A slow start is worth it to avoid a premature end.

If you get sick on the trail, you may need to take an on-trail zero day to recover—even when conditions are less than ideal.

TOP DISEASES THRU-HIKERS SHOULD KNOW ABOUT

Of course thru-hikers, like regular people, can come down with all sorts of bugs, but here are the ones that are the most common for hikers or for which hikers are at an especially high risk.

NOROVIRUS

Noroviruses (stomach bug) can cause people to have gastroenteritis, an inflammation of the stomach and the intestines. This illness often begins suddenly and lasts about one to two days. Common symptoms include vomiting, diarrhea, and some stomach cramping. Less common symptoms include low-grade fever, chills, headache, muscle aches, nausea, and tiredness. This is of special concern for AT hikers. An unofficial poll of recent thru-hikers indicates fully half of

AT hikers get norovirus, aka "food poisoning" or "the stomach flu." The following information is adapted from the Appalachian Trail Conservancy (ATC).

Noroviruses are found in the stool or vomit of infected people and on infected surfaces that have been touched by ill people. Outbreaks are more likely in areas with multiple people in small spaces, like shelters and hostels. Norovirus can stay on surfaces and objects and still infect people after days or weeks. It can be spread by:

- Eating food or drinking liquids that are contaminated with norovirus (untreated water sources can be contaminated).
- Touching contaminated surfaces and then touching your mouth, nose, or eyes.
- Not washing hands after using the bathroom and before eating or preparing food.

Prevent getting and spreading norovirus (stomach bug) through good hygiene practices. Wash your hands with soap and water often, especially after using the bathroom and before handling food or eating. Alcohol-based hand sanitizers are not as effective against norovirus, but may be used if soap and water are not available. Wash with biodegradable soap at least 200 feet (80 steps) from a water source. Boil water (rolling boil for at least 1 minute) or use chemical disinfectant (iodine, chlorine, or chlorine dioxide). Most filters do not remove viruses, but can be used effectively in combination with chemical disinfection against a broad range of pathogens. Bury human waste 8 inches deep in soil and at least 200 feet away from natural water if a privy is not available. Avoid sharing water bottles, eating utensils, and other personal items. Avoid shaking hands with other thru-hikers. Consider avoiding shelters and washing up after signing trail registers.

If you find yourself with the norovirus, first drink plenty of fluids and wash your hands often. Avoid contamination of common areas (e.g., shelters); consider camping or staying off the trail, if possible.

Limit contact with others and avoid preparing food and drinks for others for two to three days after recovery. Seek medical treatment, especially if you become dehydrated or illness lasts more than a few days (norovirus usually lasts one to two days). Report the date and location of any cases or outbreaks of vomiting and diarrhea on the AT or at places used by AT hikers (e.g., hostels) to the local health department and ATC at stomachbug@appalachiantrail.org. Your prompt report will help stop potential outbreaks.

When hikers drink the green and brown chunks found in cattle troughs, they can't help but wonder why they feel sick afterwards.

GIARDIA

Giardia might be the most famous—or should I say, infamous—of hiking diseases. Giardiasis is a diarrheal disease caused by the microscopic parasite Giardia. A parasite is an organism that feeds off another to survive. Once a person or animal (e.g., cats, dogs, cattle, deer, and beavers) has been infected, the Giardia parasite lives in the intestines and is passed in feces (poop). Once outside the body, Giardia can sometimes survive for weeks or months. Giardia can be found within every region of the United States and around the world. Symptoms include diarrhea, gas or flatulence (often with a sulfur-like odor), greasy stool that can float, stomach or abdominal cramps, upset stomach or nausea, and dehydration. It usually takes one to three weeks for symptoms to appear after being infected with giardia.

The disease can be spread by swallowing Giardia picked up from surfaces that contain feces (poop) from an infected person or animal. It can also be spread by:

- Drinking water or using ice made from water sources where Giardia may live (for example, untreated or improperly treated water from lakes, streams, or wells).
- Swallowing water while swimming or playing in water where Giardia may live, especially in lakes, rivers, springs, ponds, and streams.
- Eating uncooked food that contains Giardia organisms.
- Having contact with someone who is ill with giardiasis.
- Traveling to countries where giardiasis is common.

The best way to prevent giardia is to treat your water and make sure to clean your hands before eating. There's a lot of controversy over how much giardia really is present in the backcountry; a 2003 *BACKPACKER* study found very little, and many believe the risk is overblown. Then again, the effort of filtering is pretty minor, and giardia is very unpleasant. Plus, thru-hikers are at a relatively high risk of catching the bug, because they are out for so long and in areas that can be pretty popular or well-trodden (like the AT). My take: Why risk it?

Since giardia is spread by having contact with those who are ill with (or carrying) giardiasis, be careful in the ways you interact with other hikers. Avoid sharing food with other thru-hikers, especially if they are ill. If you do share food, place it in the other person's hand—don't let them put their hand in your foodbag. Don't share utensils. You never know whether another person cleans up properly after pooping. As I've been saying for years, never shake a thru-hiker's hand.

If you think you've contracted giardia, see a doctor. He'll ask you to submit a stool sample, and will give you prescribed medicine if you do have the disease.

LYME DISEASE

An unofficial poll says about one-third of all AT hikers get Lyme disease, but it's also prevalent on other trails. Research is still being done to understand Lyme disease, but the consequences can be dire. It is worth knowing the warning signs and symptoms before you hike. According to the Centers for Disease Control (CDC), Lyme disease is caused by the bacterium *Borrelia burgdorferi* and is transmitted to humans through the bite of infected blacklegged ticks (aka deer ticks). If caught early, it's treated by antibiotics, but catching it is the tricky part. Typical symptoms include fever, headache, fatigue, achy joints and a characteristic bulls-eye-shaped skin rash called erythema migrans. If left untreated, infection can spread to joints, the heart, and the nervous system. For more on Lyme, visit cdc.gov/lyme.

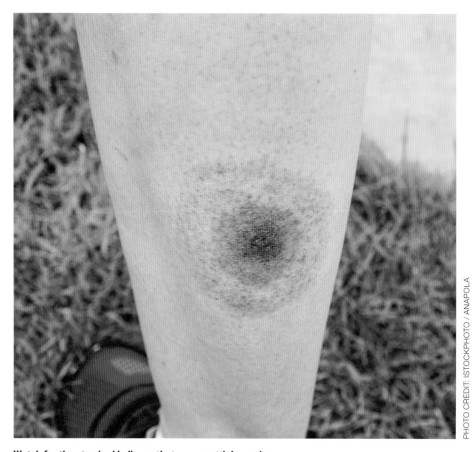

PHOTO CREDIT: ISTOCKPHOTO / ANAPOLA

Watch for the standard bullseye that comes with Lyme disease.

The way to prevent Lyme disease is to prevent tick bites. There are two ways to do that: repellent and vigilance. Here's what the CDC recommends:

- Use repellents that contain 20 to 30 percent DEET on exposed skin and clothing for protection that lasts up to several hours. Always follow product instructions.
- Use products that contain permethrin on clothing. Treat clothing and gear, such as boots, pants, socks, and tents with products containing 0.5 percent permethrin. It remains protective through several washings. Pre-treated clothing is available and may provide longer-lasting protection.
- Wear pants and long sleeves—even if it's warm. Better hot than sick!
- Tuck your shirt into your pants. Tuck your pants into your socks.
- Wear light colors to see ticks on your clothes more easily.
- Consider a hat with a flap behind the neck in serious tick country.

It's also important to find and remove ticks. That's trickier for a hiker in the field for days at a time than for day hikers, but here's some advice from my friend Justin "Trauma" Lichter on the subject. I recommend reading his whole post about Lyme disease frequency on the AT at his website www.justinlichter.com.

Do daily body checks. If you are thru-hiking, get in the routine of doing body checks every evening before you go to sleep and quick scans at breaks. Make sure to check warm areas, like armpits, head, behind your knees, and groin. Often you can find ticks crawling on you before they bite you.

Check yourself when you are in town. Even most gas stations have bathrooms with mirrors that can help you check those hard-to-see spots.

If you find the tick and remove it within about 24 hours, you're very unlikely to contract Lyme. If the tick has been in you for more than 48 hours and has Lyme, the chances of the tick transmitting Lyme to you are much higher. The incubation period for Lyme can be as long as a month after an infected bite. If you know you were bitten, keep an eye out for the bulls-eye rash or any flu-like symptoms, even without a rash.

Next, you need to know how to remove the tick. Here's the proven way:

- Use fine-tipped tweezers to grasp the tick as close to the skin's surface as possible.
- Pull upward with steady, even pressure. Don't twist or jerk the tick; this can cause the mouthparts to break off and remain in the skin. If this happens, remove the mouthparts with tweezers. If you are unable to remove the mouth easily with clean tweezers, leave it alone and let the skin heal.
- After removing the tick, thoroughly clean the bite area and your hands with rubbing alcohol, an iodine scrub, or soap and water.

Dispose of a live tick by submersing it in alcohol, placing it in a sealed bag/container, wrapping it tightly in tape, or flushing it down the toilet. Never crush a tick with your fingers.

If you think you have Lyme, get off the trail and go to a doctor immediately, ideally one with experience around Lyme, which is a bit of a tricky disease. There are blood tests to diagnose it, but they aren't always reliable. If you do have Lyme but catch it early, antibiotics should clear it up.

Even if you don't think you have Lyme, if you are hiking the AT or have removed many ticks from your body over your thru-hike, it is worth getting yourself tested for Lyme after you finish your hike. Budget some extra cash for this test, as it can be expensive. Although the tests are not always reliable, I did this after my first AT hike and ended up taking a round of antibiotics.

ROCKY MOUNTAIN SPOTTED FEVER

This is another tick-borne illness. In general it's pretty rare (way less common than Lyme disease), but due to the fact that it can kill you if not treated quickly, it is worth knowing about. It is most prevalent in North Carolina, Oklahoma, Arkansas, Tennessee, and Missouri. However, at least one CDT hiker has contracted it. According to the CDC, Rocky Mountain Spotted Fever (RMSF) is a tick-borne disease caused by the bacterium *Rickettsia rickettsii*. Typical symptoms include fever, headache, abdominal pain, vomiting, and muscle pain. A rash may also develop, but is often absent in the first few days, and in some patients never develops. To prevent the disease, follow all the same tick precautions mentioned in the previous section on Lyme.

RMSF is a serious disease that can kill you if not treated quickly. Symptoms vary widely, but if you have a fever, headache, nausea, vomiting, and muscle pain, with or without a spotted rash, get to a doctor as fast as possible. RMSF is treated with the antibiotic doxycycline.

WHAT TO DO ABOUT DISEASES ON THE TRAIL

Before you go, it's worth talking to your doctor about your trip and discussing the possible diseases that are known to exist on specific trails. She or he will help you determine whether carrying prophylactic drugs is worth it for you, including antibiotics and painkillers in case of emergency.

While on the trail, use soap and/or hand sanitizer after pooping in the woods or shaking other hikers' hands. Be careful when interacting with other hikers. Don't share food with your hand or reach into bags of trail mix or other foods with your hand. Check yourself for ticks every night and ask others (if available) to check places you cannot see. Wear long sleeves and light-colored clothes.

If you notice something not feeling right on the trail, get off the trail and take a few rest days to see an urgent-care doctor. You can find them in trail towns, and most guidebooks will list clinics along with other town services. In extreme cases, some people go home to rest. Request a test for the disease you think you may have. If you are away from the trail (e.g., hiking the AT, but went back home to the West Coast to rest up), you may need to explain to your doctor the prevalence of the disease in the region where you were hiking. This is especially true for tick-borne diseases. Be consistent about taking any drugs issued to you, and do as much research as you can about your ailment. It may save your hike, if not the quality of the rest of your life.

When you finish hiking, reserve part of your budget for getting tested for diseases afterward, especially Lyme disease. The tests for this can cost up to

$500, but if you have symptoms, you want to make sure you can afford to get the test.

NAVIGATION

I could write a whole book just on the navigation on long distance trails, but here are a few pieces of hard won advice that apply to any trail. Even if you have a GPS or phone app that aids with navigation (more information on this is available in the trail specific data), always carry a map and compass. Your phone can get wet or its battery could die. Plus, checking your map and finding where you are on it forces you to identify and appreciate the natural features around you. If you aren't sure how to use a map and compass, many local outdoor clubs and stores offer classes.

PHOTO CREDIT: LIZ THOMAS

Even with obvious trail, using a map can prevent you from taking the wrong trail at an intersection.

Even well-marked trails can sometimes be confusing (Appalachian Trail, 2008).

Experienced hikers frequently check their map and track where they are on it—especially at intersections.

The AT is usually well-marked with white blazes (6-inch paint marks on trees). The PCT is sometimes marked at intersections, as is the Colorado Trail. However, snow can obscure even obvious paths. Trails can become overgrown quickly, and after a storm, blown down trees may obscure the path. Signs may be removed, stolen, or damaged and can't be counted on. This is why carrying a map and compass is important.

Some long trails require cross country sections. Other times, it may appear as if a cross country route may be a more direct route than taking the trail. Cross country routes typically take hikers twice as long as trail to cover the same distance.

Forest fires, landslides, and other natural disasters frequently close trails. In the American West, wildfires seem to close parts of the PCT and CDT each year. It'll be up to you to figure out detours to reconnect to where the trail is open (some organizations post re-route suggestions on their websites).

CONQUERING MENTAL CHALLENGES AND STAYING MOTIVATED

A huge part of the challenge of finishing a thru-hike is the mental game. There were times during many of my first few thru-hikes when I thought about quitting. About ninety days into my first thru-hike of the Appalachian Trail, I found that much of the initial excitement of the trip was gone. Hiking during the hot and humid days was uncomfortable. The scenery from the relatively small mountains of the mid-Atlantic was not inspiring me. I wasn't ready to quit yet, but I wrote home asking for encouragement.

My dad—usually a relatively taciturn person—wrote me an inspiring story of a long-distance bike trip he had taken as a teenager. A friend with whom I had gone on several day-hiking trips sent me a nice note and a pack of chocolate-covered espresso beans. Now, almost ten years later, I am so grateful that I identified the problem early and reached out to others for help. I wouldn't be the person or hiker I am today if I had quit the AT. Here are my best lessons about the signs and triggers of quitting, and how to nip problems in the bud.

SIGNS AND TRIGGERS OF QUITTING

Just like we learn history to avoid falling down the same rabbit holes that our predecessors did, I hope you can learn how to persevere from those who have quit hiking. Some of the warning signs identified here are practical (like running out of money) and some of them are symptoms of fatigue (like not eating dinner). Read and remember this list—it will help you keep better track of where you are on the hiking motivation spectrum. These are major red flags that quitting may be in your future:

☐ **Low bank account.** Hopefully, your budget (see chapter 1) will keep you on track, but running low on money is a major reason people quit. Always check your bank balance when you are in town and force yourself to stick to a town budget (I limit myself to $100 per town stop). If you know you are bad with money, have a back-up plan, and make sure your spouse or family knows about any potential additional costs on your hike well in advance.

☐ **Not eating dinner.** Eat, especially your dinner. Food fuels not only your body but also your brain, and arguably, your morale. It helps you make smarter decisions and helps your body recover. If you ever feel too tired to eat, force yourself to eat. When I'm on the trail, the number one way I know if someone is about to quit is by watching them not eat dinner. If you don't eat dinner, your chances of quitting go up significantly.

☐ **Body hurting.** Check for the symptoms of Lyme disease and, if necessary, get to a doctor immediately. Otherwise, take a good 30 minutes and stretch out your body; in fact, make sure that stretching is part of your routine. Take a zero day or three in town, if necessary. Hikers have been able to save their hike by seeing physical therapists, massage therapists, or traditional doctors, or by taking yoga classes mid-hike.

☐ **Feeling bored.** Thru-hiking can be repetitive, especially if the scenery isn't changing. In "normal" life, we are used to being bombarded with constant stimuli. On the trail, we are not.

HOW TO AVOID A DOWNWARD SPIRAL

On a long hike, success is all about making smart small decisions. One of my hiking mentors, Glen van Peski, once said that with hiking (as compared to many other outdoor sports) we are given more chances to screw up, but we still can't keep doing it repeatedly before truly bad things happen. If you do one thing wrong, it's okay. Two things wrong, and you'll be very uncomfortable. But if you do three things wrong, chances are someone will get hurt. Here's a list of small things you can do to up your chances of staying safe.

First, identify problems early and don't be afraid to change. Is your gear giving you some pain? Adjust your straps if your pack is bothering you (many experienced hikers fiddle with their straps every few hours to give their back and shoulder a different sensation). Consider getting a different piece of gear next time you are in town. Getting new gear may be pricey, but if it can stop you from quitting, it could be worth it. Are you tired all the time? Reduce your miles. Maybe your body hurts or you're finding you don't have enough time on the trail to fish and see wildlife. This is your trip, so spend it doing what you love. Pushing too hard leads to burnout. Flexibility on trail is the key to happiness. Follow your bliss.

Second, be hygienic. Always use hand sanitizer or water and biodegradable soap after pooping, using privies, or shaking other hikers' hands. When sharing food, pour it into your hand or others' hands; don't reach into your food

Tips to Avoid Boredom

Talk and walk with other hikers. Even if it is just for a few hours and you have to hike at a different pace than your own, this is sure to brighten your day. I have met some of the most interesting people this way—a snake handler, a possum hunter, and people from all around the world. The trail is a safe space where you can meet people from all walks of life.

Jam out. Put mp3s of your favorite music, podcasts, or audiobooks on your phone. Some hikers even carry a radio to hear the news and sports games live. Use headphones so your music does not disturb wildlife or other hikers.

Slow down and do your hobby on the trail. Chances are you dreamed that your thru-hike would involve plenty of time to enjoy a hobby and hike, but your hobby got waylaid for making miles. Go back to your roots and spend some time hiking the hike you dreamed of. Go fishing! Doodle in your sketchbook! Play your guitar! Make elaborate camp meals! Paint watercolors! Take out your tripod and do some pro-grade photography! Balance your hike with what you love.

Read. Carry a book or e-book. Sure, it makes your pack a little heavier, but some of the most accomplished hikers in the world have told me that the extra weight is worth every ounce.

Write or journal. Your writing doesn't have to be about your trip. You could be working on the next great American novel. Writing helps you process your life and can make the mundane seem interesting. If you don't want to write just for your own sake, write letters to send to folks back home.

or let others' dirty hands get into your food bag. To eat your own food, use a spoon instead of your hands, even for funny things like broken chips. For solid food, better to give another person food from your dirty utensil than to have their hands or utensil in your food. These measures may seem extreme, but help prevents the spread of disease—a major reason people get off the trail.

Third, take care of your feet. Especially watch out for blisters, which are another major reason people get off the trail. If you do get blisters, take extra care to clean and drain them, and not let them get infected.

Be appreciative of the bad times along with the good. Mother Nature isn't always going to play nice, but realize that the bad times are there to teach you things about yourself. How often do people get to walk through rainstorms? I mean, it's kind of cool, especially compared to sitting at a desk. Remember, this is what it's like to truly be living. Remember that no matter how bad things

I was super stoked to stumble across an ancient cedar tree on the Chinook Trail. I couldn't help but appreciate how lucky I was to be hiking in nature.

are now, this too will pass. Thru-hiking is exhilarating because of the contrast between highs and the lows. The trail teaches us to live in the present, but also to keep everything in perspective.

Know what to expect in upcoming sections of the hike. If you know the next section will be harder, you can prepare yourself for it mentally. Of course, you can freak yourself out a little bit, too. But sometimes knowing, visualizing, and preparing your mind and body for a difficult section can save you from a situation that feels so traumatic that you want to quit afterward.

My friend Cam "Swami" Honan, who has hiked perhaps more than anyone else in the world, suggests this mental trick: Try watching yourself from above. Pretend you're watching a movie where the star is you. You're looking at yourself from above, an omniscient audience watching the main character about to enter a daunting situation. By taking this perspective, suddenly you detach yourself

Always have something to look forward to! The miniature ponies of the Roan Highlands are a highlight of the AT.

from any pain and start thinking of the situation objectively. Whatever suffering you're feeling starts to feel like it's happening to a character. What would you yell at the screen in the movie theater? "That hiker is about to go above treeline in a storm. Dumbass should stop and hunker down in his tent for a while!" It helps you put your situation into perspective instead of just feeling sorry for yourself. It helps you realize you're not a victim of nature, the weather, or your pain. You have power in these situations and in making smart decisions. You can make things better on the trail.

Set mini landmarks to be excited about and look forward to. The trail will go on for a while. Walking will become your job. Just like you have weekends to help break up your desk job, you'll need mini vacations from your vacation. Whether it is a zero day or a visit from a loved one, or a side trip into the big city or to scale

IN PRAISE OF ZEROES

William "Pi" Murphy is a huge fan of zero days.

Many hikers name their days by how many miles they've hiked: "Phew, a 20!" "Who were you with when you did your first 30?" Some even say more extreme numbers—35, 40, even 50-plus. These numbers seem competitive. They seem progressive. But sometimes, the best progress is a zero.

Everyone needs time off. There's a temptation to characterize a long hike as a lot of time off—from your job. However, a long hike is, well, long and hiking. And neither one of those is easy. A zero isn't all about making it easy. It's about having a sustainable approach to hiking. Many will say that recovery time is as important—if not more important—than training time. Ask yourself: Would you rather get a few more miles now with the chance of injury or start the next week rested and recovered, ready to go the whole hike?

Some folks cherish their zeroes. On one hike, I accumulated over thirty zeroes. Some folks like neroes instead, where they hike a few miles away from the expenses of a hotel and other town temptations, but still take a rest day. That's not to say I always forgo hiking for days in town. I've also gone two-plus weeks without a zero, but it left me thinking about quitting.

In my experience, taking less than one zero day per week leads to injury and frustration, neither of which is good for the goal of completing a long hike. If you haven't hiked before, I suggest planning on a full zero every week, or maybe even one after every five days of hiking. Try to use that zero for resting only—not for walking back and forth across town, doing laundry, getting groceries, etc.

To me, zero days are the key to a sustainable hike. Plan them in, both for time and for budget. You'll need a break from the so-called vacation of a long hike.

—William "Pi" Murphy

a peak, give yourself some mental treats once in a while. Just like you planned your itinerary by thinking of it as a bunch of shorter hikes back to back, start thinking of your thru-hike as a bunch of shorter trips back to back.

After a hard day on the trail, think of where you started that morning and all the things you have seen and done that day. It helps you realize that one day on the trail is so much more living than you get in a week at home. Even on a

Remind yourself of why you are out here. Look back at all you have come through and ahead towards all you will see.

hard day on the trail, I feel like I experience and do so much more than in a day at home. It makes me feel accomplished. It lets me appreciate the difficulty and gives it meaning: I had to push to achieve all that I have done.

Use food as a morale booster and motivator. I've found that hikers start thinking like dogs. Give yourself food treats to motivate yourself through the lows. Whether it's a chocolate bar at the top of the hill, a special freeze-dried meal for dinner at your next camp, or a big steak dinner in town, food and treats can be a simple, easy fix to make your trip feel easier.

Change your social group. Every year, people end up quitting because they don't like the crowd of hikers they've fallen in with. An easy fix is taking a week off the trail and letting them get ahead. No one says you have to hike with certain people. Don't worry about hurting their feelings. You came to the trail with a goal, and people you don't like shouldn't be what stops you from finishing.

Remind yourself of why you're here. Look at your find your "Why Hike" answers (see the "Introduction"). If you're thinking about quitting, take a zero day (or several). After a few days of sitting, watching bad TV, and eating ice cream, your body will likely ache to get back on the trail. You'll think, "Was I really about to leave the trail for this?" This has worked for me as a helpful way to put the difficulties on the trail in context. If that doesn't work, think about your worst day at the job you left for the trail. Is the trail really harder than putting up with that copy machine again? I didn't think so.

SAVORING THE
EXPERIENCE

Take time to appreciate where you are, how far you've come, and all that is ahead.

Chapter 10

+ MAKING FRIENDS, SAVORING EXPERIENCES

I first met Pi as I was hitchhiking into the trail town of Etna, California, from the PCT. He had done his town chores and was returning to the trail just as I was heading into town to start my chores. We waved at each other, exchanged a few pleasantries, and then I forgot all about him, concluding that I wouldn't ever see him again. Some 200 miles later, in the town of Ashland, Oregon, a good family friend took me to a fancy steakhouse where I assumed no hiker would ever go. A man wearing a red silk, button-up shirt came up to my table and asked if I was hiking the PCT. How did he know? This man—Pi—insisted that he had seen me on the trail. I was quite positive I had not seen anyone wearing a red silk shirt on the trail. Clearly, this man was crazy.

Two hundred miles later near Bend, Oregon, I found myself in a horrible rainstorm for which I was underprepared. I wanted to bail off the trail and go into town to dry off and buy some warmer layers, but didn't want to do it by myself. Enter Pi. We hiked together 13 miles to the side trail where we could find shelter from the storm. His bright, cheery attitude and fun stories carried me to the restaurant near the trail. We hiked together for almost 500 more miles with his friend, sleeping in a lava castle and sharing a hotel room at the fancy Timberline Lodge in Oregon after hiking a 54-mile day. A few days later, we almost burned down Miss Info's mom's house with bacon.

Making friends on the trail can be one of the most rewarding things you can do.

These are the types of crazy up and down stories that you can't make up. Spending a week with someone on the trail can form a deep relationship that feels more real and authentic than friendships formed at home. On the trail, most hikers aren't trying to impress you or pretend to be someone they are not. We're out here to learn things about ourselves, to learn to forgive others, to forgive ourselves, and see good in humanity. You couldn't ask for a better group of people to become friends with.

A lot of us go hiking to get away from the world, but thru-hiking and section-hiking come with a vibrant social life as well, and your interactions with others can make or break your hike. In this chapter, we'll teach you the key rules of hiker social etiquette so you can be a confident, positive member of the hiking community.

MAKING FRIENDS ON THE TRAIL

During prime thru-hiker season on many long-distance trails (AT, PCT, JMT, Wonderland Trail, Tahoe Rim Trail), you really have to work hard not to have other hikers near you. You may start these trails alone, but very few people hike

HIKE YOUR OWN HIKE

SOCIAL REGRETS

Felicia "Princess of Darkness" Hermosillo talks about how she wishes she'd socialized smarter in her first hikes.

As a Triple Crowner, I have somewhere close to 10,000 miles of hiking under my belt. The thing that I wish I had known when I started thru-hiking back in 2002 was how important hiking would be in my life. As a 25-year-old with a newfound freedom, I partied a lot on the AT, and I missed a lot of opportunities to interact with other hikers who had a lot more experience than I did. I met a well-known and experienced thru-hiker on Hike Naked Day [the Summer Solstice], and I was so wrapped up in the party scene of Hike Naked Day and the fun that we were having that I missed the opportunity to interact with him and learn from him. I wish I had paid more attention to those who had more experience than me. I could've learned a lot. It would've made future hikes a little easier. I would've gotten into more difficult terrain a lot sooner in my life.

Sure, have fun on the AT—or any hike you do—but I definitely wish I had been more observant of the people who had more experience than me.

—Felicia "Princess of Darkness" Hermosillo

the trail alone the whole way. I have met some of the best people in the world hiking on trails—people who have become my best friends in real life and whom I can trust. For some reason, people who have decided to take a break from their life to hike across the country are usually the best people on the planet. People hiking trails understand you and your dream.

Even if you choose to walk alone on the AT or PCT, or any other long trail, and somehow decide you don't like any of the other hikers you meet enough to walk with them for a few hours, a few days, or a few hundred miles, the thru-hiking community still watches out for you. If you go missing or if you get hurt, people you may have never met who may have only heard of you through the giant game of telephone that is trail news, spread by word of mouth from hiker to hiker, will go to extreme lengths to come to your aid.

I spent my first few hikes being a lot less social than most hikers. Part of that was due to my speed and part of it was a choice: I thought talking to others took away from my wilderness experience. In retrospect, one of the biggest regrets I have from those thru-hikes is that I did not make more friends and take advantage of the wealth of experience, knowledge, and expertise other hikers have. In subsequent hikes, I looked forward to the friendships I knew I would form. It's one of the greatest gifts of the trail.

GROUPTHINK—THE DARK SIDE OF SOCIALIZING

Group mentality can get in the way of your growth and safety. Many hikers— myself included—will say that when they hike by themselves, they take extra precautions. A prime example is treating water. Some hikers always treat their water when solo. But when they are with others who don't treat, they tend also not to treat. Someone gets an alpha male mentality going on, and it really impacts how the group reacts. The same goes for other dangerous situations— like heading over a peak during a lightning storm. Many hikers wouldn't do it alone, but, as if the group could protect them from natural forces, will head up into the danger zone with friends nearby. Similarly, many solo hikers will always hang their food in grizzly bear country, but when camping with others will assume that a few extra human bodies are security enough from an 800-pound animal to justify sleeping with their salmon.

Think about how group mentality might impact your decisions on the trail, and choose friends and hiking partners who have similar values as you.

So what makes a bad social group?

- People who are not the same pace as you, or are not willing to go your pace, or get cranky if your pace is not the same as theirs.
- People who do things you think are not ethical or responsible, like not following Leave No Trace principles or having bad trail etiquette.
- People who annoy you, are mean, and whom you genuinely dislike. This one sounds obvious, but it happens on the trail more often than you would think. Hikers sometime stick with folks they genuinely find distasteful because they are afraid to hike alone, especially in high snow years. My advice is that if you are concerned about entering a section of trail alone, take a few zeroes and wait for a new group of hikers to catch up with you. Maybe you will like that group more, and you can hike together.

Signing a trail register allows hikers behind you to know where you are. A lot of trail names are the same, so if you sign with your trail name, also leave another piece of information like what city you are from. If you get lost, this could be an important way for rescuers to find you, like those found in AT shelters above.

KEEP IN TOUCH WITH LOVED ONES

Keeping in touch while on the trail is a theme we touch upon a lot in this book, but it's so important that it bears repeating here. Your decision to hike the trail does not make you an island of one. There are people who care about what you are doing and will worry about you if you don't let them know you are okay every so often. You get cell reception more often than you might expect on most long trails in the United States, so that's one option. If you don't want to carry a cell phone, here are some other ways you can stay in touch with the folks at home and on the trail:

- SPOT/DeLorme devices allow your family to track you on a map each night.
- Libraries in town are a great way to get Internet access if you do not have a smartphone.

Social Media and the Trail

Many hikers I meet admit afterward that they became so engaged in blogging or keeping up with their social media on the trail that they found it hard to stay "present" during their hike. "I just spent all day on the trail thinking about what my next blog post will be about," one blogger told me. "I focused more on what would make a beautiful picture than on savoring being in that beauty," a photographer told me. Is that how you want to spend your hike? Think about how big a role you want your communication with the outside to be before you start your blog.

Thru-hiking is a great opportunity—one of the last opportunities we have left—to turn it all off. I urge you to experiment with turning your phone off and escaping your regular life while you are on the trail and only using your phone in town. You may find the experience makes your hike more rewarding and helps you engage with nature, yourself, and other hikers better. If you do decide to blog, get a wifi-enabled camera or SD card for your camera. It will save you a lot of time sorting photos in the library.

It's easy from the comfort of your home to think you'll have the energy to blog every night. But the truth is that thru-hiking is exhausting, and it gets to be hard to blog or even post photos every night. I know bloggers who sometimes stay up past midnight and then have to get up and hike the next day. You get into the groove of not being connected to social media 24-7. Tell friends and family you expect to blog once a week, but don't make any promises.

PHOTO CREDIT: LIZ THOMAS

Trail selfies!

- Many hikers send themselves a cheap netbook or tablet that they use and then bounce up the trail.
- Use pay phones or bring a calling card.
- Send postcards or letters from the trail.
- Ask day hikers, trail angels, or those you meet in towns to call or email your home.
- Use social media/blogging.

FINAL WORDS OF WISDOM

Now it's time for you to experience your journey. Soon you will feel the cool breeze on your face as you look down on the world from a sweeping ridge. You started your trail as far as you could see in one direction. You will continue on as far as you can see in another. Your body will become accustomed to being outdoors all day. Sleeping on the ground will become restful. You'll find that you don't miss TV, constant updates from your phone, or so many similar aspects of your old life.

When I headed off on my first hike on the AT, I was so anxious about the journey ahead that I could barely sleep the night before starting. Despite all the research and preparation I had done, there were still so many unknowns. I felt like there were so many questions that I didn't even know I should have asked.

Before I end this book, though, I do want to leave you with three simple but important takeaways.

First: Although this is the end of the book, it's definitely not the end of your learning process. In fact, one of the reasons I love thru-hiking is because I learn something new every single day. Maybe it's about myself, and how I react when conditions are tough. Maybe it's about my gear or the areas I'm walking through. The point is, don't feel like you have to already know every single thing before setting out. Discovery is part of the adventure.

Second: If whatever you're doing on your hike feels difficult, stop, sit, and eat something. It seems simple, but eating is your number one defense against injury, your number one source of recovery, and your number one way of getting along better with others.

Third: At this point you've heard the phrase "Hike Your Own Hike" a million times—and you'll hear it a million times more once you hit the trail. But seriously: Reflect often on what it means, and don't judge yourself compared to others. The trail isn't a race, competition, or sporting event. It's an exploration, where you get out of it what you came for.

As you come to the end of this book, I hope you have found the answers to many of your questions—plus the answers to questions you didn't even know you had when you started. But if there's a big topic you still feel fuzzy on, I'm here to help. Email me at liz@eathomas.com to schedule personal, one-on-one consultations with me or visit my website at www.eathomas.com. Visit www.facebook.com/TrainWithAnish to schedule a consultation for personal training with Heather Anderson. I'd also like to personally invite you to come to one of the live events put on by the long-distance hiking community. They're a lot of fun and a great place to learn more.

And finally, I just want to say thank you. Thanks for giving me this opportunity to share what I've learned. Thanks for the hard work you're putting in to making sure you're truly prepared for a long hike. And most importantly, thank you for daring to dream of a big outdoor adventure. I truly believe that this world needs thru-hikers. The more people who get to experience hiking a long trail, who risk facing their fears and come out stronger for it, who love the natural wonder of this ever-surprising planet, the better our world can be. So thank you. And see you on the trail!

A gorgeous view of the White Mountains, New Hampshire

While the route ahead may be daunting for both these CDT hikers and hikers just starting to plan their trip, use these resources to figure out what next steps you need to take.

PHOTO CREDIT: JOHANNA CARR

RESOURCES

Now that you know the ins and outs of thru-hiking long trails, here is some additional helpful information that you may want to check out as you prep for your big adventure.

This book just skims the surface of the wealth of knowledge that is available for distance hikers.

TRAIL ORGANIZATIONS

Every winter, snow and winds knock trees onto the trail. Vegetation grows over the trail. Landslides, floods, and wildfires obscure the path. Every year it takes hours of dedicated volunteer work to maintain the trails. And while volunteer work is free, their food, permits, and port-o-potties are not. Trail organizations maintain and protect the trail. They make sure that the views we have from the trail aren't obscured by a new mini-mall being built 100 feet away. They work to build trails through natural areas instead of along roads. Before you hit the trail, I encourage you to donate to the trail organizations that work hard not only to gather all the information a thru-hiker needs, but also make sure the trail is in top shape and working order.

Check out these trail organizations and show your thanks:

- Appalachian Trail Conservancy, www.appalachiantrail.org
- Pacific Crest Trail Association, www.pcta.org
- Continental Divide Trail Coalition, www.continentaldividetrail.org
- Tahoe Rim Trail, www.tahoerimtrail.org
- Colorado Trail Foundation, www.coloradotrail.org
- Pacific Northwest Trail, www.pnt.org
- Friends of the Ouachita Trail, www.friendsot.org
- Benton MacKaye Trail Association, www.bmta.org
- Superior Hiking Trail Association, www.shta.org
- Florida Trail Association, www.floridatrail.org
- Green Mountain Club (which maintains the Long Trail in Vermont), www.greenmountainclub.org
- Ice Age Trail Alliance, www.iceagetrail.org
- North Country Trail Association, www.northcountrytrail.org
- American Hiking Society, www.americanhiking.org

BRUSH UP ON BACKPACKING 101

I deliberately focused on thru-hiker-specific content in this book and not on skills that a totally beginning backpacker would need for any trip. But I want to make sure you know where to start if you have any gaps in your knowledge. Check out BACKPACKER's *The Complete Guide to Backpacking* for more.

FURTHER RESOURCES

If you're interested in further one-on-one coaching with me, Liz Thomas, go to my website at www.eathomas.com to schedule a personal consultation with me about your upcoming hike. You'll also find all sorts of tips for the trail there.

Here are some additional resources for you to check out as you prep for your upcoming trip. Please note that this is by no means an exhaustive list, but it will get you started on your journey.

PHOTO CREDIT: CAVEMAN COLLECTIVE

Liz Thomas

THRU-HIKER TRAINING TIPS

Here are five at-home strength exercises that you can do to help prepare for life on the trail, courtesy of Heather "Anish" Anderson, unassisted speed record holder on the Pacific Crest Trail, Appalachian Trail, and Arizona Trail.

EQUIPMENT YOU'LL NEED:

- Bench/Sturdy Chair/Bed/etc
- Backpack with gear (no more than 10lbs) or another weight

EXERCISE 1: INCLINE PUSH-UPS

Incline push-ups work the muscles of the lower chest, triceps, shoulders, and back muscles. They are essential for strengthening the muscles used to carry a backpack or using trekking poles.

INSTRUCTIONS:

- Stand a few feet away from a secure, hip-height object (bench, anchored chair, bed, desk, etc).
- Lean against the edge with hands shoulder width apart, keeping straight arms. Play with footing (wide, hip-width, narrow, single legged, etc. for varying levels of challenge).
- Keeping your torso straight and firm, lower down until your chest touches the edge. Hold for a second, then push yourself back up. Repeat ten times.

EXERCISE 2: LEG LIFTS

This exercise strengthens the support muscles of the pelvic region. This is essential to maintain control and form when running and walking. Having proper pelvic alignment can help prevent tight iliotibial band syndrome.

INSTRUCTIONS:

- Lie on your side with legs slightly bent. Rest your head on your lower arm (extended straight) and lightly rest the fingers of your other hand on the floor in front of your stomach for balance. Don't lean on your hand. The control needs to come from an engaged core.

- Throughout the movement maintain a stable pelvic area. Keep hips stacked, no wobbling. Your top hip should be in a vertical line above the lower one.
- Straighten upper leg and lift it slowly as high as you can without your pelvis shifting out of alignment. Lower and repeat ten times. Switch sides and repeat.

EXERCISE 3: DOUBLE LEG SQUAT

Squats are an entire body workout with special focus on the major muscle groups in the legs. Having powerful leg muscles enables you to climb steadily.

INSTRUCTIONS:

- Stand with feet shoulder width apart, arms outstretched.
- Lower yourself toward the ground by bending your knees and pushing your hips backward.
- Go as low as you can without bending your knees more than 90 degrees or letting your knees drift out to the sides or extend beyond your toes.
- Hold for a second and contract your glutes to rise back to standing. Repeat ten times.
  - For additional challenge wear your weighted backpack.

EXERCISE 4: OVERHEAD REACH

This exercise works the oblique core muscles as well as the supportive muscles of the torso to enable efficient energy transfer from upper to lower body. A strong core is also necessary to carry a backpack long distances.

INSTRUCTIONS:

- Start at the bottom of the Double Leg Squat with your backpack or weight held overhead with extended arms.
- Stand to vertical and lean to one side without leaning forward or back.
- Lower back into the squat and repeat leaning to the other side. Repeat ten times on each side.

EXERCISE 5: DYNAMIC GLUTE BRIDGE

By engaging your abs, as well as your glutes to make the movement, you gain power and control in those muscle groups. This will make you stronger for climbing and carrying.

INSTRUCTIONS:

- Lie on your back with your weight on your upper back between the shoulder blades and your feet. Keep your arms at your sides or cross them over your chest. Lower your butt almost to the ground and thrust upward by activating your glutes and driving your heels into the ground. Perform twenty reps.
  - Advanced Version #1: A more advanced version is to do a single leg variation. Lift one leg so your weight is all on one leg and your back. Repeat the same movement, making sure you drive your heel into the ground and keep a stable pelvis.
  - Advanced Version #2: Complete either one or two legged version holding your pack with weight in it held close to your chest.

Heather "Anish" Anderson is an American Council on Exercise certified personal trainer specializing in working with all levels of current and aspiring endurance athletes. As someone who didn't begin exercising until adulthood and has subsequently run half a dozen 100 mile ultra-marathons and completed nearly 20,000 miles of hiking in the backcountry since 2001 (including setting overall self-supported fastest known times on 3 National Scenic Trails), she has insight into how to get from where you are to where you want to go. Whether you're preparing for a long backpacking trip or an ultra-marathon, Heather can tailor an individual program that works for you. For more information or to contact her check out www.facebook.com/TrainWithAnish

APPALACHIAN TRAIL RESOURCES

Consider this your best starting point for all specific, logistical details regarding the Appalachian Trail.

GENERAL RESOURCES

Pmags.com
Candid advice, journals, and ramblings from outdoor enthusiast Paul Magnanti

Thehikinglife.com
Tips, tales, and trip reports from Cam "the most traveled hiker on Earth" Honan

Trailjournals.com
Journal entries from various AT hikers, which provide a good idea of what day-to-day of trail life is like

Postholer.com
Blogs and journals from hikers, as well as maps, trail planners, and gear lists

Whiteblaze.com
Extremely active forum for all things Appalachian Trail.

Walkingwithwired.com
Daily blog from a thru-hiker with extremely detailed how-to and planning information

GUIDEBOOKS AND MAPS

The Appalachian Trials, by Zach Davis
A psychological and emotional guide to successfully thru-hiking the Appalachian Trail.

Appalachian Trail Data Book 2015, by Appalachian Trail Conservancy
This book includes mileage with codes for water, shelters, road crossings, etc. It's bare bones, lightweight, and data-only (no descriptions, maps). It is keyed to ATC Appalachian Trail maps.

The A.T. Guide: A Handbook for Hiking the Appalachian Trail, by David "AWOL" Miller
This is smaller and lighter than other books. It has less data but lots of detailed descriptions.

AT Thru-Hikers' Companion, by Appalachian Long Distance Hikers Association
This offers up great elevation profiles and town maps, and different sections ca be easily separated into smaller booklets. Descriptions are included for services, shelters, and regulations.

National Geographic Topographic Maps
These can get expensive if you buy them for the whole trail, but they are top-notch topographic maps and also include trail towns and resupply information.

APPS

AT Hiker: Guthook's Guide

This app includes hundreds of waypoints with photos and descriptions, an interactive map with up-to-date information of the trail and elevation, plus many important side trails. It includes virtual trail registers and forums where hikers can share real-time updates on trail re-routes, water availability, etc.

Appalachian Trail Notebook

This app enables recording and emailing of AT locations (more than 1500 locations listed by the fourteen states). Photos can be integrated in the notecard posts.

WEBSITES AND FORUMS

Appalachian Trail Conservancy (appalachiantrail.org)
Go-to information on everything AT

The Appalachian Long Distance Hikers Association (aldha.org)
Community of thru-hikers and updated announcements and newsletters

BACKPACKER (backpacker.com)
Interesting AT news articles and general tips on thru-hiking

Appalachian Trail (appalachiantrail.com)
Curates AT news articles and thru-hiker stories

Whiteblaze.net
Access to forums and journals to get all of your questions answered

Appalachian Trials (appalachiantrials.com)
Started by a former thru-hiker and includes hiker blogs and articles

PERMITS

No fees or paid permits are required to access the AT for simply walking, but some New England campsites require fees (Green Mountain National Forest, White Mountain National Forest, and Baxter State Park), and you must obtain permits for backcountry camping in two national parks on the AT (Great Smoky Mountains National Park and Shenandoah National Park).

SHUTTLES

Appalachian Trail Conservancy Shuttle Guide (appalachiantrail.org)
A comprehensive list of shuttles by state

WHEN AND WHERE TO START

Appalachian Trail Distance calculator (atdist.com)
Calculate the walking distance between dozens of different points on the AT

Thru-hiker registration to avoid overcrowding (appalachiantrail.org)

Voluntary tool to share your start date with other thru-hikers and minimize the social and ecological impacts of overcrowding on the AT

Outdoors.org

Includes advice on when to start, depending on hiking direction and area closings

WEATHER AND TRAIL UPDATES

Appalachian Trail Conservancy (appalachiantrail.org)

Stay up-to-date with trail closures and warnings

AT Weather (atweather.org)

Check the weather in various locations along the AT

PACIFIC CREST TRAIL RESOURCES

Consider this list your best starting point for all specific, logistical details regarding the Pacific Crest Trail.

GENERAL RESOURCES

Pmags.com

Candid advice, journals, and ramblings from outdoor enthusiast Paul Magnanti

Thehikinglife.com

Tips, tales, and trip reports from Cam "the most traveled hiker on Earth" Honan

Trailjournals.com

Journal entries from various PCT hikers, which provide a good idea of what day-to-day of trail life is like

Postholer.com

Blogs and journals from hikers, as well as maps, trail planners, and gear lists

Walkingwithwired.com

Daily blog from a thru-hiker with extremely detailed how-to and planning information

GUIDEBOOKS AND MAPS

Yogi's Pacific Crest Trail Handbook, by Jackie McDonnell

Advice from PCT legend veterans, including valuable information for 108 hiker stops, and broken out into advice to read before you leave and on-trail tips on perforated paper to tear out and carry with you

Pacific Crest Trail Atlas, by Erik the Black

This lightweight guide is full of color topographic maps and elevation profiles, but it's only for southern California (not the whole trail).

Halfmile's PCT Maps (pctmap.net)

This free resource offers printable maps with accurate mileages and waypoints.

APPS

ETrails

Free for iOS users, includes photos and detailed descriptions of intersections, water, campsites, and natural history.

Guthook's PCT Hiker

Includes hundreds of waypoints with photos, and you can search for trail sections or popular locations.

Halfmile's PCT

This is a companion to the free printable maps. You can turn the app into simulation mode for hike planning and hiker support, and it includes a live trail diagram and a powerful search function. Best of all? It's free.

WEBSITES AND FORUMS

Pacific Crest Trail Association (pcta.org)

Advice on maps and guidebooks, and information on trail updates and permits

As the Crow Flies (asthecrowflies.org)

Comprehensive, free list of all the trail towns and services

Craig's PCT Planner (pctplanner.com)

Walk through choosing resupply locations, allocating food, and arriving in towns, and you can adjust your hiking time based on terrain.

BACKPACKER (backpacker.com)

Interesting PCT news articles and general tips on thru-hiking

PERMITS

Get your free interagency long-distance PCT permit from the Pacific Crest Trail Association. This permit does not cover campgrounds, park entrances, and other special use fees. Research trailheads and dates, as you'll need to provide exact campsites and dates you plan to be at locations. Obtain a self-issued trailhead wilderness permit in North Cascades National Park. Get more details at pcta.org.

SHUTTLES

Southern terminus: long-distance hikers are invited to request rides from San Diego trail angels; public buses are also available.

Northern terminus: hire the Classic Mountain Cabby or fly in on a private plane; from the west/east, Greyhound and Amtrak combined with hitchhiking are good options.

WHEN AND WHERE TO START

Ninety percent of thru-hikers hike northbound, starting in late April or early May and ending in October at the latest (the first snows in Washington can be deadly). Starting a southbound hike is a little bit of a logistical problem, as it's illegal to enter the United States from Canada via the PCT.

WEATHER AND TRAIL UPDATES

Pacific Crest Trail Water Report (pctwater.com)
Offers mileage and waypoints for all water sources on the trail

PCTA Trail Conditions and Closures (pcta.org)

NOHRSC Interactive Snow Information (nohrsc.noaa.gov)

CONTINENTAL DIVIDE TRAIL RESOURCES

Consider this list your best starting point for all specific, logistical details regarding the Continental Divide Trail.

GENERAL RESOURCES

Pmags.com
Candid advice, journals, and ramblings from outdoor enthusiast Paul Magnanti

Thehikinglife.com
Tips, tales, and trip reports from Cam "the most traveled hiker on Earth" Honan

Trailjournals.com
Journal entries from various CDT hikers, which provide a good idea of what day-to-day of trail life is like

Postholer.com
Blogs and journals from hikers, as well as maps, trail planners, and gear lists

Walkingwithwired.com
Daily blog from a thru-hiker with extremely detailed how-to and planning information

GUIDEBOOKS AND MAPS

Bear Creek Survey Maps (bearcreeksurvey.com)
Full-color maps for Colorado, New Mexico, Montana, and Wyoming, available as downloadable PDF files and unbound printed sheets

Johnathan Ley Maps (phlumf.com)
Annotated detailed map with alternate routes, originally from crowdsourced information, so it allows for annual on-the-ground updates

Continental Divide Trail Society / Jim Wolf Guidebooks (cdtsociety.org)

Includes mile-to-mile trail descriptions for the entire trail, as well as natural and cultural history of the areas near the trail

Yogi's CDT Handbook

Includes a section for planning and one for the trail, although the on-trail section only contains a town guide, not trail-specific information, since no two hikers walk the same CDT

Beacon's Data Book

Free information, including water and resupply presented in data book style, and the crowdsourced information allows for annual updates

APPS

Guthook's CDT Hiker

Includes hundreds of waypoints with photos, and you can search for trail sections or popular locations.

WEBSITES AND FORUMS

Continental Divide Trail Coalition (continentaldividetrail.org)

Includes an interactive map resource and general CDT trip planning (as well as information on permits and shuttles)

BACKPACKER (backpacker.com)

Interesting CDT news articles and general tips on thru-hiking

Spirit Eagle CDT (spiriteaglehome.com)

Information on planning, journals, resources, maps, and route information

PERMITS

Permits are not needed to hike the CDT, with the exception of within the National Parks. Permits are needed in Glacier National Park, Blackfeet Tribal Lands, Yellowstone National Park, Grand Teton National Park, Rocky Mountain National Park, Indian Peaks Wilderness, and El Malpais National Monument. For more on permits, visit continentaldividetrail.org.

SHUTTLES

CDTC operates a shuttle to and from the southern terminus.

WHEN AND WHERE TO START

This depends on your schedule, snow levels, and weather. Most thru-hikers hike northbound and start in March or April to avoid hitting Colorado too early when snow is still heavy. Others hike southbound starting in late June, but this can get delayed well into July due to high snow levels, spring run-off, and avalanche dangers.

WEATHER AND TRAIL UPDATES

CDTC Incidents and CDTC Interactive Weather Map (continentaldividetrail.org)
    Provides information on trail closures

InciWeb (inciweb.nwcg.gov)
    Provides information on forest fires and impact on trail segments

JOHN MUIR TRAIL RESOURCES

Consider this list your best starting point for all specific, logistical details regarding the John Muir Trail.

GENERAL RESOURCES

Pmags.com
    Candid advice, journals, and ramblings from outdoor enthusiast Paul Magnanti

Thehikinglife.com
    Tips, tales, and trip reports from Cam "the most traveled hiker on Earth" Honan

Trailjournals.com
    Journal entries from various JMT hikers, which provide a good idea of what day-to-day of trail life is like

Postholer.com
    Blogs and journals from hikers, as well as maps, trail planners, and gear lists

Walkingwithwired.com
    Daily blog from a thru-hiker with extremely detailed how-to and planning information

GUIDEBOOKS AND MAPS

John Muir Trail: The Essential Guide to Hiking America's Most Famous Trail, by Elizabeth Wenk
    Includes custom-made topo maps, elevation profiles, data tables, and labeled panoramas from prominent passes, as well as detailed information on campsites

John Muir Pocket Atlas, by Erik the Black
    This lightweight atlas offers improved maps and elevation profiles, with trail data and a resupply guide

Tom Harrison Maps
    Includes shaded relief topo maps and is broken into sections of one day's worth of hiking, and it's lightweight and compact

National Geographic Map Book

Includes trail profiles and elevation profiles, resupply options, trail towns, and bailout points—all on waterproof paper and stapled so maps do not get lost

APPS

Guthook's JMT Guide (aka John Muir Trail Hiker)

Includes photos and descriptions of interesting points along the trail, with elevation profiles and the option to leave messages at waypoints for other hikers

WEBSITES AND FORUMS

The Complete Guide to the John Muir Trail (johnmuirtrail.org)

Includes descriptions of trail segments and advice on preparations

BACKPACKER (backpacker.com)

Interesting CDT news articles and general tips on thru-hiking

Hiking the John Muir Trail (jmt-hiker.com)

Includes lots of photos, that allows for a "virtual hike" experience

The Muir Project (themuirproject.com)

Interesting film that gives good day-to-day of life on the trail

JMT Hikers Yahoo Group (groups.yahoo.com/neo/groups/johnmuirtrail/info)

Helpful forum members with prompt answers

PERMITS

Plan ahead, as JMT permits are under a quota system to prevent trail crowding and to protect the environment. A different permit is required, depending on which trailhead you use to access the JMT. Most hikers start at the northern terminus (Yosemite National Park), and those permit reservations are available 24 weeks in advance—but they go quickly. Others who start at Mt. Whitney are also subject to the Mt. Whitney Portal quota system. For more on permits, visit pcta.org.

SHUTTLES

Climber.org Sierra Nevada Shuttles

A comprehensive list of transportation for trailheads

WHERE AND WHEN TO START

Generally, the trail is accessible from July through September. Hiking north to south is the most popular option.

WEATHER AND TRAIL UPDATES

Pacific Crest Trail Association (pcta.org)

This includes trail updates for the entirety of the PCT, not just the JMT

NOHRSC Interactive Snow Information (nohrsc.noaa.gov)

Detailed, interactive hydrologic map

ROUTE PLANNING TEMPLATE

Use the following template to plan out your route, including your daily mileage, campsites, and costs.

Instructions: Use the example row to start filling in the information for your trip!

Trail name:

Start date and predicted end date:

Average daily miles:

Approximate total cost:

Likely weather:

Date	Planned day of trip	Daily miles	Total miles into the trip	Camping spot for the night	Services available?	Camp costs	Amount	Resupply today? (Y/N)	Pounds of food needed?	Address to send?	Meal today? (Y/N)	Meal cost	Shower today? (Y/N)	Shower cost	Approximate cost for day
3/28	1	18.2	18.2	Laurel Gap Shelter, Smoky Mountain NP	bear cables, required to camp in designated spots	Camp Fee	$5	N	11 pounds	n/a	Y	$7	N	$0	$12
	2														
	3														
	4														
	5														

GEAR CHECKLIST

Use the following template to plan out the gear needed for your trip.

	Weight	Check box
Big Three		
Backpack		
Pack Cover or Liner		
Sleeping Pad		
Shelter		
Shelter Poles (or hiking poles)		
Stakes and guylines		
Ground sheet or bivy sack		
Stuff sacks for Big Three items (optional)		
Clothing		
Sunhat or visor		
Extra Underwear		
Insulating layer (down or synthetic puffy jacket or vest)		
Rain jacket		
Rain pants or skirt/kilt		
Windshirt/windjacket		
Gloves		
Beanie or warm hat		
Extra socks (_____ pair)		
Sleep clothes (optional)		
Stuff sack for clothing		
Food and cooking		
Food bag stuff sack		
Windscreen		
Pot and Lid		
Utensils		
Stove		
Fuel bottle or canister		
Lighter and firestarter		
Bear bag system or canister		
Water filter or treatment		
Extra water storage		
Health and Safety		
Flashlight/headlamp		
Whistle		
Umbrella		
Toilet kit (trowel and TP)		
Toothbrush/toothpaste/floss		
Bug protection: spray/lotion, net (if necessary)		
Sunscreen		
Hand sanitizer		
Sunglasses		
Prescription glasses/contact lenses and solution		
Tampons/menstrual cup		
Maps, trail info, permits		
Pen and journal		
Wallet (cash, credit card, ID, insurance cards, etc.)		
Compass		
GPS/Satellite Phone/Locator Device		
Phone and charger		
Camera, SD cards, and extra battery		
Gear repair: needle and thread, patches, etc.		
Knife and mini scissors		
Wash and laundry kit (biodegradable soap, laundry bags) (optional)		
Ditty bags to hold this stuff		
Meds		
Everyday Prescription Meds		
Blister care (Leukotape, med tape, etc.)		
Triple antibiotic		
Anti-itch		
Crazy glue mini		
Safety pin or needle		
Anti-allergy meds		
Anti diarrhea		
Pain killers		
Heartburn meds		
Salt tablets		
Prophylactic Rx meds for Giardia, Norovirus, etc.		
Consumables	# days	Weight Per Day
Food		
Fuel (bottle or canister)		
Water		

CREDITS

A huge thanks to the following people who helped contribute to this book in various ways:

Rachel Zurer—editing, writing, research, and project management
Andrew Bydlon, Ben Fullerton, and Will Rochfort—photography, art direction, and project management
Genny Fullerton and Jenny Jakubowski—photo research

Thru-hikers who contributed their voices and gear:
Paul "PMags" Magnanti
William "Pi" Murphy
Dean "Ghost" Krakel
Amanda "Zuul" Jameson
John "Cactus" McKinney
Whitney "Allgood" LaRuffa
Felicia "Princess of Darkness" Hermosillo
Phil "Nowhere Man" Hough
Deb "Walking Carrot" Hunsacker
Naomi "The Punisher" Hudetz
Kate "Drop 'N Roll" Hoch
Ted "Scarecrow" Warren
Heather "Anish" Anderson

Additional writing and research help from:
Erik Johnson
Emelie Frojen
Sarah Stewart
Corey Buhay
Matt Hayes
Maggie Wallace
Cat Leipold
Heather Balogh
Mattie Schuler

INDEX

ABOUT THE AUTHOR

Liz Thomas is among the most experienced female hikers in the country; she is known for backpacking light, fast, and solo. In 2011, she broke the women's unsupported speed record on the 2,181-mile long Appalachian Trail, besting the previous record by almost a week. She has completed the Triple Crown of hiking and has backpacked over 15,000 miles across the United States on twenty long distance hikes, including the pioneering traverse of the Chinook Trail across the Columbia River Gorge and the pioneering traverse of the Wasatch Range, which she did solo. Liz is affectionately known as the "Queen of Urban Hiking," having pioneered and completed routes in five cities across the United States.

In her time not on the trail, Liz attained a Masters in Environmental Science from the Yale School of Forestry & Environmental Studies and the prestigious Doris Duke Conservation Fellowship for her research on long distance hiking trails, conservation, and trail town communities.

Liz has been featured in *The Wall Street Journal*, *Women's Health*, *Men's Journal*, *Yahoo! News*, *Outside* online, and Gizmodo. She gives presentations about long distance hiking around the country, especially to college outdoor clubs, like the one where she first learned how to backpack. Liz is honored to serve as Vice President of the American Long Distance Hiking Association-West and as one of four ambassadors for American Hiking Society. Liz is the instructor for *BACKPACKER* magazine's six-week online course, Thru-hiking 101, and wrote *The Best Hikes on the Continental Divide Trail: Colorado* with the Continental Divide Trail coalition. When not hiking, Liz splits her time between Denver, Colorado, and Los Angeles, California, and works as an outdoor staff writer for The Wirecutter, a part of the *New York Times*.

BACKPACKER is the nation's premier brand for helping hikers, campers, and wilderness enthusiasts discover new adventures in the outdoors.